THE ESSENTIAL ADOBE ANIMATE 2024 GUIDE FOR BEGINNERS

JAZEMUNE WUALSONA

i

INTRODUCTION

In the digital age, creativity knows no bounds. With the ever-expanding possibilities of animation and interactive design, the tools we use play a crucial role in shaping our creative visions. Imagine a world where your ideas, no matter how fantastical, can be brought to life with precision, fluidity, and a touch of magic. This world is not just a distant dream but a reality within reach, thanks to the advancements in animation software.

Adobe Animate stands as a testament to the evolution of animation tools, bridging the gap between traditional animation techniques and the demands of modern multimedia projects. As a powerhouse of creativity, this software provides artists, designers, and developers with the ability to craft intricate animations, build interactive content, and create visually stunning graphics that captivate audiences across various platforms.

The journey into the world of animation is one of discovery and mastery. It is a path filled with experimentation, learning, and the eventual realization of one's creative potential. Adobe Animate serves as both a guide and a companion on this journey, offering a robust set of features that cater to both beginners and seasoned professionals alike.

At its core, Adobe Animate is a tool that respects the traditions of classic animation while embracing the innovations of digital technology. It is a versatile platform that allows users to create animations frame by frame, just as traditional animators have done for decades, but with the added advantage of digital precision and efficiency. This combination of old and new makes it an essential tool for anyone looking to explore the depths of animation.

The beauty of Adobe Animate lies in its ability to adapt to the needs of its users. Whether you are an aspiring animator looking to create your first project or a seasoned professional seeking to refine your skills, Adobe Animate offers the tools and flexibility to bring your ideas to life. From simple motion graphics to complex interactive experiences, the possibilities are endless.

One of the key strengths of Adobe Animate is its intuitive interface, designed to make the animation process as smooth and efficient as possible. The layout is clean, with tools and options strategically placed to minimize clutter and maximize productivity. This user-friendly environment is ideal for both learning and mastering the various aspects of animation, allowing users to focus on the creative process rather than getting bogged down by technical details.

As you delve deeper into the world of Adobe Animate, you will discover the power of its keyboard shortcuts, which streamline the animation process and enhance workflow efficiency. These shortcuts are not just time-saving tricks; they are essential tools that enable animators to work with speed and precision, ensuring that creative momentum is never lost. Mastering these shortcuts is a crucial step in becoming proficient with the software and unlocking its full potential.

The journey of mastering animation begins with a solid understanding of the basics, and Adobe Animate provides a comprehensive foundation upon which to build. The software's introductory features offer a gateway into the world of animation, guiding users through the initial steps of creating their first projects. This is where the magic begins, as you learn to navigate the interface, experiment with different tools, and start to bring your ideas to life.

As your skills progress, Adobe Animate introduces you to more advanced techniques, such as classic tweens and motion tweens, which form the backbone of many animations. These tools allow you to create smooth, fluid movements that breathe life into your characters and designs. The ability to control timing, spacing, and motion is a fundamental aspect of animation, and Adobe Animate provides the precision needed to achieve these effects with ease.

Beyond the basics, Adobe Animate offers a wealth of features for creating graphics and text, allowing you to add depth and dimension to your projects. The software's robust design tools enable you to craft intricate visuals that enhance the overall aesthetic of your animations. Whether you are designing characters, backgrounds, or interactive elements, Adobe Animate provides the flexibility and control needed to achieve professional-quality results.

As you continue to explore the capabilities of Adobe Animate, you will encounter more complex animation techniques, such as shape animation and masking. These advanced features allow you to push the boundaries of your creativity, experimenting with different effects and transitions to create unique and dynamic animations. The ability to animate shapes and apply masks opens up a world of possibilities, enabling you to create intricate designs that are both visually stunning and technically sophisticated.

One of the most powerful features of Adobe Animate is its Inverse Kinematics (IK) and Bone Tool, which provide a new level of control over character animation. These tools allow you to create realistic movements by defining the relationships between different parts of a character's body. The Bone Tool enables you to create skeletons that control the movement of characters, while Inverse Kinematics ensures that these movements are smooth and natural. This level of control is essential for creating lifelike animations that resonate with audiences.

Adobe Animate is not just a tool for creating animations; it is a platform for building interactive media that engages and captivates users. The software's interactive features allow you to create content that responds to user input, making it ideal for games, websites, and other interactive projects. The ability to combine animation with interactivity opens up new possibilities for creative expression, allowing you to craft experiences that are both immersive and engaging.

As you journey through the world of Adobe Animate, you will discover the vast potential that lies within this powerful software. It is a tool that empowers you to bring your creative visions to life, offering the flexibility, control, and precision needed to create animations and interactive media that stand out in a crowded digital landscape.

The path to mastering Adobe Animate is one of continuous learning and growth. It is a journey that challenges you to push the boundaries of your creativity, experiment with new techniques, and refine your skills with each project. Along the way, you will discover the joy of bringing your ideas to life, the satisfaction of seeing your animations move and interact as you envisioned them, and the fulfillment that comes from creating content that resonates with others.

In this ever-evolving digital world, the ability to create compelling animations and interactive media is a valuable skill that opens doors to countless opportunities. Whether you are pursuing a career in animation, looking to enhance your design skills, or simply exploring a new hobby, Adobe Animate provides the tools and resources needed to succeed.

As you embark on this journey, remember that the key to mastering Adobe Animate lies in practice, experimentation, and a willingness to learn. The more you use the software, the more you will discover its potential, and the more confident you will become in your abilities. Each project you undertake is an opportunity to refine your skills, push the boundaries of your creativity, and bring your ideas to life in new and exciting ways.

Adobe Animate is more than just a tool; it is a gateway to a world of creative possibilities. It is a platform that empowers you to tell stories, create experiences, and connect with audiences in meaningful ways. With each animation you create, you are not just crafting a visual experience; you are bringing your imagination to life, one frame at a time.

As you continue to explore the features and capabilities of Adobe Animate, you will find that the possibilities are truly endless. From simple animations to complex interactive projects, the software provides the tools and flexibility needed to achieve your creative goals. Whether you are just starting out or looking to take your skills to the next level, Adobe Animate offers a world of possibilities waiting to be explored.

The journey ahead is one of discovery, creativity, and growth. It is a journey that will challenge you, inspire you, and ultimately lead you to new heights of creative expression. As you delve deeper into the world of animation and interactive media, remember that the only limit is your imagination. Adobe Animate is your guide, your tool, and your canvas. The rest is up to you.

CONTENTS

INTRODUCTION iii

CONTENTS ix

Chapter 1: Introducing to Adobe Animate.................................1

Chapter 2: Keyboard shortcuts in Adobe Animate.....................25

Chapter 3: Getting Started with Adobe Animate.......................31

Chapter 4: Mastering Classic Tweens....................................73

Chapter 5: Crafting Graphics and Text..................................115

Chapter 6: Motion Tweens Unleashed 179

Chapter 7: Advanced Shape Animation and Masking 198

Chapter 8: Inverse Kinematics and Bone Tool 231

Chapter 9: Building Interactive Media..................................263

CONCLUSION...297

CHAPTER 1: INTRODUCING TO ADOBE ANIMATE

I. WHAT IS ADOBE ANIMATE?

Overview of Adobe Animate

Adobe Animate, formerly known as Flash Professional, is a multimedia authoring and computer animation program developed by Adobe Systems. It is widely used for creating vector graphics, animation, games, and interactive content that can be published on multiple platforms, including web, mobile, and desktop applications. The software is part of Adobe's Creative Cloud suite, which provides a range of tools for design, development, and multimedia production.

Adobe Animate stands out for its versatility and ease of use, making it accessible to beginners while providing advanced features for professional animators and developers. Its intuitive interface allows users to create animations and interactive content through a combination of timeline-based animation and frame-by-frame animation techniques. This makes it an excellent choice for producing everything from simple animations to complex interactive applications.

One of the core strengths of Adobe Animate is its support for various export formats, including HTML5 Canvas, WebGL, Flash (SWF), and even video formats. This flexibility ensures that content created in Adobe Animate can be viewed on a wide range of devices and platforms, catering to the needs of different audiences and ensuring compatibility with modern web standards.

Over the years, Adobe Animate has evolved to meet the changing demands of digital content creation. Its robust set of tools and features enables users to produce high-quality animations and interactive experiences efficiently. Whether you're creating animated cartoons, rich web applications, or engaging mobile apps, Adobe Animate provides the tools you need to bring your vision to life.

Key Features and Capabilities

1. Vector and Bitmap Support Adobe Animate allows you to work with both vector and bitmap graphics, giving you the flexibility to create scalable artwork or detailed images. Vector graphics are particularly useful for creating animations that need to be resized without losing quality, while bitmap graphics are ideal for more detailed and textured artwork.

2. Timeline and Keyframe Animation The timeline in Adobe Animate is one of its most powerful features. It allows you to create animations by defining keyframes, which are specific points in time where you specify the properties of objects. The software then interpolates the changes between these keyframes, creating smooth animations. This method, known as tweening, can be applied to various properties such as position, scale, rotation, and opacity.

3. Motion Tweens and Classic Tweens Adobe Animate offers two primary types of tweens: motion tweens and classic tweens. Motion tweens are used for animating symbols and allow for more complex motion paths and transformations. Classic tweens, on the other hand, are typically used for simpler animations and are easier to set up. Both types of tweens provide a high degree of control over the animation process.

4. Shape Tweens Shape tweens are used to animate the transformation of one shape into another. This feature is particularly useful for creating morphing effects and other dynamic transformations. Shape tweens work by interpolating the changes between two shapes, resulting in a smooth transition from one to the other.

5. Symbols and Instances Symbols are reusable elements that you can create and animate independently from the main timeline. They can be graphics, buttons, or movie clips, and they greatly enhance the efficiency and organization of your projects. Instances of symbols can be reused multiple times, with each instance being capable of having its own properties and animations.

6. ActionScript and JavaScript Integration For those who want to add interactivity to their animations, Adobe Animate supports scripting with ActionScript (for SWF output) and JavaScript (for HTML5 Canvas output). These scripting languages allow you to create interactive buttons, control animations programmatically, and build complex interactive applications.

7. HTML5 Canvas and WebGL Support Adobe Animate provides robust support for HTML5 Canvas and WebGL, allowing you to create content that runs natively in modern web browsers without the need for plugins. This ensures that your animations and interactive content are accessible to a wide audience and comply with current web standards.

8. Bone Tool and Inverse Kinematics The Bone tool in Adobe Animate allows you to create and animate skeletal structures for characters and objects. This feature, known as inverse kinematics (IK), makes it easier to animate complex motions such as walking, running, or other articulated movements. By defining a bone structure, you can create more natural and fluid animations.

9. Audio Support Adobe Animate provides extensive support for audio, enabling you to synchronize sound with your animations. You can import audio files, place them on the timeline, and control their playback properties. This is particularly useful for creating animated videos, interactive presentations, and multimedia applications that require sound effects or background music.

10. Export Options One of the standout features of Adobe Animate is its wide range of export options. You can export your animations and interactive content to various formats, including HTML5 Canvas, WebGL, Flash (SWF), video formats (such as MP4), and even as animated GIFs. This flexibility ensures that your work can be viewed on different devices and platforms, from websites and mobile apps to social media and video-sharing platforms.

11. Integration with Other Adobe Products Adobe Animate seamlessly integrates with other Adobe Creative Cloud applications, such as Photoshop, Illustrator, and After Effects. This integration allows you to import assets from these applications and use them in your animations, streamlining your workflow and enhancing your creative possibilities.

12. Asset Warping Adobe Animate includes an asset warping tool that allows you to create complex deformations of vector shapes and bitmaps. This tool is particularly useful for animating characters and objects with natural and fluid movements. By defining control points and manipulating them, you can achieve detailed and expressive animations.

13. Camera Tool The camera tool in Adobe Animate lets you add depth and movement to your animations by simulating a virtual camera. You can pan, zoom, and rotate the camera to create dynamic and engaging scenes. This tool enhances the storytelling aspect of your animations and adds a professional touch to your projects.

14. Collaboration and Sharing Adobe Animate supports collaboration features that allow multiple users to work on the same project. You can share your work with colleagues and clients, gather feedback, and make revisions in real-time. This collaborative approach ensures that your projects are aligned with the vision and expectations of your team and stakeholders.

In conclusion, Adobe Animate is a powerful and versatile tool for creating animations and interactive content. Its comprehensive set of features and capabilities makes it suitable for a wide range of applications, from simple animations to complex interactive experiences. Whether you are a beginner or a seasoned professional, Adobe Animate provides the tools you need to bring your creative ideas to life.

II. DEVELOPMENT HISTORY

Evolution of Adobe Animate

Adobe Animate, formerly known as Flash Professional, has a rich and intricate history that dates back to the mid-1990s. The software has undergone significant transformations, evolving from a simple vector animation tool into a comprehensive multimedia authoring platform. This evolution has been driven by advancements in technology, changing user needs, and the dynamic landscape of digital content creation.

The Birth of Flash

The origins of Adobe Animate can be traced back to 1996 when a company named FutureWave Software developed a vector-based drawing program called FutureSplash Animator. FutureWave's software was designed to create animations that could be played back in web browsers, offering a more interactive and engaging web experience. At the time, the internet was still in its infancy, and most web content was static. FutureSplash Animator aimed to bring animations and interactivity to the web, a revolutionary concept at the time.

In 1996, Macromedia, a company known for its multimedia software, recognized the potential of FutureSplash Animator and acquired FutureWave Software. Macromedia rebranded the software as Macromedia Flash, launching the first version of what would become a cornerstone of web animation and interactive content.

The Rise of Flash

Throughout the late 1990s and early 2000s, Macromedia Flash rapidly gained popularity. It became the go-to tool for creating interactive web content, including animations, games, and advertisements. Flash's ability to deliver rich multimedia experiences through relatively small file sizes made it ideal for the bandwidth constraints of the early internet.

Flash introduced several groundbreaking features that contributed to its success. The use of vector graphics allowed for scalable animations that looked crisp at any resolution, while the timeline and keyframe-based animation system made it accessible to both novice and experienced animators. Additionally, the introduction of ActionScript, Flash's scripting language, enabled developers to create complex interactivity and functionality within their animations.

Adobe's Acquisition and Evolution

In 2005, Adobe Systems acquired Macromedia, bringing Flash into the Adobe family of products. This acquisition marked a significant turning point for Flash, as Adobe began integrating it more closely with its other creative software, such as Photoshop and Illustrator. The integration allowed users to seamlessly import assets and incorporate them into their Flash projects, enhancing their creative workflows.

Under Adobe's stewardship, Flash continued to evolve. The software saw numerous updates and improvements, including enhanced drawing tools, better performance, and expanded support for multimedia content. However, as the internet continued to evolve, so did the challenges and opportunities for Flash.

The Shift to HTML5

By the late 2000s, the internet landscape was changing rapidly. The rise of mobile devices, particularly smartphones and tablets, presented new challenges for Flash. These devices often had limited support for Flash content, leading to performance issues and compatibility problems. Moreover, the emergence of HTML5, a new web standard, offered a powerful alternative for creating interactive and multimedia-rich content without the need for plugins.

Recognizing the shift towards HTML5, Adobe began repositioning Flash to adapt to the changing environment. In 2011, Adobe announced that it would no longer develop Flash Player for mobile browsers, signaling a strategic shift towards HTML5 and other open web standards. This decision marked the beginning of a new era for Flash, as it sought to remain relevant in an increasingly mobile-centric world.

The Birth of Adobe Animate

In 2016, Adobe rebranded Flash Professional as Adobe Animate, reflecting its broader focus beyond Flash technology. The rebranding was part of a larger effort to align the software with the evolving needs of digital content creators and to emphasize its support for modern web standards, including HTML5 Canvas and WebGL.

Adobe Animate retained the powerful animation and multimedia capabilities that had made Flash so popular while expanding its support for new technologies. The software's integration with Creative Cloud enabled users to access a wide range of assets and resources, further enhancing their creative possibilities. Animate also introduced new features, such as improved vector drawing tools, enhanced motion tweening, and the ability to export animations in multiple formats, including HTML5, WebGL, and video.

Milestones in Development

FutureSplash Animator (1996) The journey began with FutureSplash Animator, a vector-based animation tool developed by FutureWave Software. Its acquisition by Macromedia and subsequent rebranding as Macromedia Flash set the stage for the software's rise to prominence.

Macromedia Flash 1.0 (1996) The first official version of Macromedia Flash introduced vector graphics and the timeline-based animation system. It quickly became a popular tool for creating web animations and interactive content.

Introduction of ActionScript (2000) Flash 5 introduced ActionScript, a powerful scripting language that enabled developers to create interactive and dynamic content. ActionScript significantly expanded the capabilities of Flash, allowing for the creation of complex applications and games.

Acquisition by Adobe (2005) Adobe's acquisition of Macromedia brought Flash into the Adobe ecosystem. This acquisition led to greater integration with other Adobe products and a focus on enhancing the software's capabilities for professional use.

Flash CS3 (2007) Flash CS3 marked a significant milestone with the introduction of Adobe's Creative Suite. This version included new features such as improved drawing tools, better integration with Photoshop and Illustrator, and support for ActionScript 3.0, which offered improved performance and functionality.

HTML5 Support (2011) As the web landscape shifted towards HTML5, Adobe announced that it would no longer develop Flash Player for mobile browsers. This decision marked the beginning of a transition towards HTML5 and other open web standards.

Rebranding as Adobe Animate (2016) The rebranding of Flash Professional as Adobe Animate signified a new era for the software. Adobe Animate embraced modern web standards, including HTML5 Canvas and WebGL, while retaining its powerful animation capabilities. The rebranding aimed to align the software with the evolving needs of digital content creators and to ensure its relevance in a changing technological landscape.

Introduction of Virtual Reality (2017) Adobe Animate introduced support for virtual reality (VR) content, allowing creators to design immersive experiences. This feature enabled the creation of interactive VR animations and games, expanding the software's capabilities into the realm of emerging technologies.

Enhanced Export Options (2018) Adobe Animate continued to evolve with enhanced export options, enabling users to publish their content in various formats, including HTML5, WebGL, and animated GIFs. These export options ensured that animations and interactive content could be viewed across a wide range of devices and platforms.

Integration with Creative Cloud Libraries (2019) The integration with Creative Cloud Libraries allowed users to access a vast collection of assets, including graphics, fonts, and templates, directly within Adobe Animate. This integration streamlined the creative process and provided users with a wealth of resources to enhance their projects.

Improved Performance and Workflow (2020) Adobe Animate received updates focused on improving performance and workflow efficiency. These updates included enhancements to the timeline, improved vector drawing tools, and better support for high-resolution displays. The goal was to provide a smoother and more efficient experience for animators and developers.

Continued Innovation (2021-Present) Adobe Animate continues to innovate, with ongoing updates and new features that address the evolving needs of digital content creators. Recent updates have focused on enhancing the software's capabilities for creating interactive and immersive experiences, as well as improving the user interface and overall performance.

In conclusion, the development history of Adobe Animate is a testament to its adaptability and resilience in the face of changing technological landscapes. From its humble beginnings as FutureSplash Animator to its current incarnation as a versatile multimedia authoring tool, Adobe Animate has consistently evolved to meet the needs of its users. Its rich history is marked by significant milestones and innovations that have shaped the way digital content is created and consumed. As Adobe Animate continues to evolve, it remains a powerful and indispensable tool for animators, designers, and developers worldwide.

III. SUBSCRIPTION PURCHASE AND PRICING

Adobe Creative Cloud Subscription

Adobe Animate is part of the Adobe Creative Cloud suite, a subscription-based service that offers a wide range of creative software and tools for professionals and enthusiasts alike. Adobe Creative Cloud provides access to over 20 desktop and mobile apps, including Photoshop, Illustrator, Premiere Pro, After Effects, and, of course, Adobe Animate. The subscription model offers several benefits, including continuous updates, cloud storage, and a collaborative environment that caters to modern workflows.

Key Benefits of Adobe Creative Cloud Subscription:

1. **Access to Latest Versions:** Subscribers always have access to the latest versions of Adobe software. Updates are rolled out regularly, ensuring that users benefit from the newest features, performance improvements, and security enhancements.

2. **Cloud Storage:** Creative Cloud subscriptions come with varying amounts of cloud storage, which allows users to save their projects, assets, and libraries online. This facilitates easy access from different devices and ensures that your work is backed up and secure.

3. **Collaboration and Sharing:** Creative Cloud includes tools for collaboration, such as shared libraries and cloud documents. These features make it easier for teams to work together on projects, share assets, and provide feedback in real time.

4. **Mobile Apps:** Many of the Creative Cloud applications have companion mobile apps that enable users to create and edit on the go. This integration between desktop and mobile apps enhances flexibility and productivity.

5. **Adobe Fonts and Stock:** A Creative Cloud subscription includes access to Adobe Fonts, which offers thousands of high-quality fonts. Additionally, users can integrate Adobe Stock, a vast library of photos, graphics, and videos, into their workflow for a fee.

6. **Learning Resources:** Adobe provides a wealth of tutorials, guides, and community support to help users get the most out of their software. This is especially beneficial for beginners looking to learn and improve their skills.

Pricing Plans and Options

Adobe Creative Cloud offers several subscription plans to cater to different needs and budgets. The pricing structure is designed to be flexible, allowing individuals, students, educators, and businesses to choose the plan that best suits their requirements.

1. Individual Plans

- **Single App Plan:** This plan allows users to subscribe to a single Adobe application, such as Adobe Animate. It is ideal for users who only need access to one specific tool. The single app plan includes 100 GB of cloud storage, Adobe Fonts, and access to Adobe Portfolio, Behance, and Adobe Spark.

- **All Apps Plan:** This comprehensive plan provides access to the entire suite of Adobe Creative Cloud applications. It is perfect for users who need multiple tools for their creative projects. The all apps plan includes 100 GB of cloud storage, Adobe Fonts, Adobe Portfolio, Behance, and Adobe Spark.

2. Student and Teacher Plans

Adobe offers discounted plans for students and teachers, making it more affordable for educational users to access the full range of Creative Cloud applications. These plans are available to both individuals and institutions.

- **Student and Teacher All Apps Plan:** This plan provides students and teachers with access to all Creative Cloud applications at a significantly reduced price. It includes the same benefits as the individual all apps plan, with additional resources tailored for educational use.

3. Business Plans

For businesses and teams, Adobe offers several plans that provide additional features and administrative tools to support collaborative workflows and enterprise needs.

- **Teams Single App Plan:** This plan allows businesses to subscribe to individual Adobe applications for each team member. It includes 1 TB of cloud storage per user, Adobe Fonts, and additional business features like centralized administration, advanced technical support, and collaboration tools.

- **Teams All Apps Plan:** This comprehensive plan provides businesses with access to all Adobe Creative Cloud applications for each team member. It includes 1 TB of cloud storage per user, Adobe Fonts, and all the additional business features mentioned above.

- **Enterprise Plans:** For larger organizations, Adobe offers customized enterprise plans that include all Creative Cloud applications, advanced security features, dedicated support, and additional storage options. Enterprise plans are tailored to meet the specific needs of large teams and organizations.

4. Free Trial and Discounts

Adobe offers a free trial for most of its Creative Cloud applications, including Adobe Animate. The free trial allows users to explore the software and its features for a limited time, usually seven days. This is an excellent way for new users to evaluate the software before committing to a subscription.

In addition to the free trial, Adobe frequently offers discounts and promotions, especially for new subscribers. Students, teachers, and educational institutions often benefit from substantial discounts, making Adobe Creative Cloud more accessible to the academic community.

Subscription Purchase Process

Purchasing an Adobe Creative Cloud subscription is straightforward and can be done through the Adobe website. Here is a step-by-step guide to the subscription purchase process:

1. **Visit the Adobe Creative Cloud Website:** Go to the official Adobe Creative Cloud website and navigate to the pricing section.

2. **Choose a Plan:** Review the available plans and select the one that best fits your needs. You can choose between individual, student and teacher, business, or enterprise plans.

3. **Create an Adobe ID:** If you don't already have an Adobe ID, you will need to create one. Your Adobe ID will be used to manage your subscription and access the Creative Cloud applications.

4. **Select Billing Options:** Choose your billing frequency (monthly or annual) and enter your payment information. Adobe accepts various payment methods, including credit cards and PayPal.

5. **Download and Install:** Once your purchase is complete, you can download and install the Creative Cloud desktop application. From the Creative Cloud app, you can install the Adobe applications included in your subscription.

6. **Access and Manage Your Subscription:** Use your Adobe ID to log in to the Creative Cloud desktop app and start using the software. You can manage your subscription, update billing information, and access your cloud storage through your Adobe account.

Conclusion

The subscription purchase and pricing structure of Adobe Creative Cloud is designed to provide flexibility and value to a wide range of users, from individual creators to large enterprises. By offering access to a comprehensive suite of creative tools, continuous updates, cloud storage, and collaborative features, Adobe Creative Cloud supports modern workflows and enhances productivity. Whether you are an individual looking to explore your creative potential, a student seeking to learn new skills, or a business aiming to streamline your creative processes, Adobe Creative Cloud offers a plan that fits your needs.

IV. INSTALLATION METHOD

System Requirements

Before installing Adobe Animate, it's crucial to ensure that your system meets the necessary requirements to run the software smoothly. Adobe provides specific system requirements for both Windows and macOS platforms. Meeting these requirements will help ensure optimal performance and avoid potential issues during installation and use.

Windows

- **Operating System:** Windows 10 (64-bit) version 1909 or later

- **Processor:** Intel Pentium 4, Intel Centrino, Intel Xeon, or Intel Core Duo (or compatible) processor

- **RAM:** 8 GB or more recommended

- **Hard Disk Space:** 4 GB of available hard-disk space for installation; additional free space required during installation (cannot install on removable flash storage devices)

- **Monitor Resolution:** 1024 x 900 display (1280 x 1024 recommended)

- **Graphics Card:** 16-bit video card

- **Internet:** Internet connection and registration are necessary for required software activation, validation of subscriptions, and access to online services.

macOS

- **Operating System:** macOS X v10.15 (Catalina) or later

- **Processor:** Multicore Intel processor

- **RAM:** 8 GB or more recommended

- **Hard Disk Space:** 4 GB of available hard-disk space for installation; additional free space required during installation (cannot install on a volume that uses a case-sensitive file system or on removable flash storage devices)

- **Monitor Resolution:** 1024 x 900 display (1280 x 1024 recommended)

- **Graphics Card:** 16-bit video card

- **Internet:** Internet connection and registration are necessary for required software activation, validation of subscriptions, and access to online services.

Additional Requirements for VR Content:

- **VR Headset and controllers (for previewing VR content)**

- **Windows 10 (64-bit) for Windows Mixed Reality, HTC Vive, or Oculus Rift**

- **Mac OS 10.15 or later for macOS with Steam VR**

Ensuring your system meets or exceeds these requirements will allow Adobe Animate to function efficiently, providing a smooth user experience.

Step-by-Step Installation Guide

Once you've confirmed that your system meets the necessary requirements, you can proceed with the installation of Adobe Animate. The following step-by-step guide will walk you through the process:

Step 1: Sign Up for an Adobe ID

If you don't already have an Adobe ID, you'll need to create one. Your Adobe ID will be used to manage your subscription and access Adobe services.

1. Go to the Adobe Account page.

2. Click on "Create Account."

3. Fill in the required information (name, email address, password, etc.).

4. Follow the prompts to complete the account creation process.

Step 2: Purchase a Subscription

1. Visit the Adobe Creative Cloud Plans page.

2. Choose the plan that best suits your needs. You can select a single app plan for Adobe Animate or an All Apps plan for access to the entire suite.

3. Follow the prompts to purchase your subscription. You'll need to provide payment information and confirm your billing details.

Step 3: Download the Creative Cloud Installer

1. Once you've purchased your subscription, go to the Creative Cloud Download page.

2. Click on "Download Creative Cloud."

3. The Creative Cloud installer will begin downloading. This application is necessary to manage all your Adobe apps, including Adobe Animate.

Step 4: Install the Creative Cloud Desktop App

1. Locate the downloaded Creative Cloud installer file on your computer (usually in the Downloads folder).

2. Double-click the installer file to begin the installation process.

3. Follow the on-screen instructions to complete the installation of the Creative Cloud desktop app.

Step 5: Sign In to Creative Cloud

1. Once the Creative Cloud desktop app is installed, launch it.

2. Sign in with your Adobe ID and password.

3. The Creative Cloud app will open, displaying a dashboard with all available Adobe applications.

Step 6: Install Adobe Animate

1. In the Creative Cloud desktop app, locate Adobe Animate in the list of available applications.

2. Click on the "Install" button next to Adobe Animate.

3. The installation process will begin, and the progress will be displayed in the Creative Cloud app.

4. Once the installation is complete, Adobe Animate will be available for use on your computer.

Step 7: Launch Adobe Animate

1. After installation, you can launch Adobe Animate directly from the Creative Cloud desktop app by clicking the "Open" button.

2. Alternatively, you can find Adobe Animate in your list of installed applications on your computer and launch it from there.

Step 8: Activate Your Subscription

1. The first time you launch Adobe Animate, you may be prompted to activate your subscription.

2. Sign in with your Adobe ID if prompted.

3. Follow any additional on-screen instructions to complete the activation process.

Step 9: Customize Your Settings

1. Once Adobe Animate is launched, you can customize the settings according to your preferences.

2. Go to "Edit" (Windows) or "Adobe Animate" (macOS) in the top menu and select "Preferences."

3. Adjust settings for general preferences, workspace layout, shortcuts, and more.

Step 10: Start Creating

You're now ready to start using Adobe Animate! Explore the interface, familiarize yourself with the tools, and begin creating your animations and interactive content.

Tips for a Smooth Installation Process:

- **Ensure Stable Internet Connection:** A stable internet connection is essential for downloading the Creative Cloud app and Adobe Animate, as well as for activating your subscription.

- **Disable Antivirus Temporarily:** Sometimes, antivirus software can interfere with the installation process. If you encounter issues, temporarily disable your antivirus software and try again.

- **Keep System Updated:** Ensure that your operating system and drivers are up to date to avoid compatibility issues.

- **Check Disk Space:** Make sure you have enough free disk space for the installation process. Adobe Animate requires at least 4 GB of available hard-disk space.

Troubleshooting Common Installation Issues:

1. **Installation Fails or Freezes:**
   - Restart your computer and try the installation again.
   - Ensure that no other applications are running during the installation.
   - Check your internet connection for stability.

2. **Creative Cloud App Not Responding:**
   - Restart the Creative Cloud app.
   - If the issue persists, uninstall and reinstall the Creative Cloud app.

3. **Activation Problems:**
   - Ensure that you're signed in with the correct Adobe ID associated with your subscription.
   - Check your subscription status in the Creative Cloud app or on the Adobe website.

4. **Compatibility Issues:**
   - Verify that your system meets the minimum requirements for Adobe Animate.
   - Update your operating system and graphics drivers if necessary.

By following this detailed installation guide and ensuring your system meets the requirements, you'll be well on your way to using Adobe Animate effectively. With the software installed and activated, you can begin exploring its features and creating dynamic animations and interactive content.

V. DESIGN CONCEPT AND MINDSET

Understanding the Design Philosophy

Adobe Animate is a powerful tool for creating animations and interactive content, but mastering it requires more than just technical knowledge. Understanding the design philosophy behind the software and adopting the right mindset is crucial for creating effective, engaging, and aesthetically pleasing animations. This section delves into the core principles that should guide your use of Adobe Animate and provides best practices for beginners to ensure a smooth and productive creative journey.

The Design Philosophy of Adobe Animate

1. **User-Centric Design:** Adobe Animate is designed with the user in mind. Its intuitive interface and comprehensive toolset cater to both beginners and seasoned professionals. The goal is to provide users with a flexible and efficient environment that enhances creativity while simplifying complex processes. This user-centric approach is evident in features like customizable workspaces, easy-to-use drawing tools, and streamlined workflows.

2. **Versatility and Flexibility:** One of the key strengths of Adobe Animate is its versatility. It supports various types of animation, including frame-by-frame, tweening, and inverse kinematics, as well as a range of output formats like HTML5, WebGL, and video. This flexibility allows creators to produce content for different platforms and audiences, from web animations and interactive games to educational content and advertisements.

3. **Integration and Interoperability:** Adobe Animate is part of the Adobe Creative Cloud suite, which means it integrates seamlessly with other Adobe applications like Photoshop, Illustrator, and After Effects. This integration fosters a cohesive workflow, allowing users to import assets, edit graphics, and enhance animations with ease. The interoperability extends to exporting animations to various formats, ensuring compatibility with modern web standards and devices.

4. **Efficiency and Productivity:** Adobe Animate is built to maximize efficiency

and productivity. Features like reusable symbols, motion presets, and a robust library system help streamline the animation process. Automation tools such as motion tweens and asset warping reduce the time and effort required to create complex animations. Additionally, the software's performance optimizations ensure smooth playback and rendering, even for resource-intensive projects.

5. **Creativity and Innovation:** At its core, Adobe Animate is a platform for creativity and innovation. It empowers users to bring their ideas to life through dynamic animations and interactive experiences. The software encourages experimentation and exploration, providing a wide array of tools and features that enable creators to push the boundaries of their imagination.

Best Practices for Beginners

For beginners, diving into Adobe Animate can be both exciting and overwhelming. Following best practices can help you navigate the learning curve and develop a solid foundation for creating high-quality animations. Here are some essential tips and guidelines to get you started:

1. **Start with the Basics:** Before diving into complex animations, take the time to familiarize yourself with the basics of Adobe Animate. Learn how to navigate the interface, use the drawing tools, and understand the timeline and keyframes. Adobe offers a wealth of tutorials and resources that can help you get started.

2. **Plan Your Animation:** Planning is a crucial step in the animation process. Before you start animating, sketch out a storyboard or create a script that outlines the key scenes and actions. This planning phase will help you visualize the flow of your animation and ensure a coherent and engaging story.

3. **Use Layers and Symbols:** Organize your animation by using layers and symbols. Layers allow you to separate different elements of your animation, making it easier to manage and edit. Symbols are reusable assets that can be animated independently from the main timeline. Using symbols helps streamline your workflow and maintain consistency throughout your project.

4. **Master the Timeline:** The timeline is the heart of Adobe Animate. Understanding how to use it effectively is essential for creating smooth and precise animations. Learn how to create keyframes, use tweens, and adjust

timing to achieve the desired effect. Practice using the timeline to control the movement, scale, rotation, and opacity of your objects.

5. **Leverage Motion Tweens:** Motion tweens are a powerful tool for animating objects between keyframes. They automate the process of creating in-between frames, saving time and effort. Experiment with motion tweens to animate position, scale, rotation, and other properties. Adjust the easing options to create more natural and dynamic movements.

6. **Explore Different Animation Techniques:** Adobe Animate supports various animation techniques, including frame-by-frame animation, shape tweens, and inverse kinematics. Experiment with these techniques to understand their strengths and applications. For example, use frame-by-frame animation for detailed and expressive movements, while shape tweens are ideal for morphing effects.

7. **Pay Attention to Timing and Spacing:** Timing and spacing are fundamental principles of animation that determine how objects move and interact. Pay attention to the timing of your animations to ensure they feel natural and engaging. Use spacing to control the speed and fluidity of movements. Practice these principles to create animations that are both visually appealing and effective.

8. **Add Sound and Interactivity:** Enhance your animations by adding sound effects and interactivity. Adobe Animate allows you to synchronize audio with your animations and add interactive elements using ActionScript or JavaScript. Sound can add depth and emotion to your animations, while interactivity can engage your audience and create a more immersive experience.

9. **Optimize for Performance:** Ensure your animations run smoothly by optimizing for performance. Use symbols and reusable assets to reduce file size and improve playback. Avoid overloading your animations with excessive detail or complex effects that can slow down performance. Test your animations on different devices and platforms to ensure compatibility and responsiveness.

10. **Seek Feedback and Iterate:** Animation is an iterative process. Seek feedback from peers, mentors, or online communities to improve your work. Use constructive criticism to refine your animations and enhance your skills. Continuously iterate and experiment with new techniques and ideas to grow

as an animator.

11. **Stay Updated and Keep Learning:** Adobe Animate is constantly evolving, with new features and updates being released regularly. Stay updated with the latest developments and continue learning through tutorials, courses, and community forums. Join online communities and participate in discussions to share knowledge and gain insights from other animators.

12. **Practice Patience and Perseverance:** Mastering animation takes time and practice. Be patient with yourself and persevere through challenges and setbacks. Every project is an opportunity to learn and improve. Celebrate your progress and keep pushing your creative boundaries.

Conclusion

Understanding the design philosophy of Adobe Animate and adopting the right mindset is essential for creating compelling animations and interactive content. By embracing a user-centric approach, leveraging the software's versatility, and following best practices, beginners can navigate the learning curve and unlock their creative potential. Adobe Animate provides a powerful platform for storytelling, creativity, and innovation, empowering users to bring their ideas to life through dynamic and engaging animations. Whether you are a novice or an experienced animator, these principles and practices will guide you in making the most of Adobe Animate and achieving your creative goals.

VI. FUTURE USE AND TRENDS

Emerging Trends in Animation

The field of animation is constantly evolving, driven by technological advancements and changing consumer preferences. As a beginner using Adobe Animate, staying informed about emerging trends will help you create relevant and cutting-edge content. Here are some of the key trends shaping the future of animation:

1. Real-Time Animation: Real-time animation is gaining traction, thanks to advancements in software and hardware. Tools like Adobe Character Animator enable animators to create and control characters in real-time using live performance capture. This trend is particularly relevant for live broadcasts, interactive applications, and virtual events, where instant animation is essential.

2. Virtual Reality (VR) and Augmented Reality (AR): VR and AR are transforming the animation landscape by providing immersive experiences. Animators are now creating content for VR headsets and AR-enabled devices, allowing users to interact with animated elements in a three-dimensional space. Adobe Animate has introduced features that support the creation of VR and AR content, making it easier for animators to explore these emerging technologies.

3. 3D Animation Integration: While Adobe Animate primarily focuses on 2D animation, the integration of 3D elements is becoming more common. Animators are combining 2D and 3D techniques to create hybrid animations that offer depth and realism. Software like Blender and Autodesk Maya can be used alongside Adobe Animate to incorporate 3D models and effects into 2D animations.

4. Artificial Intelligence (AI) and Machine Learning: AI and machine learning are revolutionizing the animation industry by automating tedious tasks and enhancing creativity. AI-powered tools can generate animations, predict motion paths, and even create facial expressions and lip-sync movements. Adobe Animate is increasingly incorporating AI features to streamline workflows and enable animators to focus on creative aspects.

5. Interactive and Responsive Animation: The demand for interactive and responsive animations is growing, especially for web and mobile applications. Interactive animations respond to user input, creating engaging and personalized experiences. Adobe Animate's support for HTML5 Canvas and JavaScript makes it an ideal tool for creating interactive content that works seamlessly across different devices and platforms.

6. Motion Graphics and Explainer Videos: Motion graphics and explainer videos are becoming more popular for marketing, education, and entertainment. These animations combine text, graphics, and movement to convey complex information in a simple and visually appealing way. Adobe Animate provides the tools needed to create compelling motion graphics that capture attention and communicate messages effectively.

7. Minimalist and Flat Design: Minimalist and flat design trends continue to influence animation styles. This approach focuses on simplicity, using clean lines, bold colors, and minimal details to create visually striking animations. Adobe Animate's vector-based tools are well-suited for creating minimalist and flat designs that are both modern and timeless.

8. Inclusive and Diverse Storytelling: There is a growing emphasis on inclusive and diverse storytelling in animation. Creators are increasingly aware of the need to represent different cultures, identities, and experiences. Adobe Animate enables animators to bring diverse characters and stories to life, contributing to a more inclusive animation landscape.

9. Animation for Social Media: With the rise of social media platforms like Instagram, TikTok, and YouTube, there is a high demand for short, engaging animations. Animators are creating content tailored to these platforms, focusing on bite-sized, shareable animations that capture viewers' attention quickly. Adobe Animate's export options make it easy to create animations optimized for social media.

10. Sustainable Animation Practices: Sustainability is becoming a priority in all industries, including animation. Animators are exploring eco-friendly practices, such as using energy-efficient hardware, minimizing waste, and promoting digital distribution. Adobe Animate supports digital workflows, reducing the environmental impact of traditional animation processes.

Potential Future Applications

As technology continues to advance, the potential applications for animation are expanding. Adobe Animate's versatility and robust feature set position it well for various future uses. Here are some potential future applications of animation:

1. Education and E-Learning: Animation is a powerful tool for education and e-learning. Animated videos and interactive content can make complex concepts more accessible and engaging for learners of all ages. Adobe Animate can be used to create educational animations, interactive quizzes, and virtual labs, enhancing the learning experience.

2. Healthcare and Medical Animation: Medical animation is an emerging field that uses animation to explain medical procedures, illustrate complex biological processes, and train healthcare professionals. Adobe Animate can be used to create detailed and accurate medical animations that improve patient understanding and support medical education.

3. Advertising and Marketing: Animation plays a crucial role in advertising and marketing, capturing attention and conveying messages effectively. As digital advertising continues to grow, the demand for high-quality animations will increase. Adobe Animate enables marketers to create engaging advertisements, promotional videos, and social media content that drives brand awareness and conversions.

4. Entertainment and Media: The entertainment industry, including film, television, and video games, relies heavily on animation. Adobe Animate's capabilities make it a valuable tool for creating animated series, feature films, and game assets. As the entertainment industry continues to evolve, animation will remain a key component of storytelling and visual effects.

5. User Interface (UI) and User Experience (UX) Design: Animation enhances UI and UX design by providing visual feedback, guiding user interactions, and creating a more enjoyable experience. Adobe Animate can be used to design animated icons, loading animations, and interactive elements that improve the usability and aesthetics of digital products.

6. Corporate Training and Communication: Corporations are increasingly using animation for training and internal communication. Animated videos can simplify complex information, making it easier for employees to understand policies, procedures, and best practices. Adobe Animate can be used to create training modules, explainer videos, and internal communications that engage and inform employees.

7. Virtual Events and Presentations: With the rise of virtual events and remote work, animation is becoming an essential tool for creating dynamic presentations and virtual experiences. Adobe Animate can be used to design animated slides, virtual backgrounds, and interactive elements that enhance virtual events and presentations.

8. Augmented Reality (AR) Applications: AR applications are expanding across various industries, from retail and real estate to education and entertainment. Adobe Animate can be used to create AR content that overlays digital animations onto the real world, providing interactive and immersive experiences.

9. Accessibility and Assistive Technologies: Animation can improve accessibility by creating content that is easier to understand for people with disabilities. For example, animated sign language interpreters can assist deaf users, while animated instructions can help users with cognitive impairments. Adobe Animate can be used to develop accessible content that meets the needs of diverse audiences.

10. Scientific Visualization: Scientists and researchers use animation to visualize complex data and phenomena, making them easier to understand and analyze. Adobe Animate can be used to create scientific visualizations that illustrate processes such as molecular interactions, climate change, and astronomical events.

Conclusion

The future of animation is bright, with emerging trends and technologies opening up new possibilities for creative expression and practical applications. Adobe Animate is well-equipped to meet the demands of these evolving trends, providing animators with the tools they need to create innovative and engaging content. By staying informed about the latest trends and exploring potential future applications, beginners can position themselves at the forefront of the animation industry. Whether you are creating for education, entertainment, marketing, or any other field, Adobe Animate offers the flexibility and power to bring your ideas to life.

CHAPTER 2: KEYBOARD SHORTCUTS IN ADOBE ANIMATE

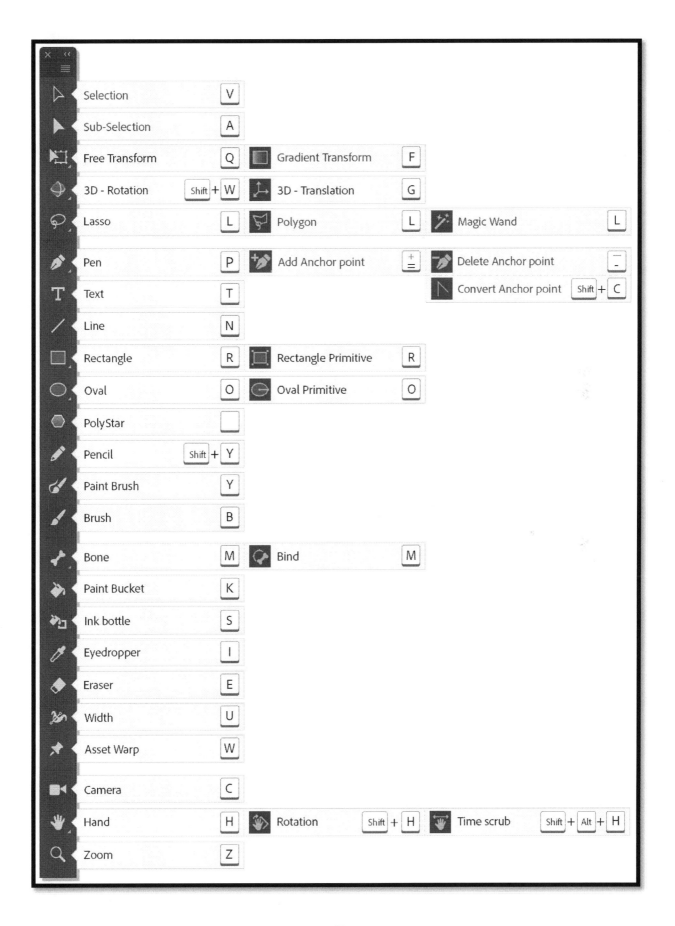

Selection	V				
Sub-Selection	A				
Free Transform	Q	Gradient Transform	F		
3D - Rotation	Shift + W	3D - Translation	G		
Lasso	L	Polygon	L	Magic Wand	L
Pen	P	Add Anchor point	+ =	Delete Anchor point	-
				Convert Anchor point	Shift + C
Text	T				
Line	N				
Rectangle	R	Rectangle Primitive	R		
Oval	O	Oval Primitive	O		
PolyStar					
Pencil	Shift + Y				
Paint Brush	Y				
Brush	B				
Bone	M	Bind	M		
Paint Bucket	K				
Ink bottle	S				
Eyedropper	I				
Eraser	E				
Width	U				
Asset Warp	W				
Camera	C				
Hand	H	Rotation	Shift + H	Time scrub	Shift + Alt + H
Zoom	Z				

File

Action	Mac	Windows
Import Image/Sound/etc...	Command ⌘ + R	Ctrl + R
Export Movie	Command ⌘ + Shift + Option Alt + S	Ctrl + Shift + Alt + S
Open as Library	Command ⌘ + Shift + O	Ctrl + Shift + O

View

Action	Mac	Windows
View movie at 100% size	Command ⌘ + 1	Ctrl + 1
Show Frame	Command ⌘ + 2	Ctrl + 2
Show All	Command ⌘ + 3	Ctrl + 3

Windows

Action	Mac	Windows
Show/Hide Library	Command ⌘ + L	Ctrl + L
Comment selection	Command ⌘ + M	Ctrl + M
Toggle between Edit Movie and Edit Symbol Mode	Command ⌘ + E	Ctrl + E
Show/Hide Timeline	Command ⌘ + Option Alt + T	Ctrl + Alt + T

Edit and modify

Action	Mac	Windows
Group	Command + G	Ctrl + G
Ungroup	Command + Shift + G	Ctrl + Shift + G
Break Apart	Command + B	Ctrl + B
Paste in Place	Command + Shift + V	Ctrl + Shift + V
Duplicate	Command + D	Ctrl + D
Select All	Command + A	Ctrl + A
Deselect All	Command + Shift + A	Ctrl + Shift + A
Import Library	Command + Shift + O	Ctrl + Shift + O
Align Window	Command + K	Ctrl + K
Save As	Command + Shift + S	Ctrl + Shift + S
Scale and Rotate	Command + Option + S	Ctrl + Alt + S
Remove Transform	Command + Shift + Z	Ctrl + Shift + Z
Move Ahead	Command + ▲	Ctrl + ▲
Move Behind	Command + ▼	Ctrl + ▼
Bring to Front	Command + Shift + ▲	Ctrl + Shift + ▲
Send to Back	Command + Shift + ▼	Ctrl + Shift + ▼
Show or hide Transform Panel	Command + T	Ctrl + T
Narrower letterspacing (kerning)	Command + Option + ◄	Ctrl + Alt + ◄
Wider letterspacing (kerning)	Command + Option + ►	Ctrl + Alt + ►

Miscellaneous actions

Action	Mac	Windows
Remove rotation or scaling from the selected objects	Command + Shift + Z	Ctrl + Shift + Z
Rotate the selection to 90 degrees left	Command + Shift + 7	Ctrl + Shift + 7
Scale and/or rotate the selection using numeric values	Command + Option + S	Ctrl + Alt + S
Auto formats the editor code	Command + Shift + F	Ctrl + Shift + F
Show hidden characters	Command + Shift + 8	Ctrl + Shift + 8
suppresses highlighting of selected items	Command + Shift + E	Ctrl + Shift + E
Show or hide the rulers	Command + Shift + Option + R	Ctrl + Shift + Alt + R
Show Frame Script Navigator	Command + Option + [	Ctrl + Alt + [
Show or hide the tweening shape hints	Command + Option + I	Ctrl + Alt + I
Show a smaller area of the drawing with more detail	Command + =	Ctrl + =
Show a larger area of the drawing with less detail	Command + -	Ctrl + -
Show or hide the Align panel	Command + K	Ctrl + K
Show or hide the Color panel	Command + Shift + F9	Ctrl + Shift + F9
Show or hide the Compiler Errors panel	Option + F2	Alt + F2

Open a new window in the front most simulation that is a duplicate of the active window	Command + Option + K	Ctrl + Alt + K
Show or hide the History panel	Command + F10	Ctrl + F10
Show or hide Info Panel	Command + I	Ctrl + I
Show or hide the Library panel for this document	Command + L	Ctrl + L
Show or hide the Property Inspector	Command + F3	Ctrl + F3
Show or change a list of the scenes in the current movie	Shift + F2	Shift + F2
Select colors from swatches and manage swatches	Command + F9	Ctrl + F9
Show or hide the animation timeline and layers controls	Command + Option + T	Ctrl + Alt + T
Show or hide the drawing toolbar	Command + F2	Ctrl + F2
Increase onion skin marker size on both directions equally	Command + drag towards right/left	Ctrl + drag towards right/left
Shifts the entire range of onion skin markers to the right/left respectively.	Shift + drag towards right/left	Shift + drag towards right/left

CHAPTER 3: GETTING STARTED WITH ADOBE ANIMATE

OVERVIEW

Chapter One introduces us to the steps required to install the new Adobe Animate 2024 including learning the required requirements, how to open Adobe Animate, and carry out basic file design.

LAUNCHING ADOBE ANIMATE AND OPENING A FILE

When you first use Adobe Animate, you'll see the Home page, which also allows you to create a new document or access one that has al-ready been saved. It shows the several types of projects you can create, as well as any recently opened files.

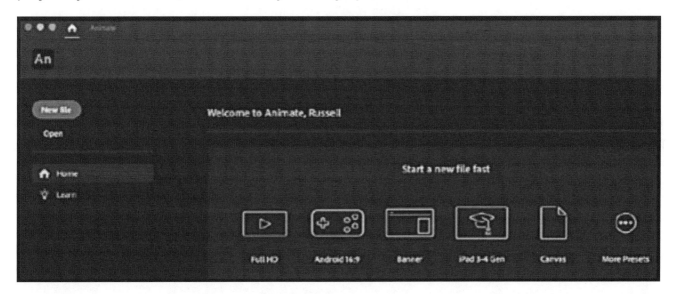

You can also launch Animate by double-clicking an Animate file (*.fla or *.xfl), such as the 01End.fla file, which displays the finished project. In this example guide, you'll develop a basic slideshow animation to display a few vacation photos. You'll add a background, pho- to graphs, and other ornamental components, and you'll learn how to place objects on the Stage and along the animation's timeline so that they display one at a time, in order. You'll start learning how to Use the Stage to arrange your visual components geographically and the Timeline panel to manage them chronologically.

Here are the steps:

1. First of all, open Animate. In macOS, double-click the Adobe Animate 2024 folder in the Applications folder. In Windows, choose **Start > Programs > Adobe Animate**.
2. Click the Open button or choose **File > Open**(Command+0/Ctrl+O). To see the completed project, in the Open dialog box, choose the 01 End.fla file from the 01 / 01 End folder and click **Open.**
3. Click the **Test Movie button** in the upper-right corner of the program interface or choose **Control > Test.**

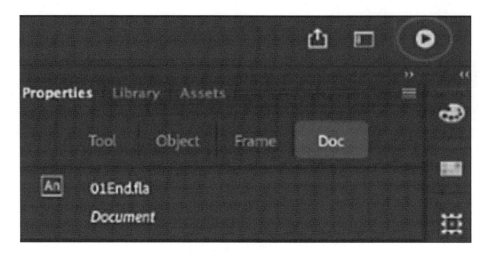

Animate exports the project and launches it in a new window.

An animation plays. While the animation is ongoing, multiple overlapping photos are displayed one after the other, with stars emerging at the conclusion. As fresh photographs arrive, the preceding ones get hazy and fade into the background.

4. Close both the preview window and the FLA file.

HOW TO UNDERSTAND DOCUMENT TYPES AND CREATING A NEW DOCUMENT

Animate is an animation and multimedia production tool that generates content for a variety of platforms and playback technologies. When creating a new file, you'll pick the kind of document based on where your finished animation will play.

PLAYBACK ENVIRONMENT

The playback, or runtime, environment is the technology that allows your final published files to play. Your animation might run on a browser that supports HTML5 and JavaScript. Perhaps your animation will be exported as a video to be shared on YouTube or as an

animated GIF on social media. Alternatively, your concept might be implemented as a smartphone app or a virtual reality immersive ex-perience. You should make that choice first, so you can choose the proper document type. No tall functionalities are compatible with all document types. For example, HTML5 Canvas documents do not support the 30 Rot ati on or 30 Translation tools. Tools that do not work with the current document type are darkened in the Animate interface.

DOCUMENT TYPES

There are nine categories of papers, but you'll probably just deal with the first two or three outlined here since they're the most prevalent. The nine papers address various playback contexts, which influence some of the animation and interactive aspects. Your options for An-imate documents are as follows: The ActionScript 3.0 document now allows you to publish material as a projector on either Windows or macOS. **A projector functions as a standalone program on the desktop, eliminating the need for a browser.**

- Use ActionScript 3.0 to output animations to video or images, including sprite sheets and PNG sequences. Action Script is Animate's native scripting language, and it is comparable to JavaScript; however, selecting an ActionScript 3.0 document does not require you to include ActionScript code.
- Use HTML5Canvas to develop contemporary browser-compatible projects using HTML5 and JavaScript. You can add interaction by using JavaScript inside Animate or in the final published files.
- Select WebGL glTF Extended or WebGL glTF Standard for hardware-accelerated 30 visuals or interactive animation elements.
- Use AIR for Desktop to develop animations that run as standalone applications on Windows and macOS desktops, eliminating the need for a web browser. Use ActionScript 3.0 to add interaction to an AIR document.
- Use AIR for Android or AIR for iOS to publish an app for Android or Apple mobile devices. You can use ActionScript 3.0 to make your mobile app more interactive.
- Use VR Panorama or VR 360 to create a 360-degree virtual reality project for web browsers. You may include animation or interac-tion in your immersive surroundings.

You can quickly swap between document types. If you wish to update an old Flash banner ad animation, you can convert it from an ActionScript 3.0 document to an HTML5 Canvas document. Choose **File > Convert To > [New Document Type].** Some functionality and features may be lost during the migration. For example, converting to an HTML5 Canvas page will result in ActionScript code being com-mented out. Regardless of the viewing environment or document type, all documents are stored in FLA or XFL (Animate) format. The dis-tinction is that each document type is set up to produce different final published files.

HOW TO CREATE A NEW DOCUMENT

Starting a new document will allow you to build the basic animation that you previewed before.

Here are the steps to accomplish that:

1. Navigate to the Home screen in Animate, the default workspace after startup. You can also access the Home screen by hitting the Home button in the upper left corner of the interface. The Home screen provides presets for various playing contexts and layout sizes.

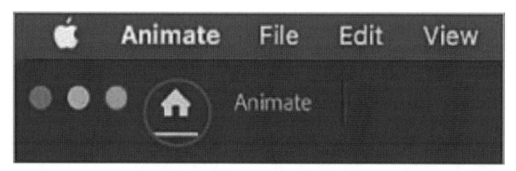

For example, when you pick More Presets and the Full HD option under Character Animation, Animate generates a new ActionScript 3.0 document designed to output video at I 920xl080 resolution. The Square option in the Ads menu generates a new HTML Canvas docu-ment with a size of 250x250 pixels designed for browser playing.

2. Select **More Presets or Create New (File> New).**

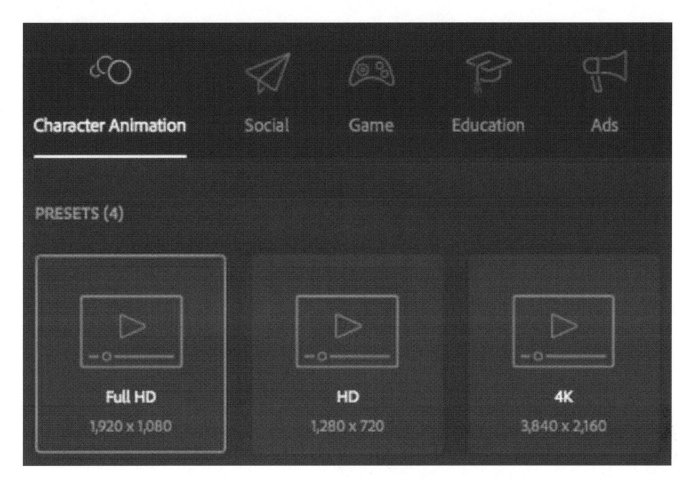

The "New Document" dialog box will be displayed. The top row has six categories of intended usage; choose a category to see the preset size layouts in the middle of the dialog box. You can use the presets as is or adjust their parameters in the Details section on the right side of the dialog box.

3. Select the Advanced category on the right-hand side of your screen.

The platform list is now shown in the middle of the dialog box. You can pick a document type and enter your document's dimensions in the Width and Height boxes.

4. In the Platforms section of the dialog box, choose **ActionScript 3.0**. In the Details section on the right side of the dialog box, add new pixel values for the Stage's Width and Height. Enter 800 for the width and 600for the height. Enter 30 as the frame rate.
5. Select **Create**. Animate generates a new ActionScript 3.0 document with the given Stage dimensions.
6. Select **File > Save**. Create a file named 01 _working copy.fla and choose Animate Document (*.fla) from the File Format/Save as Type option. Although the software program is named Animate, be mindful that the file extension is .fla or. XFL, both of which

are echoes of the name of Animate's progenitor, Flash. Navigate to the O1 Start folder and choose Save.

Saving your file immediately away is a good working habit since it assures that your work is not lost if the program or machine dies. To identify your Animate source file, always save it with the.fla extension (or.xfl if you save it as an Animate Uncompressed Document).

When you save an Animate document as an Animate Uncompressed Document (.xfl), you are saving a collection of files in folders rather than a single document. This exposes the contents of your document to both you and other developers, allowing for easy asset swapping.

UNDERSTANDING THE WORKSPACE

On starting Adobe Animate 2024, you'll be asked whether you're a novice or an experienced user. Your response will affect how the inter-face is set up. Don't be concerned about your decision; you may personalize your workstation to suit your preferences. The Animate Work area has command options at the top of the screen, as well as a range of tools and panels for editing and adding parts to your video. You can use Animate to build all of your animation's objects, or you can import components from Adobe Illustrator, Photoshop, After Effects, or other compatible tools. There are other interface options, but in the Essentials workspace, Animate shows the navigation bar, Timeline panel, Stage, Tools panel, Properties panel, and Edit bar, among other panels. As you work with Animate, you may open, shut, group, un-group, dock, undock, and move panels across the screen to suit your workflow or screen size.

CHOOSING A NEW WORKSPACE

Animate also has a few pre-configured panel layouts ("workspaces") that may better meet the demands of certain users. To move between workspaces or create a new one, use the **Window > Workspaces** submenu or the workspace switcher in the top right of the interface.

Here are the steps:

1. **Access** the workspace switcher and choose a new workspace.

The different panels are reorganized and scaled based on their value in the selected workspace. For example, in the Animator and Designer workspaces, the Timeline panel is located at the top of the work area for quick and simple access.

2. Choose the Essentials workspace.
3. To return to a pre-arranged workspace after rearranging panels, select **Window > Workspaces > Reset [preset name]** and confirm with Yes. Alternatively, from the workspace switcher, choose the reset icon to the right of the workspace name.

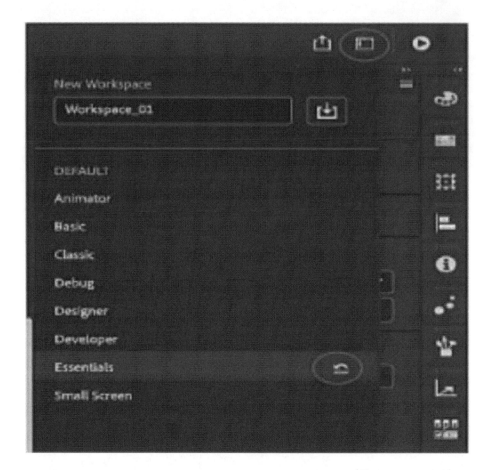

If you specify that you are a new user, the default workspace will be Basic; otherwise, it will be Essential.

HOW TO SAVE YOUR WORKSPACE

If you discover a panel configuration that works well for you, save it as a custom workspace and return to it later.

The steps:

1. In the workspace switcher, choose **New Workspace** and name it.

2. Click the **Save Workspace icon** under the new name. Animate preserves the current panel layout and adds it to the Workspace menu, which may be accessed at any time.

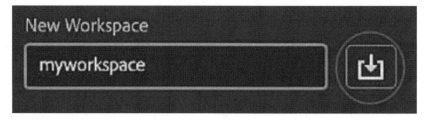

You can store and share your workspace settings, as well as other adjustments, by exporting them as an ANP file. Animate > Settings > Export Preferences will save a file that others may import.

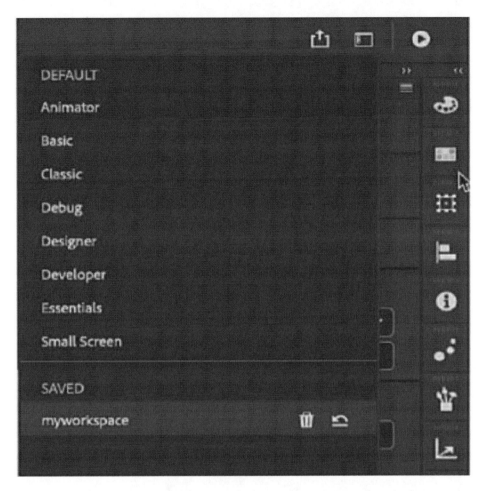

3. The Animate interface defaults to dark gray. However, you can change the interface color to a lighter gray if you want. Select **Animate > Settings> Edit Preferences (macOS) or Edit > Preferences (Windows),** and then change the gray level in the Interface preferences category.

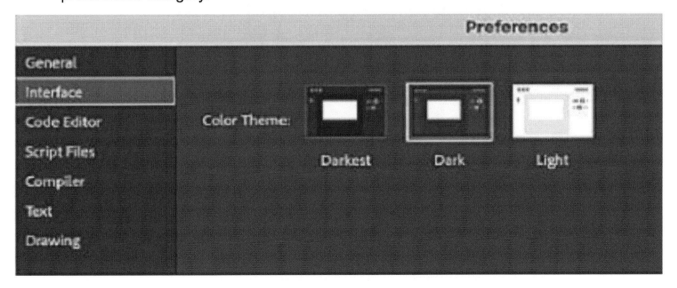

ABOUT THE STAGE

The large white rectangle in the center of your screen is known as the Stage. The Stage in Animate, like a theatrical stage, is the area that spectators see when a movie is playing. It holds the text, graphics, and video that are shown on the screen. You move items on and off the stage to bring them into and out of view. You may use rulers (**View> Rulers) or grids (View > Grid> Show Grid)** to arrange things on the stage. Other positioning tools include guidelines (drawn from the top or side rulers; **View > Guides**) and the Align panel, among others. By default, you'll notice a gray space on the Stage where you may insert components that will not be seen by the audience. The gray area is known as the pasteboard. To view just the Stage, go to **View > Magnification** and choose **Clip to Stage.** For the time being, leave Clip to Stage de selected so that the pasteboard remains visible. You can also click the Clip Content outside the Stage button to crop visual compo-nents that extend beyond the Stage area, allowing you to preview how your audience will see your finished creation.

Select **View > Screen Mode > Full-Screen Mode** to observe the Stage without being distracted by the numerous panels. To switch between panels, use F4, and then return to Standard Screen Mode by pressing **Esc**. To fit the Stage entirely in the application window, choose **View > Magnification > Fit In Window**. You can also choose other magnification view settings from the menu located directly above the stage.

HOW TO CHANGE THE STAGE PROPERTIES

You can adjust the color of the Stage. The Stage color, as well as other document attributes such as Stage size and frame rate, can be found in the attributes panel, which is located vertically to the right of the Stage.

Here are the steps:

1. In the Document Settings area of the Properties panel, notice that the current Stage's dimensions (the Size parameters) are set to 800x600 pixels, as you specified when creating the new document.

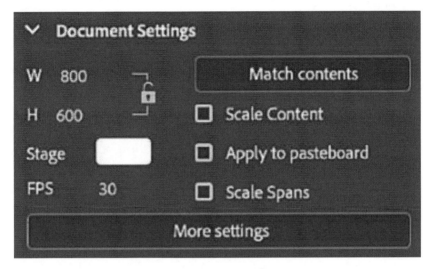

2. In the Properties tab, click the **Background Color box** next to the Stage and choose a new color from the palette. Select **dark grey (#333333)**.

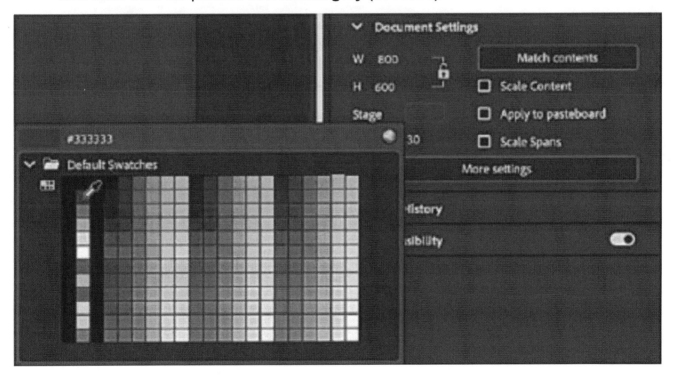

From this moment on, your stage is now another color entirely. You can always opt to change the stage properties whenever you want.

WORKING WITH THE LIBRARY PANEL

The Library panel is accessed via a tab located immediately to the right of the Properties panel. The Library panel shows the contents of your document's library, which is where you store and manage Animate symbols, distorted materials, and imported files such as bitmaps, images, sound files, and specific video clips. Symbols and distorted assets are visuals used in animation.

ABOUT THE LIBRARY PANEL

The Library panel allows you to arrange library objects into folders, see how often an item is used in a document, and filter things by kind. You can also create folders in your Library panel to help you organize your goods. When you import things into Animate, you may place them immediately on the Stage or in the Library. Any objects you import into the Stage, as well as any symbols you develop, are automati-cally added to the library. You can then quickly re-add the objects to the Stage, change them, or see their characteristics. Store assets in the Assets panel **(Window > Assets)** or share them across Adobe applications by selecting the CC Libraries button **(Window > CC Libraries)** and saving them to your Creative Cloud account. To open the Library panel, click **Window > Library** or press **Command+L / Ctrl+L.**

IMPORTING AN ITEM INTO THE LIBRARY PANEL

Animate's drawing capabilities are often used to generate visuals that are then saved as symbols in the library. At other times, you'll Use the Asset Warp tool to build a rig around imported visuals that are also saved in the library. You can also import media, such as JPEG pho-tos or MP3 music files, which are saved in the library. If the Enable menu is not displayed, click the Options button to open it.

Here are the steps to import an item into the library panel:

1. Select **File >Import> Import to Library**. In the Import to Library dialog box, choose the background. pngfile from the 01/ 01 Start folder and click Open. If the picture files appear muted, choose **All Files** (*.*)from the Enable option. Animate imports the chosen PNG image and adds it to the Library panel.
2. Continue to import photos l. jpg, 2.jpg, and 3.jpg from the 01 Start folder. You can also import all photographs at once by holding down the Shift key while selecting several files. The Library panel displays the filenames of all imported photos and a thumbnail preview of each chosen file. These pictures are now ready to use in your Animate document.

ADD AN ITEM FROM THE LIBRARY PANEL TO THE STAGE

To Use an imported picture, drag it from the Library panel to the Stage. You can also choose **File > Import > Import To Stage**, or press **Com-mand+R/Ctrl+R**, to import an image file to the library and then place it on the Stage in one step.

1. If the Library panel is not currently open, choose **Window > Library** to open it.
2. Drag the **background.Png item** onto the Stage and position it about in the middle.

HOW TO UNDERSTAND THE TIMELINE PANEL

In the Essentials workspace, the Timeline panel is positioned underneath the Stage. The Timeline panel includes both playback controls for your animation and the timeline itself, which shows the animation's events in order from left to right. Animate movies, like filmstrips, measure time in frames. As the movie plays, the play head, represented by a blue vertical line, moves through the frames in the timeline.

You can change the information on the Stage to fit various frames. Move the play head to the frame in the timeline that contains the ma-terial you want to show on the Stage at a certain moment. Animate appears at the top of the Timeline panel, indicating the chosen frame number as well as the current frame rate.

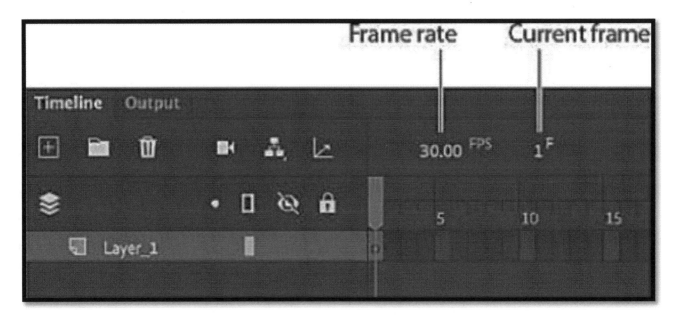

Layers, which help you arrange the artwork in your project, are also shown in the Timeline panel's timeline area. At present, your project just contains one layer, which is named Layer_1. Layers are like many film strips piled on top of each other. Each layer may display a sepa-rate picture on the Stage, and you can create and modify items on one layer without impacting those on another. The layers are layered in the order in which they overlap, such that items on the bottom layer of the timeline appear at the bottom of the stack on the Stage. You can hide, lock, or expose the contents of layers as outlined by clicking the dots or squares in the layer's layer options icon. If you have many layers, select the View Only Active Layer option above the timeline to display only the currently chosen layer.

HOW TO CHANGE THE APPEARANCE OF THE TIMELINE

You can customize the timeline's design to fit your workflow. To show additional layers, choose Short from the Frame View option in the upper-right corner of the Timeline window. The Short option lowers the height of the frame cell rows. The Preview and Preview In Context options show thumbnail copies of your key frames in the timeline.

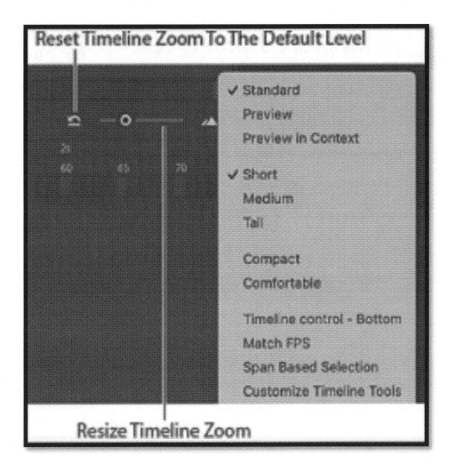

Reset Timeline Zoom To The Default Level

✓ Standard
Preview
Preview in Context

✓ Short
Medium
Tall

Compact
Comfortable

Timeline control - Bottom
Match FPS
Span Based Selection
Customize Timeline Tools

Resize Timeline Zoom

Drag the Resize Timeline Zoom slider to adjust the timeline frame sizes more precisely. The slider controls the size of the frames, allowing you to view more or less of the timeline. To return the timeline view to normal size, click the Reset Timeline Zoom to the Default Level button. To easily access various animation settings on your timeline, click the options menu in the timeline's corner and choose Custom-ize Timeline Tools. The Customize Timeline menu displays all of the various tools that can be shown or hidden. The highlighted icons are those that are normally shown at the top of the timeline.

Click to add or delete a tool. Click the **Reset Timeline Controls button** to restore the timeline to its original state.

RENAMING A LAYER

It is overly important to break your information into layers and label each layer to describe its contents so you can simply locate the one you need later.

Here's how to rename a layer in Adobe Animate 2024:

1. To rename an existing layer, double-click its name, Layer_1, and type background.
2. Click outside the name box to use the new name.

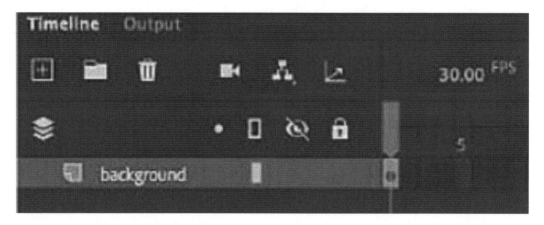

3. To lock the layer, click just below the lock symbol. Locking a layer stops you from mistakenly moving or changing any- thing within it.

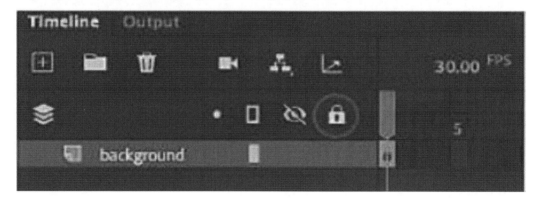

A lock symbol appears in the layer. The lock symbol shows that you cannot change the layer since it is locked.

HOW TO ADD A LAYER

A new Animate document only has one layer, but you may add as many as you like. Unless you use the Layer Depth panel to modify the layer depth, items in the upper levels will overlap things in the lower ones.

The steps:

1. Select the background layer from the timeline.

2. Select **Insert > Timeline >Layer**. You can also use the New Layer button above the timeline. Anew layer emerges over the background layer.

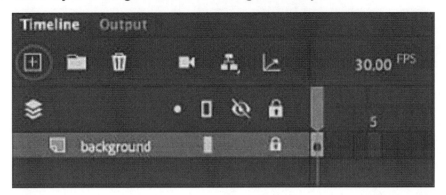

3. Double-click the new layer to rename it, then type photo1. Click outside the name box to use the new name. Your timeline now has two tiers. The background layer holds the background picture, but the newly formed photo1 layer above it is empty.
4. Select the top layer, photo1.
5. If the Library panel is not currently open, choose **Window > Library** to open it.
6. Drag the library item photo1.jpgfrom the library to the stage.

As you add additional layers and your overlapping visuals get more complex, click the dot underneath the eye symbol in any layer to conceal its contents. Alternatively, hold down the Shift key and click the dot below the eye symbol to make the layer partly transparent, allowing you to see what's behind it. Hiding or making a layer translucent changes just how you view your project in Animate, not the final exported file. To change the amount of transparency, double-click the Layer icon in the Layer Properties dialog box. The photo1 pic-ture emerges on the stage, overlapping the background image.

7. Add a third layer by selecting **Insert > Timeline > Layer** or clicking the New Layer icon above the timeline.
8. Rename the third layer, photo 2.

WORKING WITH LAYERS

If you don't want a layer, just pick it and click the Delete button above the timeline.

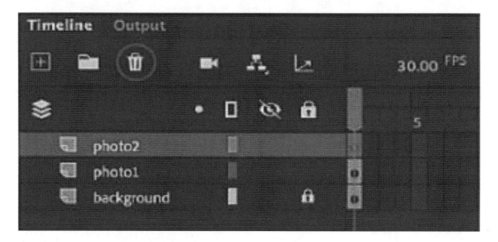

To reorganize your layers and modify the way your graphics overlap, just drag any layer up or down to a new place in the layer stack.

HOW TO INSERT FRAMES

At this point, you have a background picture and another overlaying photo on the Stage, but the whole animation lasts just one frame or a fraction of a second. You must add more frames to the timeline to extend the length of this animation.

Here are the steps:

1. Select **frame 48** from the background layer. Use the Resize Timeline View slider in the upper-right corner of the Timeline panel to enlarge the timeline frames and make frame 48 easier to find.

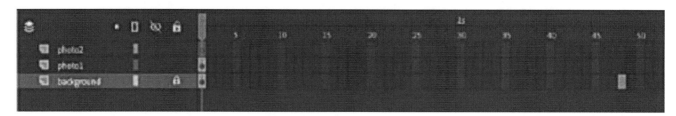

2. Select **Insert > Timeline > Frame** (FS). You can also pick Frame from the menu above the timeline (if the Frames Group option is selected in Customize Timeline Tools), or right-click frame 48 and choose Insert Frame from the context menu that opens. Animate adds frames to the background layer up to the specified frame, frame 48.

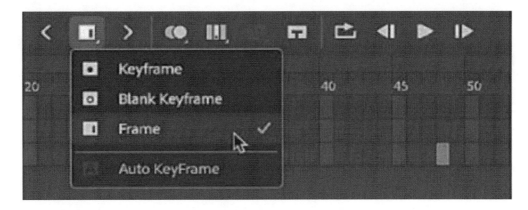

3. Select frame 48 from the photo 1 layer.
4. Choose **Insert > Timeline > Frame** (FS), Insert Frame above the timeline, or right-click and choose Insert Frame to add frames in the photo 1 layer up to frame 48.
5. Select frame 48 on the photo2 layer and add frames to it.

You now have three layers, each with 48 frames in the timeline. Because your Animate document has a framerate of 24 frames per second, your current animation is 2 seconds long.

HOW TO SELECT MULTIPLE FRAMES

Holding down the Shift key allows you to pick several files on your desktop, as well as many frames on the Animate timeline. If you have numerous layers and wish to put frames into each of them, choose a frame in the first layer and then Shift-click the same frame in the final layer to select all the frames in the layers in between or drag to select multiple layers. Then, choose **Insert > Timeline > Frame.**

CREATING A KEYFRAME

A keyframe represent s a change in material on the Stage. Keyframes are shown on the timeline by a circle. An empty circle indicates that there is nothing in that specific stratum at that moment. A filled-in black circle indicates that there was anything in that layer at the time. The background layer, for example, has a filled keyframe (black circle) in the first frame. In addition, the photo1 layer's first frame has a filled keyframe. Both levels include photos. In contrast, the photo2 layer includes an empty keyframe in the first frame, suggesting that it is presently empty.

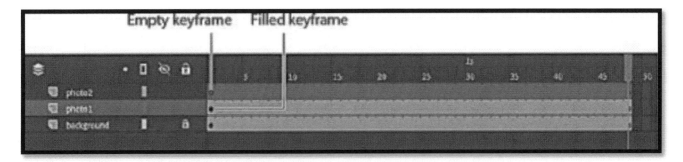

UNDERSTANDING AUTO-KEYFRAME MODE

There are two options for making keyframes. The Auto Keyframe option located above your timeline may be activated or disabled.

If it is enabled (the keyframe icon is a letter "A"), adding or changing material on the Stage generates a new keyframe at that moment. If it is disabled, you must construct keyframes manually. In the subsequent task, you'll add a keyframe to the photo2 layer at the moment you want the next picture to appear. To enable or disable Auto Keyframe, go to the Customize Timeline Tools option in the upper-right corner of the timeline. To add and activate the Auto Keyframe icon in your Timeline controls, pick it; to remove and disable it, deselect it.

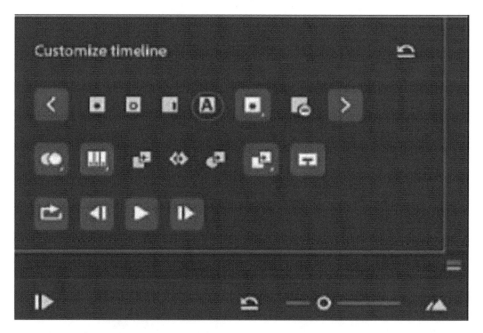

Here, the Auto Keyframe option is disabled (unless otherwise indicated), and the Frames Group above your timeline is created using the Customize Timeline Tools option in the upper-right corner of your timeline.

1. Ensure the Auto Keyframe option is turned off. Select frame 24 from the photo2 layer. The frame number of a chosen frame appears above the timeline's left end.

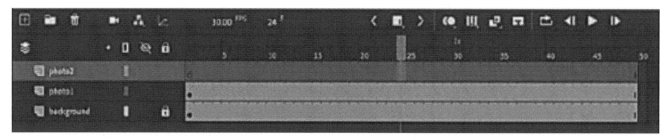

2. Select **Insert Keyframe** from the menu above the timeline, or **Insert > Timeline > Keyframe** (F6). In frame 24, a new keyframe arrives in the photo2 layer, represented by an empty circle.

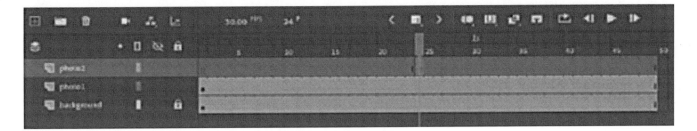

3. Drag photo 2.jpg from your collection to the stage.

In frame 24, the empty circle fills up, indicating that the photo2 layer now has material. When your animation runs, your picture will display on the Stage in frame 24. Drag the blue play head along the top of the timeline to "scrub," or display what's occurring on the Stage, at any point in time. You'll see that the background picture and photo1 stay n the Stage throughout the timeframe, while photo2 only shows in frame 24.

Understanding frames and keyframes is vital for learning Animate. Make sure you understand how the photo 2 layer has 48 frames and two keyframes: an empty keyframe at frame 1 and a filled keyframe at frame 24.

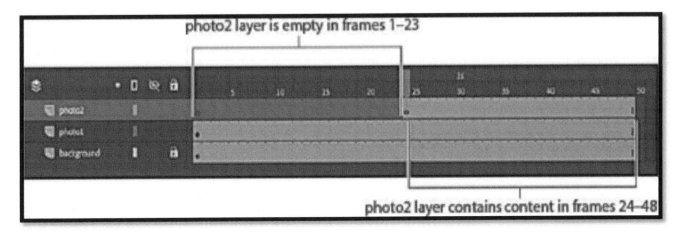

HOW TO MOVE A KEYFRAME

If you want photo2.jpg to appear later or earlier, you must change the keyframe such that it appears closer to or further from the right on the timeline. You can easily shift any keyframe by dragging it to a different location.

Here are the steps:

1. Select the keyframe in frame 24 of the photo2layer.
2. Drag the keyframe to frame 12 of the photo2 layer. As you drag, a box symbol will appear beneath your mouse to indicate that you are relocating the keyframe.

The photo2.jpg file is now visible on the stage considerably earlier in the animation.

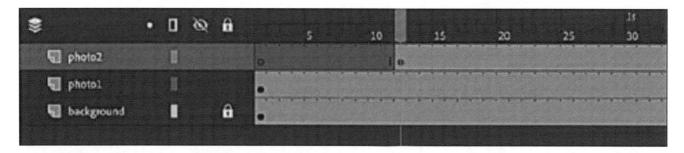

HOW TO REMOVE A KEYFRAME

If you wish to erase a keyframe, do not use the **Delete/ Backspace keys.** This will eliminate just the contents of that keyframe from the Stage, leaving you with an empty keyframe. In its place, select the keyframe and then **Modify > Timeline > Clear Keyframe** (Shift +F6). Your keyframe (with its contents) will be erased from the timeline.

ORGANIZING LAYERS INSIDE A TIMELINE

At this time, your working Animate file consists of simply three layers: a background layer, a photo1 layer, and a photo2 layer. You will be adding additional levels to this project, and as with most other projects, you will need to handle many layers. Layer folders, like folders for similar documents on your desktop, let you organize and control your timeline by grouping relevant layers. Although creating the folders may take some time, you will save time in the long run since you will know precisely where to search for a certain layer.

CREATING LAYER FOLDERS

For this project, you will continue to build layers for more photos and save them in a layer folder.

The steps:

1. Select the photo2 layer and then click the **New Layer icon** above the timeline.
2. Name the layer **"photo 3."**
3. Add a keyframe at frame 24.
4. Drag photo3.jpg from the library to the stage. You've now got four layers. The top three photographs are sights from Coney Island that occur at various keyframes.

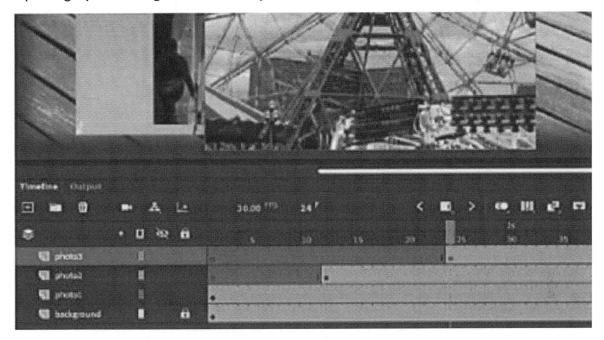

5. Select the photo3 layer and then click the New Folder button at the top of the Timeline panel. Anew layer folder emerges above the photo 3 layer.

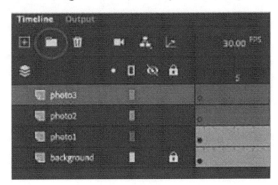

6. Name the folder **photos.**

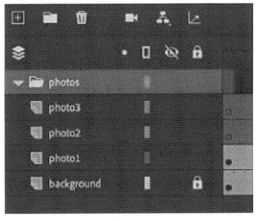

53

ADDING LAYERS INTO LAYER FOLDERS

Proceed to add the picture layers to the photos folder. When arranging layers, keep in mind that Animate shows the information in the layers in the order that it appears in the timeline, with the top layer's content at the front and the bottom layer's content at the back.

Here are the steps:

1. Drag or reposition the photo1 layer to the photos folder. Be sure to check how the bold line shows your layer's destination. When you put a layer within a folder, Animate indents its name.

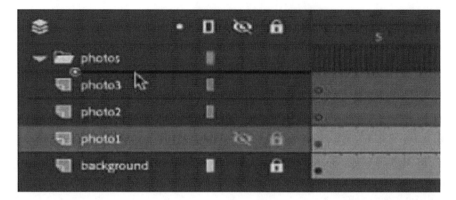

2. Drag layers photo2 and photo3 into the photographs folder. All three picture layers should be in the images folder, stacked in the same order as they were outside.

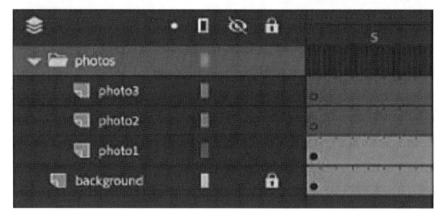

To collapse the folder, click the arrow immediately to the left of the folder name. To expand the folder, click the arrow again. Be cautious that deleting a layer folder also deletes all of the layers contained inside it.

LAYER HIGHLIGHTING

When working on a project, it might be good to highlight certain levels to emphasize that something significant is included inside them.

1. Click the dot in the layer underneath the Highlight Layers indication.

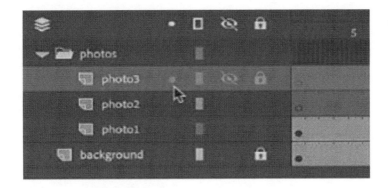

2. The chosen layer is highlighted in a color that matches the color used for outlines and bounding boxes in the Show Layers as Outlines option.

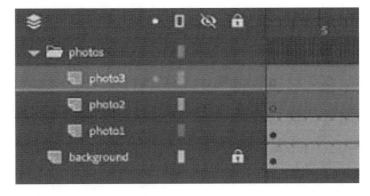

3. To remove the highlight, just click the dot in the layer again. You won 't need to highlight it for the remainder of this challenge.

CUT, COPY, PASTE, AND DUPLICATE LAYERS

Cut, copy, paste, and duplicate layer commands can help you manage many layers and layer folders more easily and efficiently. The entire chosen layer's characteristics are copied and pasted, including its frames, keyframes, animations, and even the layer name and type. You may also copy and paste layer folders and their contents. To cut or copy a layer or layer folder, just pick it, right-click its name, and choose **Cut Layers or Copy Layers.**

Right-click the timeline once more and choose Paste Layers. The layer(s) that you cut or copied are inserted into the timeline. Use Duplicate Layers to copy and paste in a single action. The application's navigation bar also allows you to cut, copy, paste, and duplicate layers. Select Edit> Timeline, and then Cut, Copy, Paste, or Duplicate Layers.

USING THE PROPERTIES PANEL

The Properties tab provides rapid access to the properties that you will most likely need to change as you build your animation. What is displayed in the Properties window is determined by the options you select. For example, if nothing is chosen, the Properties panel dis- plays typical Animate document choices, such as altering the Stage color or size. If you choose an item on the Stage, the Proper ties panel displays its x and y coordinates, width, and height, among other details. If you pick a frame or keyframe on the timeline, as shown in the image below, the Properties panel displays information about that keyframe, such as its name and whether it includes sound. Different qualities are organized into parts that may be compacted or enlarged.

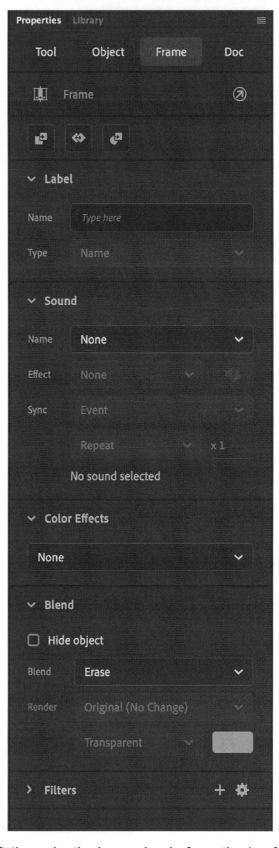

The Properties tab also allows you to quickly shift the selection's emphasis from the keyframe to items on the Stage. For example, clicking the Object tab at the top of the Properties panel changes the view from the keyframe's properties to the characteristics of the chosen object on the Stage in that keyframe.

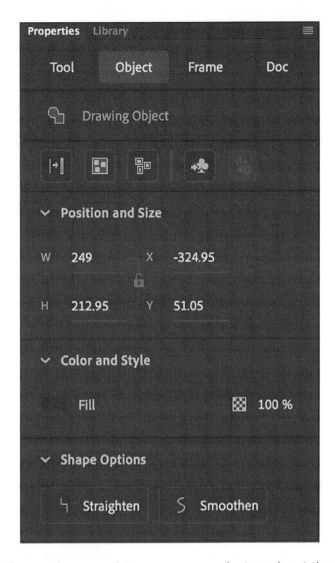

You can opt to Use the Properties panel to move your photos about the Stage.

HOW TO POSITION AN OBJECT ON THE STAGE

To begin, use the Properties panel to relocate the photographs. You will also Use the Transform panel to rotate the images. Note that if the Properties window is not visible, click **Window > Properties** or press **Command+F3/Ctrl+F3.**

1. Move the play head to frame 1 of the timeline and select the photol.jpg picture you put into the Stage's photo1 layer. An extremely thin blue outline shows that the item has been picked.
2. In the Properties window, enter 50for the X and Y values. To apply the settings, press Return on macOS or Enter on Win-dows. Drag over the X and Y numbers to alter them. The photo goes to the left side of the stage.

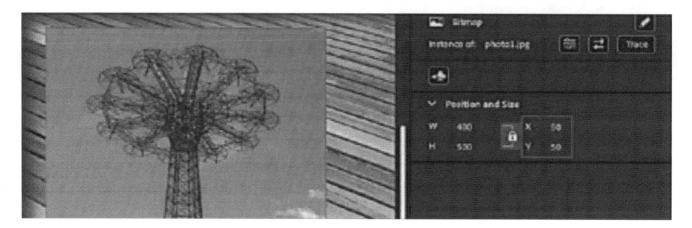

The X and Y values are measured on the Stage starting from the upper-left corner. X starts at zero and grows to the right, whereas Y starts at zero and increases downward. The registration point (from which Animate takes measurements) for imported photographs is in the upper-left corner.

3. To access the Transform panel, choose **Window > Transform**. The Trans form panel may also be accessed via the Proper- ties panel's icon column on the side.
4. In the Transform panel, choose Rotate and enter-12 into the Rotate box, or drag the number to modify the rotation. To apply the value, press **Return or Enter**. The chosen picture on the stage rotates 12 degrees counterclockwise.

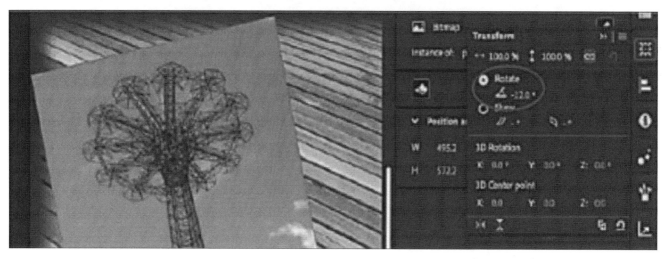

5. Select frame 12 from the photo2 layer. Click photo2.jpg on the Stage to pick it.
6. Use the Properties and Transform panels to place and rotate the second image intriguingly. To give it some contrast with the previous shot, set X=200, Y=40, and Rotate to 6.

7. Select frame 24 from the photo3 layer. Click photo3.jpg on the Stage to pick it.
8. Use the Properties and Transform panels to place and rotate the third picture uniquely. To ensure that all of your photo- graphs have visual variation, set X=36 0, Y=65, and Rotate to -2.

When pictures are resized or rotated in Animate, they might seem ragged. You can use the Bitmap Properties dialog box to smooth out each picture. To open the dialog box, double-click the bitmap icon or picture thumbnail in the Library panel, and then choose Allow Smoothing.

WORKING WITH PANELS

Almost everything you do with Animate includes a panel. Here, you'll Use the Library, Tools, Properties, Transform, History, and Timeline panels. Since panels are such an important aspect of the Animate workplace, it helps to understand how to handle them. To open a panel in Animate, choose its name from the window menu. Individual panels float freely and may be arranged in docks, groups, or stacks.

- A dock consists of panels or groups arranged vertically. Docks are attached to the left or right edges of the user interface.
- A group consists of panels that can either be docked or float freely.
- Stacks, similar to docks, can be put anywhere in the interface.

The Essentials workspace's panels are divided into three docks on the right side of the screen. The Timeline and Output panels are clus-tered at the bottom, with the Stage at the top. However, you can relocate a panel to any location that is convenient for you.

- To relocate a panel, drag its tab to a new spot.
- To relocate a panel group or stack, drag it by the tabs.

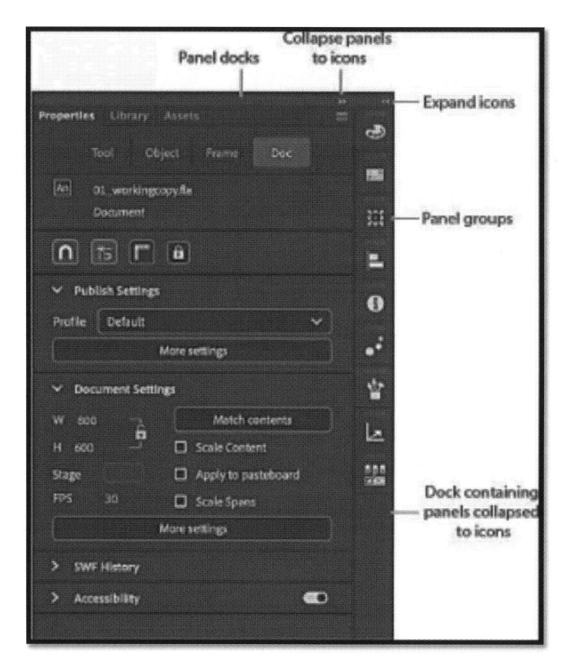

As the panel, group, or stack moves over other panels, groups, docks, or stacks, a blue highlighted drop zone appears. When you remove the mouse button while a drop zone is visible, the panel is added to the group, dock, or stack.

- To dock a panel, move its tab to the left or right side of the screen. If you slide it over the top or bottom of an existing dock, a hor-izontal drop zone will show you the panel's new placement. If a vertical drop zone occurs, lowering the panel will form a new dock.
- To group a panel, drag its tab onto the tab of another panel or the drop zone at the top of an existing group.
- To construct a stack, move a group off of a dock or an existing stack so that it floats freely. Alternatively, slide one free-floating panel onto the tab of another free-floating panel.

You also have the option of showing most of the panels as icons to conserve space but still keep rapid access. Click the t wo arrowheads in the upper-right corner of a dock or stack to collapse the panels into icons. Click the two arrowheads again to expand the icons into panels.

USING THE TOOLS PANEL

The Tools panel- the long, thin panel on the far-left side of the Essentials work area- contains selection tools, drawing and type tools, painting and editing tools, navigation tools, and tool choices. You'll Use the Tools panel often to switch between tools suitable for the work at hand. Most typically you'll use the Selection tool, which is the black arrow tool at the top of the Tools panel, for choosing and clicking anything on the Stage or the timeline.

SELECTING AND USING A TOOL

When you choose a tool, the choices accessible at the bottom of the Tools panel and the Properties panel change. For example, when you choose the Rectangle tool, the Object Drawing Mode option shows. When you pick the Zoom tool, the Enlarge and Reduce options display. The Tools panel has too many tools to show all at once. Some tools are grouped in hidden groups in the Tools panel; only the tool you last picked from a group is visible. A little triangle in the lower-right corner of the tool's button shows that there are additional tools in the group. Press and hold the symbol for the visible tool to view the other available tools, and then choose one from the menu.

TEARING OFF TOOLS

Many lesser-used tools are accessible, but they are kept away and you need to add them to your Tools panel to access them. You may tailor the Tools panel to show just the tools you need or the ones you use most frequently. You may also organize the tools to your preference.

Here are the steps:

1. Click the **Edit Toolbar option** at the bottom of the Tools panel.

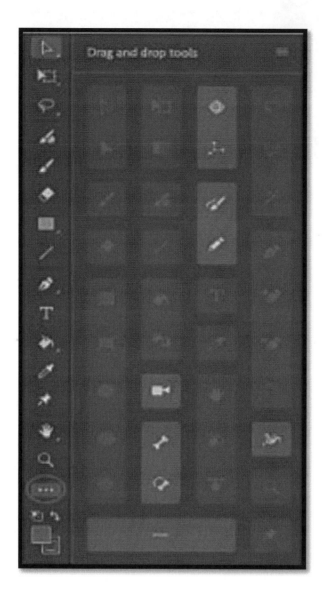

You cannot pick a tool for usage from the Drag and Drop Tools menu. You must add the tool to the Toolbar for it to become accessible for usage.

2. Additional tools are shown in an adjacent Drag and Drop Tools window. Drag the tools that you want into the Tools panel. You can add spacers (horizontal separators) to construct groupings of tools, which can be ripped off from the main Tools panel to form a floating panel.

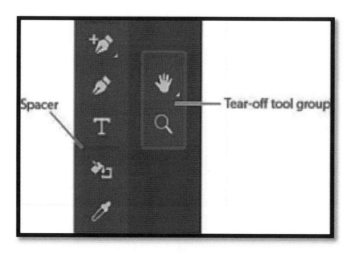

If you're working with a smaller monitor, the bottom of the Tools panel may be cut off. That renders some of the tools and buttons invisi-ble. But there's a simple method to address the problem: slide the right border of the Tools panel to broaden it so that it can display numer-ous columns of tools.

3. Choose the choices from the upper-right corner to return the Toolbar to its default workspace setup, pick a new size icon for the tools, or cancel the Drag and Drop Tools menu.

HOW TO ADD LAYER EFFECTS

You can use various visual effects to modify the look of things in a certain layer. These layer effects include color effects and filters, which can be found in the Properties window when a keyframe is chosen.

Brightness, Tin t, and Alpha are all settings under the Style menu in the Color Effect s area.

- Brightness determines the layer's relative darkness or brightness.
- Tint determines the amount of color given to a layer.
- Alpha regulates the layer's transparency.
- Advanced lets you adjust brightness, hue, and alpha all at once.

Filters are special effects that alter or distort an image in more dramatic ways, such as adding a drop shadow or blur.

ADDING LAYER EFFECTS TO KEYFRAMES

Layer effects are keyframe-based. That is, a single layer might have several layer effects at different keyframes. You'll apply a filter and a color effect to various keyframes in your layers to provide depth to the slideshow and make new photos stand out as they're introduced.

Here are the steps:

1. To pick frame 12 in both the photo1 and background layers, move the play head to frame 12 on the timeline and press Shift while clicking. Frame 12 is where picture 2 appears in the slideshow.

2. Select the Insert Keyframe button above the timeline (F6). Both layers include a keyframe in frame 12.

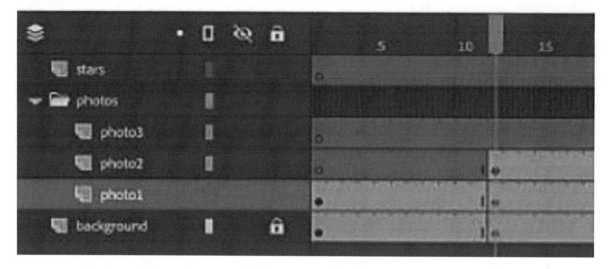

3. To apply a blur filter to two keyframes, select them and click the Add Filter button in the Properties box. Choose Blur.

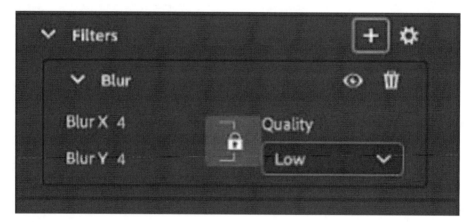

4. Increase the Blur X and Blur Y settings to 8 pixels. The background and first photos grow fuzzy, highlighting the new picture that emerges in the photo2 layer. The keyframes on your timeline turn white, indicating that a layered effect has been applied.

5. Select frame 24 on the photo2 layer, where photo3 appears.
6. Select Insert Keyframe from above the timeline(F6). This keyframe enables you to apply a filter to the layer, modifying its look at that moment in time.

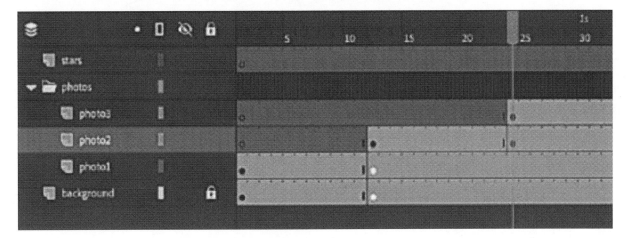

7. In the Properties panel, click **Add Filter** and choose **Blur.** Increase the Blur X and Blur Y to 8 pixels. The picture in the sec-ond layer blurs, allowing your viewers to concentrate on the new image in the third layer.

8. Insert a keyframe (F6) at frame 36of the photo 1, photo 2, photo 3, and background layers.

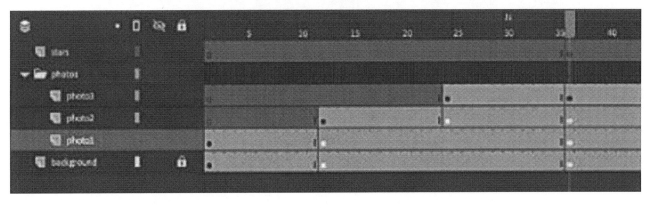

9. In the Color Effects section of the Properties panel, choose Brightness from the Style menu and set it to -30%. The chosen layers darken somewhat, adding drama to the brilliant yellow stars in the stars layer.

UNDOING STEPS IN ADOBE ANIMATE

In an ideal world, everything would proceed as planned. However, there are instances when you need to back up a step or two and restart.

Animate allows you to undo steps using the Undo command or the History panel. To undo a single step in Animate, click **Edit > Undo** or hit **Command +Z/Ctrl+Z.** To redo an undone step, choose **Edit> Redo.** To undo several steps in Animate, Use the History panel, which shows a record of the previous 100 steps you've taken. Closing a document removes its history. To open the History panel, choose **Window > History**. For example, if you are dissatisfied with the newly added stars, you may reverse your changes and reset your Animate docu-ment to its prior configuration.

1. Select **Edit > Undo** to undo your previous action. You can use the Undo command many times to go back as many steps as are indicated in the History window. To modify the maximum amount of Undo commands, choose **Animate > Settings (macOS) or Edit > Preferences (Windows)**. If you remove steps from the History panel and subsequently conduct new steps, the deleted steps will no longer be visible.
2. Select **Window > History** to see the History panel.
3. Move the slider in the History window to the previous step where you made the error. Steps below that point are muted in the History panel and deleted from the project. To add a step back, slide the slider back down.

4. Return the History panel slider to its original position, adjacent to the bottom step.

PREVIEWING AND EXPORTING YOUR MOVIE

When working on a project, it's a good idea to preview it periodically to verify that you're getting the right results.

HOW TO TEST YOUR MOVIE

To quickly see your animation, choose **Control > Play** or just hit the **Return/ Enter key.**

To preview how an animation or movie will seem to a spectator, click the **Test Movie button** in the upper-right corner of the Animate workspace, or choose **Control > Test**. You can also use **Command+Return/Ctrl+Enter** to preview your video.

The steps:

1. Select **Control > Test** or the Test Movie button from the upper-right comer of the Animate workspace. Animate displays the animation in a new panel. Animate loops your movie in this preview mode.

2. Close the **Test Movie panel.**

USE QUICK SHARE AND PUBLISH

When you're finished with your product, you can quickly and simply export and share it on your preferred social networking channels. Adobe offers a seamless workflow from Animate to X (formerly Twitter), YouTube, video, and animated GIF.

The steps:

1. Select **Social Share** from the Quick Share and Publish menu in Animate's upper-right corner.
2. Select your target platform. Here, we'll look at how Quick Share works with X, often known as Twitter and identified by its bird emblem in the user interface.

3. The preview pane shows the first frame of your project as it would look on X. Include a description. You can retain, change, or delete the recommended hashtags. The number above the description represents the number of characters remaining in your post.

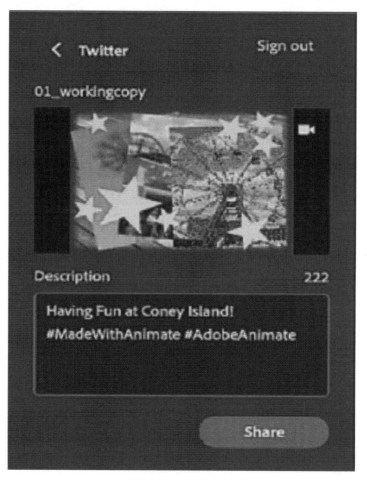

4. Click **Share.**
5. Adobe Media Encoder launches immediately and converts your project to the appropriate media format. If you are not logged in to X, Animate will request permission to access X to upload your exported animation. You will be requested to sign in using your handle and password. Keep a watch on the Quick Share and Publish choices, as Adobe will continue to introduce more social media outlets. Once allowed, you may publish straight from Animate.

6. Go to X to see your post and associated animation.

MODIFYING THE CONTENT AND STAGE

When you initially began this course, you generated a new file with the Stage set to 800x600 pixels. However, your customer may sub-sequently inform you that they want the animation in a variety of sizes to fit various layouts. For example, they want to make a smaller version with a different aspect ratio for a banner ad. Alternatively, they may wish to design a version that runs on AIR for Android devices with certain dimensions. Fortunately, you can change the Stage even after all of your material is in place. When you modify the size of the Stage, Animate automatically shrinks or enlarges all of your material following the new dimensions.

RESIZE THE STAGE AND SCALE THE CONTENT

You will develop a new version of this animation project with changed Stage dimensions. To save your progress, choose **File > Save**.

Here are the steps:

1. In the Properties panel's Document Settings, the current Stage's dimensions are set to 800x600 pixels. The Document Set- tings dialog box may be opened by clicking the **More Settings button.**

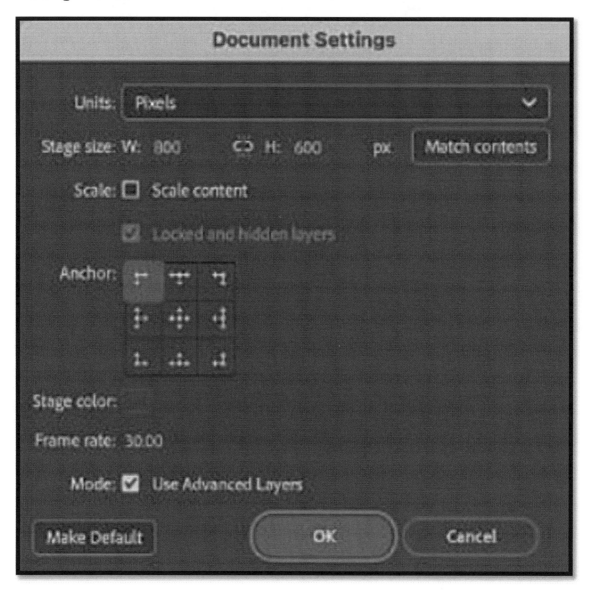

2. Enter new pixel dimensions into the Width and Height boxes. Enter 400 for the width and 300for the height. To confine the Stage's proportions, click the link symbol between the Width and Height boxes. With the connection icon chosen, al-tering one dimension changes the other correspondingly.

3. Choose the **Scale Content** option. Leave the Anchor option as is. If the new Stage's proportions change, you can use the Anchor option to specify the origin from which your content is scaled.

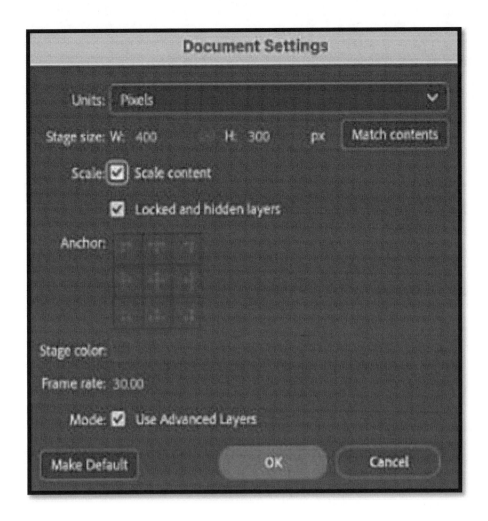

4. Click "OK."

Animate changes the dimensions of the Stage and automatically resizes all of the content. If your new dimensions are not proportionate to the original size, Animate will adjust everything to ensure that the content fits. This implies that if your new Stage size is larger than the previous there will be more Stage space on the right. If your new Stage size is higher than the previous, there will be more Stage space at the bottom.

1. Select **File > Save as.**
2. In the Save dialog box, choose Animate Document (*.fla) from the File Format selection. Name the file 10 _workingcopy_re- sized.fla. Save the file.

You now have two Animate files with similar content but differing Stage dimensions.

HOW TO SAVE YOUR MOVIE

"Save early, save often" is a multimedia production slogan. Applications, operating systems, and hardware fail more often than anybody wishes, especially at inconvenient and unexpected times. You should constantly save your video at regular intervals so that if it crashes, you don't lose too much time. If you have unsaved changes in an open document, Animate will put an asterisk at the end of the filename at the top of the document window as a polite reminder. Anime can also help ease most of the stress associated with missing work. The Auto- Recovery function produces a backup file in the event of a crash.

USING AUTO-RECOVERY TO MAKE BACKUPS

The Auto-Recovery functionality is a preference option that affects all Animate documents. It creates a backup file in case of a crash, giving you an alternative file to return to.

Follow the steps below:

1. Select **Animate > Settings > Edit** Preferences (macOS) or **Edit > Preferences** (Windows).
2. Select the General category in the left column.
3. Enable Auto-Recovery and choose a time interval (in minutes) for Animate to produce backup files.

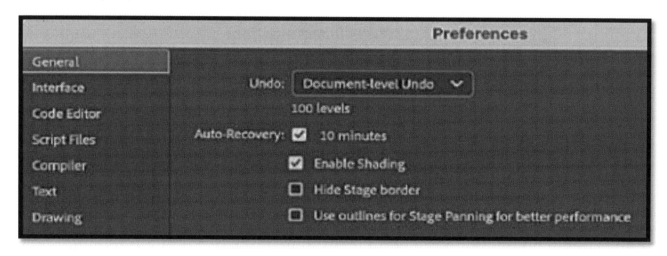

4. Click" **OK."**

If you make modifications to your file but do not save them during the Auto-Recovery time, Animate produces a new file in the same directory as your FLA, with RECOVER_ at the beginning of the filename. The file persists as long as the document is open. When you dis- miss the document or exit Animate safely, the file is destroyed.

FREQUENTLY ASKED QUESTIONS

1. How do you download and install the new Adobe Animate 2024?
2. How do you launch and open a file?
3. How do you choose and save a new workspace?
4. How do you work with the library panel?
5. How do you import an item into the library panel?
6. How do you change the stage properties?
7. How do you work with keyframes?
8. How do you organize layers inside a timeline?
9. How do you work with panels?
10. How do you add layer effects to your projects?

CHAPTER 4: MASTERING CLASSIC TWEENS

OVERVIEW

In chapter two, you will learn how to animate symbols with classic tweens in Adobe Animate 2024. Also, you will understand what ani-mation is all about, how to import Photoshop assets, how to animate scale, how to add a 3D title, and so much more. Let's get started then.

GETTING STARTED

Using a sample and exercise file

The steps:

1. To play the final animation, which has been exported as a high-definition video file, double-click on the 03End.mp4 file located in the 03/03End folder.

The project entails the creation of an animated opener that can be seamlessly integrated into a website, serving as an introduction to a fictitious motion picture that is yet to be released. Within this instructional module, you will be employing motion tweens to effectively animate various elements present on the webpage. These elements include the background, the bandits, the primary male character, the secondary female character, and the revolver that gracefully slides across the entirety of the page.

2. Proceed with closing the 03End.mp4 file.
3. In Adobe Animate, navigate to the **File menu** and select **New**. The New Document dialog box is displayed.
4. Select the first category, which is Character Animation. In the details section located on the right-hand side, input the value of 1800for Width and 1024 for Height. It is recommended to maintain the Frame Rate at 30.00 and select the Plat- form Type as ActionScript 3.0. Click on the **"Create"** button. The user will Use the complete range of animation capabili-ties offered by an ActionScript 3.0 document, followed by exporting the resulting content as an MP4 video file.

5. To ensure optimal visibility, select the **"Fit In Window"** option from the view options located above the Stage. Alterna-tively, you can navigate to the **"View"** menu and choose **"Magnification"** followed by **"Fit In Window"**. This will allow you to comfortably view the entirety of the Stage on your computer screen.

6. Select the "File" option from the menu and then choose "Save As". Assign the file the name "03_workingcopy.fla" and proceed to save it in the designated folder named "03Start". Creating a backup copy guarantees the preservation of the ini-tial source file, allowing for a fresh start if desired.

UNDERSTANDING ANIMATION

Animation refers to the process of altering the visual characteristics of an object sequentially, resulting in a transformation of its appearance over a specific period. Animation can be described as the process of creating the illusion of motion by manipulating objects on the Stage. A basic example of animation involves moving a ball from one position to another, thereby changing its position. Furthermore, it has the potential to become significantly more intricate. As demonstrated in this lesson, it is possible to animate various properties of an object. Furthermore, apart from altering an object's position, it is possible to modify its color or transparency, adjust its size or rota-tion, and even animate the filters demonstrated in the preceding lesson. Additionally, you possess the ability to manipulate an object's trajectory and its easing, which refers to how an object alters its properties by either accelerating or decelerating. The use of classic tweens allows for the creation of animation to depict changes in various aspects, including position, rotation, size, color or transparency, and fil-ters. To create classic tweens, it is necessary to Use a symbol instance. If the object you have chosen is not a symbol instance, Animate will promptly prompt you to convert the selection into a symbol.

When working in Animate, the fundamental workflow for animation using classic tweens is as follows: Commence by placing a symbol instance on the Stage. Initiate the creation of an initial keyframe and a concluding keyframe on the timeline, subsequently modifying the properties of the symbol instance within one of these keyframes. Choose one of the frames located between the initial and final keyframes, and then proceed to select the option to Create Classic Tween. The Animate function handles the remaining tasks by seam-lessly interpolating the modifications between the two temporal points. There exist only two fundamental rules that must be adhered to. There are two important rules to consider. Firstly, each layer can only have one tween. Secondly, no element other than the symbol in- stance should be present on that layer.

IMPORTING ADOBE PHOTOSHOP ASSETS

Occasionally, it may be necessary to generate graphics directly within Animate, as demonstrated in the preceding lesson. On certain occa-sions, graphics may be generated using software applications like Adobe Photoshop or Illustrator. Alternatively, graphics may be supplied to be incorporated into an animation. There is no need to be concerned. Animate offers a streamlined procedure for importing graphic as- sets, offering a wide range of choices to maintain layers, transparencies, and other essential data.

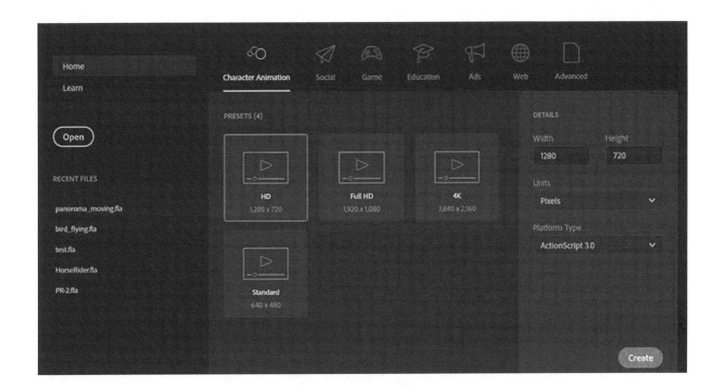

IMPORTING ADOBE PHOTO SHOP LAYERS

Within the 03Start folder, there is a Photoshop file titled 03_assets.psd. This file encompasses all the necessary images required for the animation here.

Follow the steps below:

1. Within the Animate software, navigate to the File menu and select the **Import option**. From the dropdown menu, choose the Import To Stage option. Alternatively, you can use the keyboard shortcut **Command+R (Mac)** or **Ctrl+R (Windows)** to achieve the same result.
2. Select the file named **"03_assets.psd"**located in the **"0.3Start"** folder. Click on the **"Open"** button. The Import To Stage dialog box is displayed. Within the interface, Animate conveniently displays previews of individual layers from the Pho-toshop file on the left-hand side. Import options for each individually selected layer can be set on the right side. Within the Animate software, there is an option available to determine the arrangement of Photoshop layers. This option can be found at the bottom of the interface.

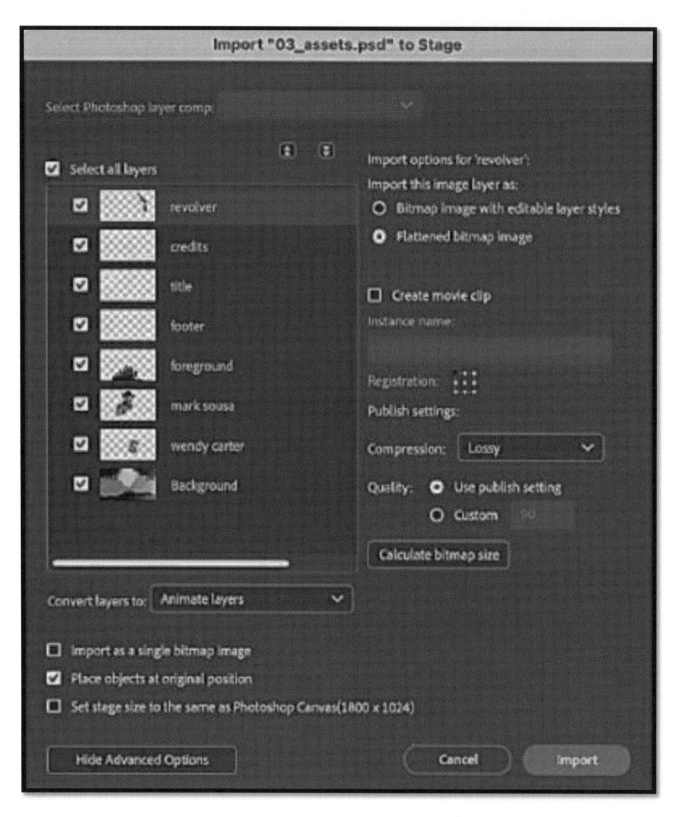

Import "03_assets.psd" to Stage

Select Photoshop layer comp:

☑ Select all layers

☑ revolver

☑ credits

☑ title

☑ footer

☑ foreground

☑ mark sousa

☑ wendy carter

☑ Background

Import options for 'revolver':
Import this image layer as:
○ Bitmap image with editable layer styles
◉ Flattened bitmap image

☐ Create movie clip
Instance name:

Registration: ⦙⦙⦙
Publish settings:

Compression: Lossy ▾

Quality: ◉ Use publish setting
○ Custom

Calculate bitmap size

Convert layers to: Animate layers ▾

☐ Import as a single bitmap image
☑ Place objects at original position
☐ Set stage size to the same as Photoshop Canvas(1800 x 1024)

Hide Advanced Options   Cancel   Import

3. To apply the same action to multiple layers, hold down the Shift key and select all the desired layers. Then, choose the option **"Bitmap Image with Editable Layer Styles"** from the available options. This particular option effectively maintains transparency within the layers. The lowermost layer lacks transparency, thus enabling you to import it as a consolidated bitmap.

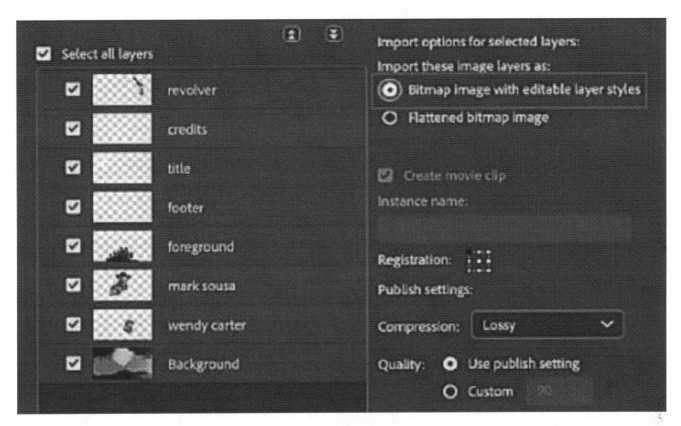

4. Ensure that the **"Convert Layers To"** option in the dialog box is set to **"Animate Layers"** and choose the **"Place Objects At Original Position"** setting. Proceed by clicking on the **"Import"** button.

The Animate software imports each layer from Photoshop as a distinct bitmap and subsequently organizes them into separate Animate layers, maintaining the original layer names. The relative positioning of the images within the layers is preserved.

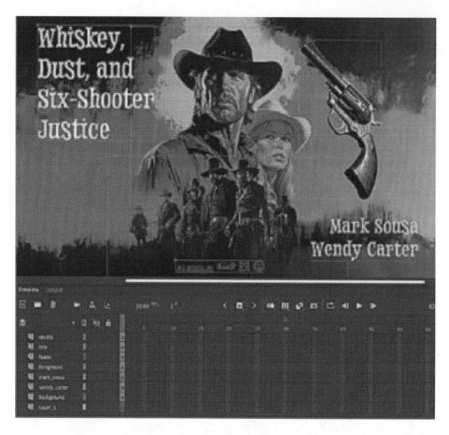

The bitmap assets in the Library panel are stored within a designated folder named "03_asset.psd Asset". Furthermore, each bitmap is transformed into a movie clip symbol.

5. Remove the empty Layer_1 from the Timeline panel.

ANIMATING POSITION

The initial step of this project involves animating the vibrant background. It is recommended to increase the size of the background slightly larger than the Stage to allow for animation, specifically a slow scrolling effect from left to right.

Follow the steps:

1. To begin, choose frame 100 for each layer and proceed to insert additional frames (F5) to allow for ample space to manipu-late all moving elements.

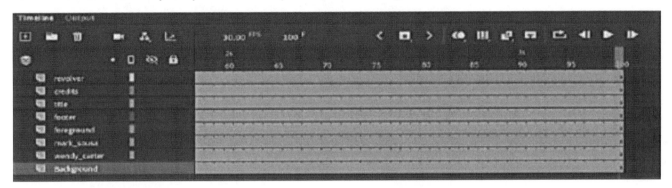

2. It is recommended to lock all layers except the background layer to prevent any accidental modifications.
3. Locate and select the background instance. Then, proceed to modify its dimensions using the Properties panel. input a value of2000 for the width. It is recommended to maintain the lock icon in its original state to ensure that the Height ad-justs proportionally. The background graphic expands slightly beyond the dimensions of the Stage.

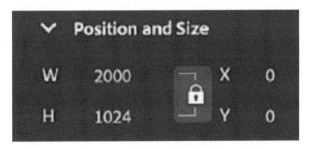

4. To insert a new keyframe at frame 100, press the F6 key. The background layer now contains two keyframes: an initial keyframe at frame 1 and a final keyframe at frame 100.
5. At frame 100, proceed to select the instance of the background located on the Stage. While holding down the Shift key, proceed to move the instance towards the left until its right edge is aligned with the right edge of the Stage. The two keyframes currently feature an identical symbol instance situated at distinct positions on the Stage.

6. Choose a frame between the two keyframes and then select the option **"Create Classic Tween"** located above the timeline. Alternatively, you can right-click and choose **"Create Classic Tween"**.

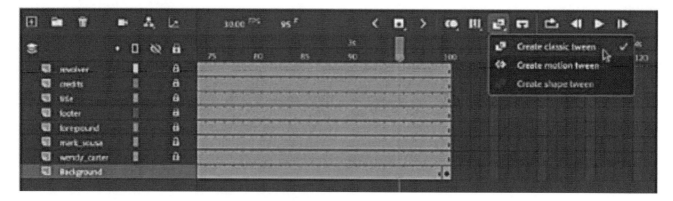

A traditional tween is Used to transition between the two keyframes, denoted by a black arrow positioned over a purple background.

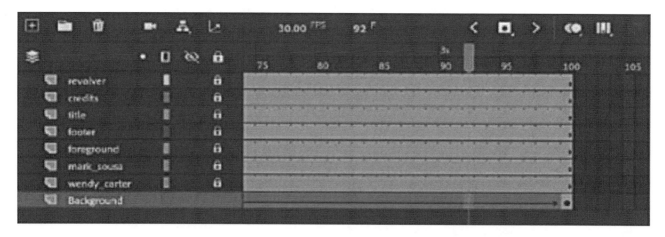

The process of animation involves the smooth interpolation of position changes between frame

1 and frame 100.The background gradu-ally moves in a rolling motion, creating a captivating background for the characters in the foreground.

The tween in question meets all the requirements for achieving success: it Uses a symbol instance, occupies a separate layer, and is posi-tioned between two keyframes.

7. Use the play head by dragging it along the top of the timeline to observe the seamless motion. Alternatively, users have the option to select **Control > Play** or Use the keyboard shortcuts **Return (macOS)** or **Enter (Windows)** to initiate playback of the animation in Animate.

To remove a motion tween, the user should first select the desired tween and then proceed to click on the **"Remove Tween"** option located in the Fra me tab of the Properties panel. An alternative method to remove the classic tween is by right-clicking on the tween located on the timeline or the Stage and selecting the option **"Remove Classic Tween"**.

PREVIEWING THE ANIMATION

The Timeline panel features a comprehensive set of playback controls. The provided controls enable the user to engage in various actions such as playing, rewinding, looping, or incrementally navigating through the timeline to carefully examine the animation. Addition- ally, the playback commands located on the Control menu can be used.

1. Use any of the playback buttons located on the controller positioned above the timeline to initiate playback, stop the playback, or navigate forward or backward one frame. To

navigate to the last or first frame, simply press and hold the Step Forward or Step Backward button to move the play head accordingly.

2. Select the **Loop button** located to the left of the controller. Afterward, proceed to click the **Play button**. An alternative method is to Use the Time Scrub tool, which can be found by accessing the Hand tool's hidden features. This tool allows you to navigate along the timeline, enabling you to preview your animation by moving both forward and backward. Use the Time Scrub tool by either selecting it or holding down the Space bar +T combination, then proceed to drag the tool hori-zontally across the Stage. The play head is designed to loop, enabling users to repeatedly view the animation for meticulous analysis purposes.

3. To define the range of frames that you wish to loop, simply adjust the start or end marker in the timeline header.

The playhead will continuously repeat playback within the designated frames. Click the Loop but to n once more to deactivate it.

ANIMATING THE SCALE

Subsequently, the bandits in the foreground will be animated to increase in size, thereby conveying a sense of imminent danger.

1. First of all, ensure that the background layer is locked and proceed to unlock the foreground layer.
2. Proceed to insert a new keyframe by pressing the F6 key at frame 100 in the foreground layer. The initial keyframe is set at frame 1, while the final keyframe is positioned at frame 100.

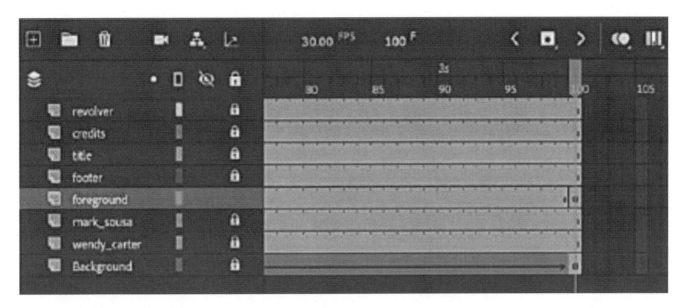

3. At frame 100, proceed to select the instance of the bandits on the Stage and then opt for the Free Transform tool. The transform control handles are visible surrounding the instance.

4. To maintain the aspect ratio of the bandit's instance, hold down the Shift key while dragging the corner control point to increase the size of the graphic. It is not necessary to be precise, but it is recommended to target a new Width of approxi-mately 1320.Ifdesired, you have the option to Use the Properties panel to input the desired width value.
5. Choose a frame between the two keyframes and select the option **"Create Classic Tween"** located above the timeline.

The Animate function smoothly interpolates the scale change between frame 1 and frame 100. As the background gradually moves across the background layer, the image of the bandits in the foreground becomes more prominent.

ANIMATING MULTIPLE PROPERTIES

In the previous assignments, you animated just two properties: position and scale. However, you may simply animate several properties without retweening the animation. If you alter the instance's properties in any keyframe, Animate will automatically include the changes in the animation.

Follow the steps:

1. Select frame 1 from the foreground layer.
2. Use the Selection tool to shift the bandit's instance on the Stage slightly to the left. In this example, the instance is located at X=270.

3. To preview your animation, hit **Return/ Enter.**

The bandits in the front get bigger and travel slightly left to right across the stage. The conflicting motion of the background sky high- lights the movement of the foreground characters.

CHANGING THE PACING AND TIMING

You can adjust the length of the full tween span or the timing of the animation by dragging keyframes on the timeline.

CHANGING ANIMATION LENGTH

If you want the animation to move at a slower speed (and hence last longer), you must prolong the whole tween between the starting and finishing keyframes. If you want to abbreviate the animation, reduce the amount of frames between the keyframes.

The steps:

1. Drag the last keyframe from frame 100 to frame 65. Your tween shrinks to 65 frames, shortening the time it takes the ban-dits to move and resulting in speedier movement.

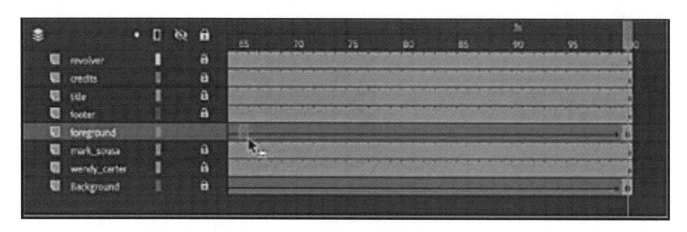

2. Drag the first keyframe ahead from frame 1 to frame 10.

Your motion tween starts later, thus it now only plays from frames 10 to 65. However, because you moved the keyframe, frame 1 now has an empty keyframe.

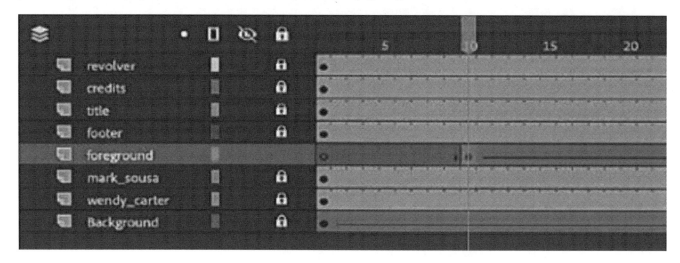

3. Copy (Command+C/Ctrl+C) the ban di t s' instance in frame 10 and paste it in frame 1 using Command +Shift+V/Ctrl+Shift+V.

Paste in Place places the copied instance in the same location that it was copied from. Your Stage now displays the bandits' static images from frames 1 through 9. In frame 10, they start their animation.

UNDERSTANDING FRAME RATE

The frame rate of your document determines the pace of your animation. However, you should not vary the frame rate to control the pace or length of your animation. The frame rate specifies how many frames on the timeline comprise one second. The default is 30 or 24 frames per second (fps). The seconds are indicated on the timeline. Fr am e rate is a measure of how fluid an animation seems; the greater the framerate, the more frames are used to depict the action. Animations with decreased frame rates seem choppy because there are fewer frames to depict the action. Slow-motion videography relies on very high frame rates to capture action that occurs very fast, such as a speeding bullet or a falling water droplet.

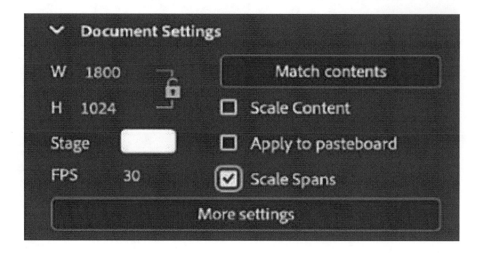

If you want to change the overall length or pace of your animation, do not adjust the frame rate. Instead, add or remove frames from your timeline. If you wish to adjust the frame rate while keeping the total time the same, first pick the Scale Spans option in the Properties box.

ANIMATE THE MAIN CHARACTER

Using the supposed example, animate the main figure, performed by fictitious actor Mark Sousa, such that he rises above the foreground robbers.

Follow the steps:

1. Lock all layers except the mark_sousa layer.
2. Add a new keyframe (F6) at frame 65.
3. In frame 1, shift the Sousa instance to about X=501 and Y=1 50.
4. Add a new keyframe at frame 30. You now have two keyframes with the main figure lower on the Stage (at frames 1 and 30), as well as a third keyframe with him higher on the Stage in his original location (at frame 65).

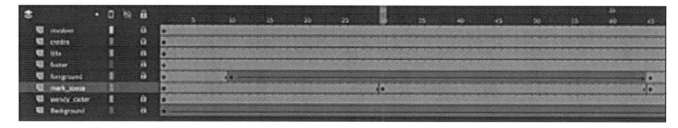

5. Select a frame between two keyframes and click Create Classic Tween above the timeline.

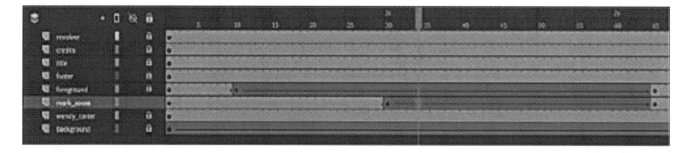

Animate generates the smooth motion of the main figure boldly ascending from the middle of the stage. Feel free to play with the timing, pace, and even location of the different moving parts in the composition thus far.

ANIMATING TRANSPARENCY

You can modify the color effect of an instance in one keyframe and the value of the color effect in another keyframe, and Animate will show a seamless transition, just as it does with position or scale changes. You will alter the transparency of the secondary character, per- formed by the fictitious Wendy Carter, who stands behind the main character. She will begin translucent, but as she emerges, she will be- come opaque. Animate produces a seamless fade-in effect.

1. Lock all layers except the Wendy_Carter layer.
2. Select the Carter instance and select **Alpha** from the Style menu in the Color Effects section of the Properties panel (Object tab).
3. Change the Alpha value to 0%.

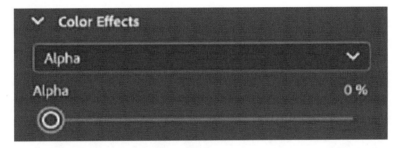

The secondary figure turns translucent and disappears from view on stage. The instance's blue bounding box remains visible and selectable.

4. Insert new keyframes (F6) at frames 50 and 65. The secondary character's animation will begin after the main characters, but both will complete their tweens at the same point.

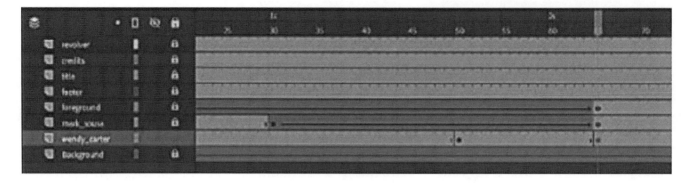

5. In frame 50, slide the translucent Carter instance to the left to partly hide the secondary character at X=740.
6. At frame 65, choose the Carter instance.
7. In the Color Effects area of the Properties panel, choose **Alpha** from the Style option.
8. Set Alpha to 100%. The secondary character becomes obscure. You now have two keyframes: one in frame 50, where the secondary figure is translucent and behind the main character, and one in frame 65, where she is opaque and to the right of him.

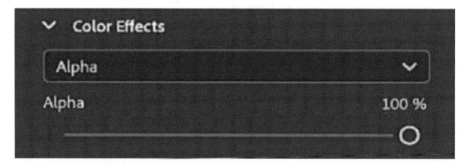

9. Choose a frame between two keyframes and click Create Classic Tween above the timeline. Then animate the secondary character fading in as she comes into view.

EASING

At this time, you've animated four elements: the background, foreground bandits, main character, and secondary character. However, the way they begin and conclude their animation makes their movements look rather mechanical. Easing might help to give the action a more organic, genuine feel. Easing relates to how a motion tween moves. Easing for position changes may be thought of as either acceleration or deceleration. An item moving from one side of the Stage to the other may begin slowly, gain speed, and then abruptly halt. Alternatively, the item may begin moving swiftly and then gradually come to a stop. Your keyframes mark the start and finish points of the motion, but the ease controls how your object moves from one keyframe to the next. Easing gives your items a sensation of weight, which increases realism. To add easing to a motion tween, choose the Effect option from the Tweening section of the Properties panel. You may choose Classic Ease, which offers easing values from -100 to 100.A negative number results in a slow rise in speed from the beginning position (known as ease-in). A positive number causes a steady reduction in speed (known as ease-out). Alternatively, you may choose more com-plicated ease effects that affect both ease-in and ease-out.

ADDING EASE TO MOTION

You will ease the motions of your primary and minor characters; however, ease may be applied to any property modification, including size, transparency, and color. **Follow he steps:**

1. In the mark_sousa layer, select any tweened frames between the animation's initial and end keyframes.
2. In the Properties panel's Tweening section, choose the **Classic Ease button** next to Effect. The pop-up menu displays a variety of eases. The easing curve in the graph on the right depicts on the vertical axis how the property (in this example, the location) changes with each interval of time on the horizontal axis.
3. Select Ease in out in the first menu and Cubic in the second option.

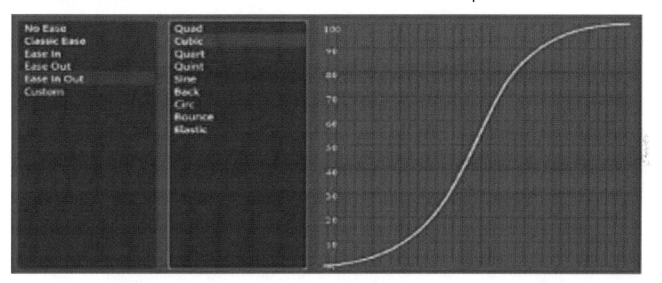

For an Ease In Out, your instance moves softly at the start and finishes. Because there is very little variation at the beginning and con-clusion of the tween, the curve is relatively shallow in the front and rear, resulting in a "S" form. The second selection controls the ease's strength and offers several more possible effects at the bottom (Elastic and Bounce).

4. Double-click the **Cubic option** to apply ease and close the panel.
5. Hit **Return/Enter** to preview your animation. The main character's animation now progressively increases (ease-in) be- fore slowing down at the finish.
6. To finish the animations, apply Ease In Out to the secondary character and the foreground bandits.

ADDING MORE COMPLEX EASES

Many more ease options can be found in the Effect menu in the Properties panel's Tweening section. Select Custom, then double-click New to create a new ease. Enter a name in the Name area for your convenience. You can create your ease profile by using Bezier curves to regu-late the curve.

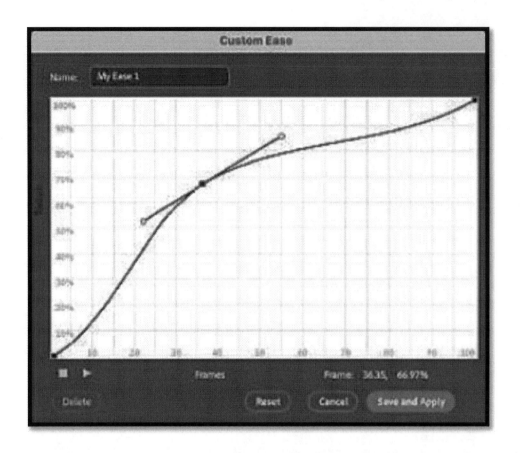

Click the ease curve to create an anchor point. Drag the anchor point to reposition it, or the handlebars to modify the curvature at that location. Select **Save** and **Apply** to store your customized ease. When you copy and paste a tween's frames, you also copy and paste the ease given to them. To remove an ease, choose **No Ease** from the Effects option in the Tweening section of the Properties panel.

ANIMATING FILTERS

Filters, which provide special effects like blurring and drop shadows, may also be animated. Filters may be animated in the same way that position or color effects can be. Simply specify the settings for a filter at one keyframe and different values at another, and Animate will generate a seamless transition. Filters can be used, but not animated, in an HTML5Canvas page.

Follow the steps:

1. Lock all layers, except the revolver layer.
2. Insert new keyframes (F6) at frames 65 and 100.The revolver will move across the screen when the actors' actions come to a stop.

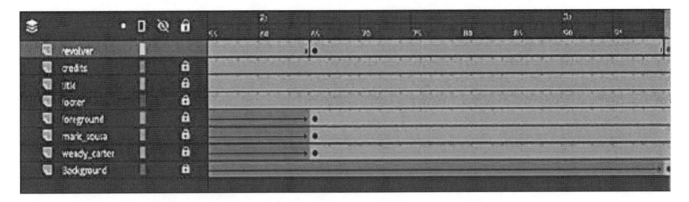

3. Remove the handgun from the stage by selecting it in frame 1 and pressing Delete.

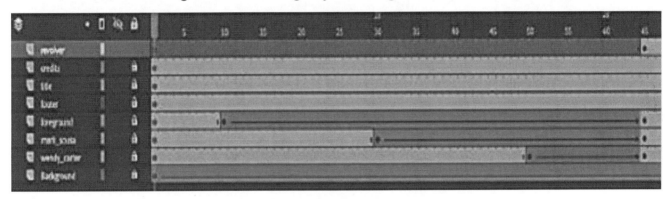

The keyframe in frame 1 is empty. Inframe 65, the revolver appears.

4. Select the revolver in frame 65 and drag it to the left border of the stage.
5. Insert a traditional tween animation between frames 65 and 100. The revolver t ravels smoothly from left to right.

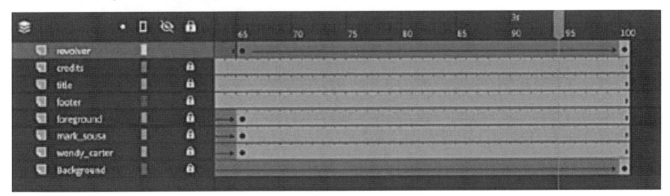

6. Add **Ease Out > Quad** to the twee n to simulate the revolver's progressive halt and inertia.

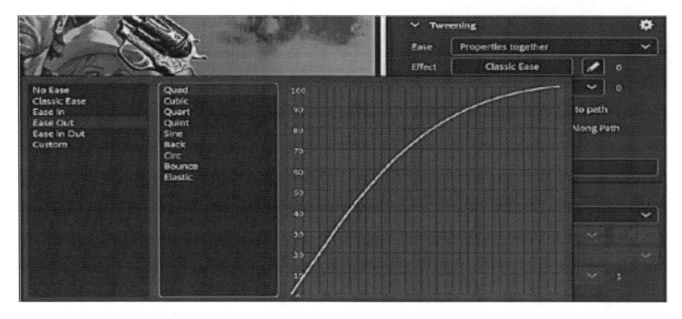

7. To apply the filter, choose the revolver in the last keyframe. Under the Properties panel, under the Filters section, click the **Add Filter (+)** button and choose **Drop Shadow** from the menu to add a drop shadow to the instance.

8. To apply equal values to the Blur X and Blur Y directions, pick the link symbol in the Filters section of the Properties panel (if not already chosen). Set the Blur X value to ten pixels. The Blur Y setting is likewise adjusted to 10 pixels.
9. Set the distance to 12 and strength to 60%.

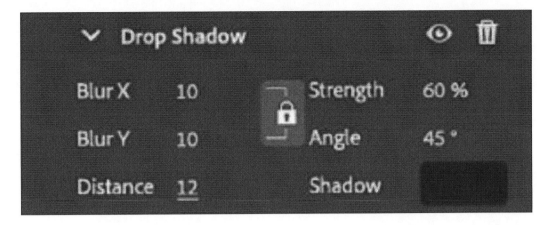

The Distance value controls the distance between the shadow and the object, the Strength value controls the intensity (opacity) of the shadow, and the Blur value controls the sharpness of the shadow's edges. You may also adjust the color and angle of the shadow.

10. To copy all filters, choose the gear symbol in the upper-right corner.

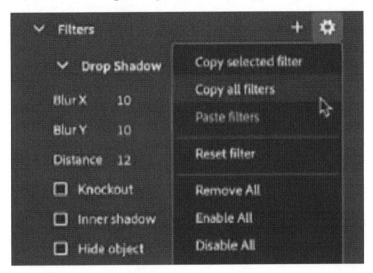

Copy the Drop Shadow filter parameters from this instance and paste them into frame 6S.

11. Choose the revolver instance at frame 65.
12. In the Filter area of the Properties panel, choose the gear icon, then Paste Filters.

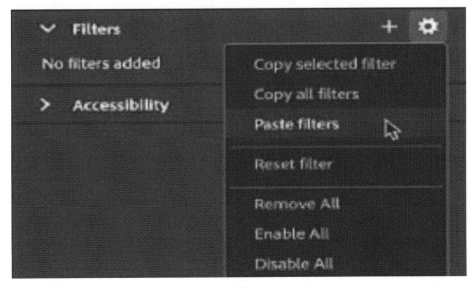

The settings from the copied filter are applied to this instance. Remember that you may apply filters to the keyframe itself (shown by a white keyframe dot), not just the instances inside it. Make sure to pick the revolver instance before pasting your filter. If you just choose the keyframe, the filter will be applied to that keyframe, not the instance.

13. Preview your animation (Return/Enter).

As the revolver glides into view, the drop shadow underneath it creates a th ree-dimensional effect, as if it is resting on top of the screen.

CARRYING OUT AUTOMATIC ROTATIONS

To enhance the visual impact of the revolver sliding into view, consider incorporating a subtle spinning motion. Within the Animate software, there exists the capability to manually manipulate the rotation of an instance at either the initial or final keyframe. Alterna-tively, one may opt to employ the Rotate option, which conveniently automates the rotation of instances throughout a tween.

The steps:

1. Firstly, choose the tween located within the revolver layer.
2. Within the Tweening section located in the Properties panel, proceed to select the Rotate option and opt for the Clock wise direction. Maintain the number of rotations at 1.

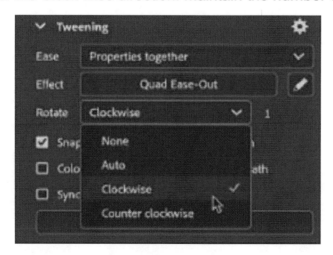

3. Preview your animation by pressing the Return or Enter key. The revolver is currently rotating in a clockwise direction as it smoothly glides across the Stage.

HOW TO CREATE A PATH FOR MOTION

To facilitate the movement of an object along a predetermined trajectory, traditional tweens necessitate the creation of a distinct layer known as a motion guide, where the desired path must be meticulously drawn. A motion guide provides instructions to an object within a classic tween, dictating its movement from the initial keyframe to the final keyframe. When a motion guide is not used, a classic tween will facilitate the animation of an object's position by moving it in a linear trajectory from the initial keyframe to the final keyframe. The user engages in the process of drawing the path within the motion guide. The trajectory may exhibit curvature, zigzagging, or various deviations provided that it does not intersect itself. It is recommended that the path be defined as a stroke rather than a fill. To effectively illustrate the process of creating the motion path, access the sample file 03MotionGuide_Start.flalocated in the 03/03Start folder. The file consists of a solitary classic tween wherein a leaf gracefully transitions from the top of the Stage to the bottom.

The steps:

1. Access the file named **"03MotionGuide_Start.fla"** located in **the "03/ 03 Start"** directory. The leaf transitions smoothly from the uppermost point to the lowermost point, undergoing a rotational movement and gradually assuming a slanted position in the process. One can devise a more intriguing trajectory for the leaf to follow during its descent.

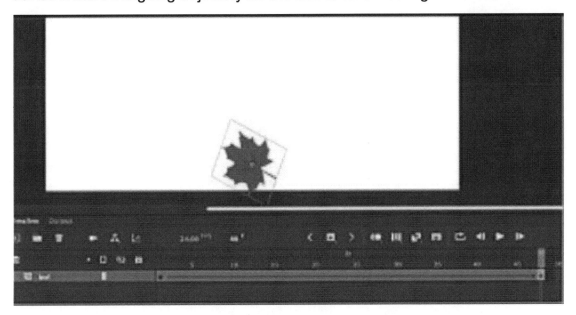

2. To add a Classic Motion Guide to the layer containing the classic tween of the falling leaf, right-click close to the layer name and select the option **"Add Classic Motion Guide"**.

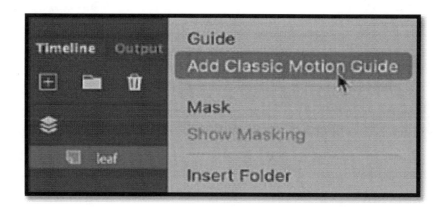

An additional layer, referred to as a classic motion guide, is introduced above the layer that encompasses your classic tween. The classic tween layer is automatically indented beneath the classic motion guide layer, signifying that it will adhere to any path that is drawn within the classic motion guide layer.

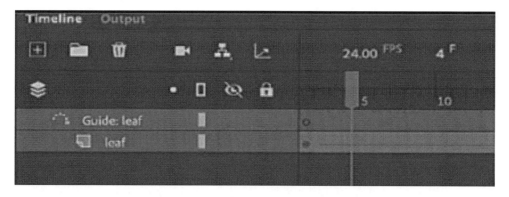

3. Use the Pencil tool and opt for the Smooth feature located in the Tool tab of the Properties panel or at the bottom of the Tools panel. It may be necessary to include the Pencil tool in the Tools panel if it is not currently presents.

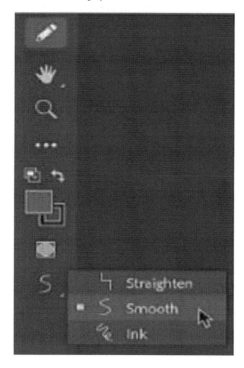

4. Begin by selecting the motion guide layer, followed by initiating the drawing process on the Stage. Create a trajectory for the leaf to traverse, originating from the uppermost point of the Stage and gracefully curving downwards in an elegant s-shape. Ensure that the path does not intersect itself. Conclude the trajectory close to the leaf's location at the final keyframe.

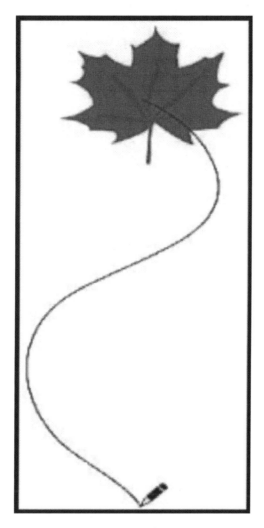

5. Use the Selection tool and ensure that the Snap to Objects feature is activated (indicated by the depressed magnet icon) in the Properties panel. The Snap to Objects feature ensures precise alignment between objects, thereby facilitating the accu-rate positioning of the registration point of the leaf on the path.

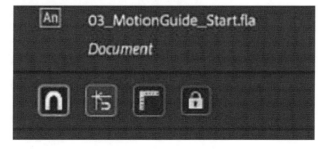

6. Adjust the play head to the initial keyframe, which is located at frame 1. Move the leaf in such a way that it aligns precisely with the initial point of the path.

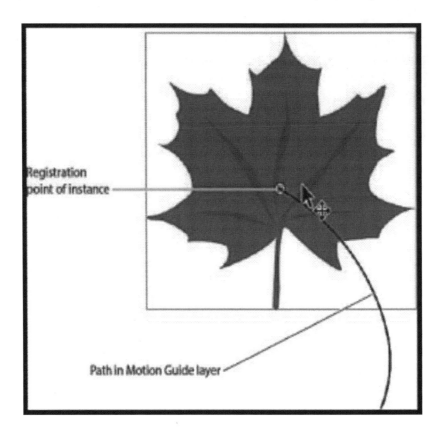

7. Adjust the position of the leaf in the final keyframe to ensure that it aligns precisely with the endpoint of the path.

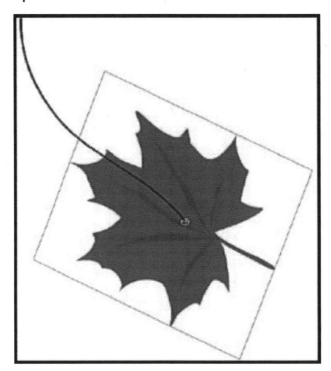

8. Press the **Return/ Enter key** to observe the impact of the motion guide on the classic tween.

The leaf gracefully descends the stage, following a path that is defined by the classic motion guide.

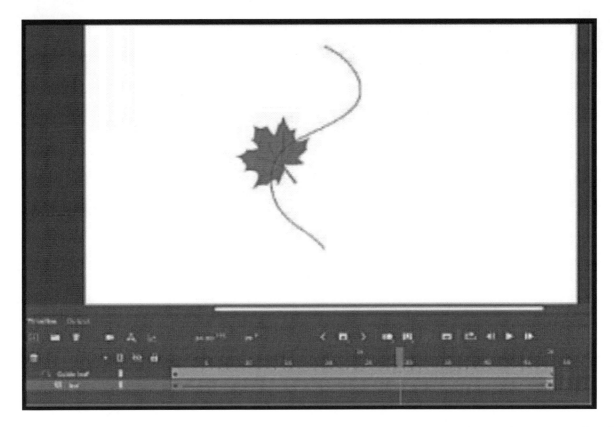

To view the animation without the motion guide path, navigate to the Control menu and select **Test Movie.**

ORIENTING OBJECTS TO THE PATH

The orientation of an object in motion along a given trajectory can be of significance in certain cases. In the previous task, the orientation of the leaf is inconsequential as it undergoes a tumbling motion during its descent. Nevertheless, when animating the movement of a rocket ship along a designated trajectory, it is imperative that the orientation of its nose constantly aligns with the direction of its motion. The option to Orient to Path can be found in the Properties panel.

1. Firstly, choose the leaf instance located in the initial keyframe of the classic tween layer.
2. To access the Swap Symbol option, navigate to the **Object tab** located in the Properties panel. The Swap Symbol dialog box is displayed.

3. Select the rocket symbol and proceed by clicking the OK button. The leaf instance has been replaced by a rocket.

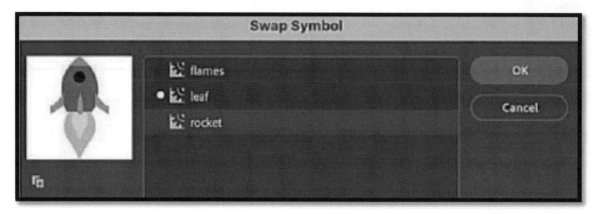

4. Locate the leaf instance within the final keyframe of the classic tween layer. Proceed to Use the Swap Symbol option to substitute the leaf with the rocket symbol. The leaf in both the initial and final keyframes of the classic tween has been substituted with a rocket.

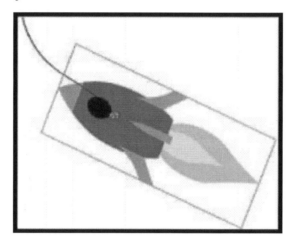

5. Click on the rocket located on the Stage in the final keyframe of the classic tween layer, and proceed to select **the Trans- form panel option**.
6. To access the Remove Transform option, navigate to the **Transform panel** and locate it at the bottom.

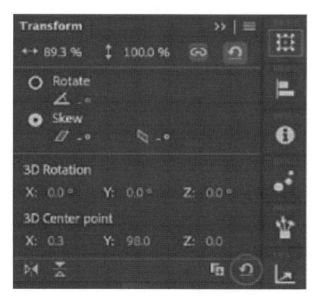

The applied transformations on the original leaf are reset, restoring the rocket to its original size and orientation.

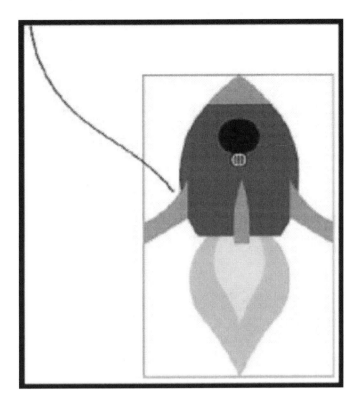

7. Use the Free Transform tool to execute a rotation on the rocket, aligning its nose with the direction of the path.
8. Use the Selection tool to relocate the rocket, ensuring that its registration point aligns precisely with the terminus of the Motion Guide path.

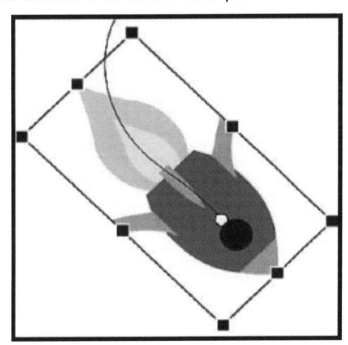

9. Use the Free Transform and Selection tools to make the necessary adjustments to the rocket in the initial keyframe. Ensure that the rocket is aligned with the designated path and appropriately rotated to match the direction of the path.

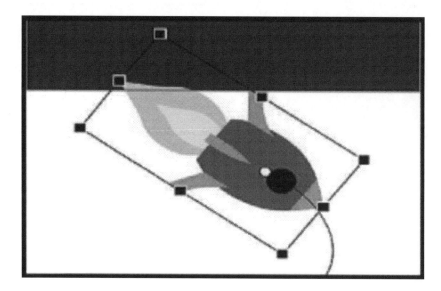

10. Choose a frame within the classic tween. To enable the Orient To Path option, navigate to the Frame tab of the Properties panel and locate the Tweening section.

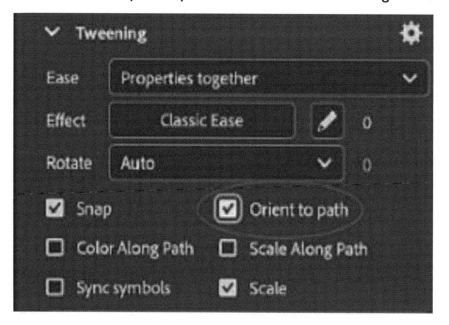

The Animate feature ensures that the rocket's orientation is consistently aligned with the direction of the path, with its nose pointing in that direction at all times.

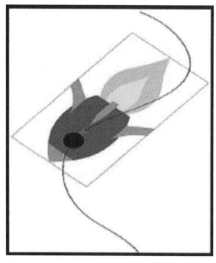

HOW TO CREATE NESTED ANIMATIONS

Frequently, an object that is animated on the Stage will possess its internal animation. As an illustration, the wings of a butterfly may undergo flapping motions as the butterfly traverses the Stage. Alternative y, the rocket with which you have previously collaborated could feature dynamically animated flames emanating from its fuselage during flight. The animations of this nature are commonly referred to as nested animations, as they are encapsulated within their respective movie clip symbols. The movie clip symbols possess their dedicated timeline, which is capable of showcasing animations that are completely separate from the main timeline. For this assignment, you will be tasked with generating an animated sequence depicting flames gracefully emanating from the rear of the rocket within the designated rocket movie clip. Once the movie clip enters a loop, the animation will commence and continue to progress along its designated path on the Stage.

CREATING ANIMATIONS INSIDE MOVIE CLIP SYMBOLS

The task at hand involves editing the rocket movie clip symbol to incorporate a tween animation of the flames.

Follow the steps:

1. Within the Library panel, proceed to double-click n the symbol representing the rocket movie clip. Entering this mode will allow you to edit the rocket symbol. The movie clip symbol consists of two layers. The rocket ship is housed within one layer, while the flames are contained within another layer.

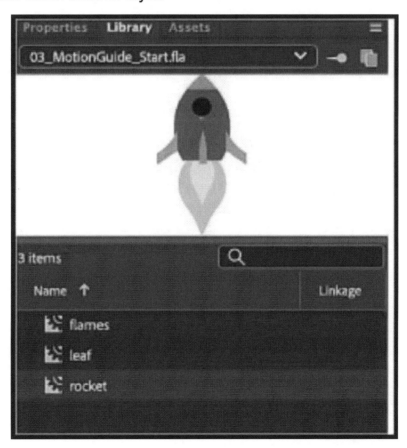

2. Apply an increment of 15 frames (F5) to each of the layers.

3. Add a keyframe (F6}to frames 5, 10, and 15 in the flames layer. The flames layer now contains a total of four keyframes. It is recommended to maintain the instance in frames 1 and 15 (the first and last frames) as identical to achieve a seamless loop in the animation. However, it is advised to modify the shape of the flames in frames 5 and 10.

4. Within frame 5, proceed to select the instance of the flame located on the Stage. Subsequently, opt to Use the Free Trans- form tool.
5. While holding the Option /Alt key, the user should proceed to drag the tip of the flame to adjust its length to a shorter size, all while ensuring that its position at the base remains unchanged.

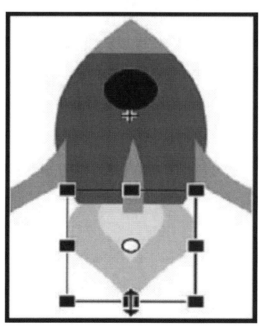

6. For frame 10, make the necessary adjustments to the shape of the flame. While holding down the **Option/ Alt key**, the user can manipulate the flame by dragging its tip to increase its length. Additionally, the user can adjust the width of the flame by dragging its sides to make it either wider or narrower.

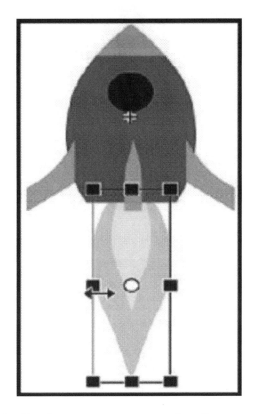

7. Apply a classic tween to the frames encompassing frames 1 to 15.
8. Using the Loop playback feature located above the timeline, proceed to adjust the markers for the starting and ending frames to encompass the entirety of the 15frames. Take a moment to preview your looping animation. The flames oscil-late within the confines of the rocket's fuselage.
9. To navigate back to the main timeline, click on the left-facing arrow located at the top corner of the Stage.
10. Test your movie by selecting **"Test Movie "**in the Animate menu, or by pressing **Command/Ctrl+Return/Enter.**

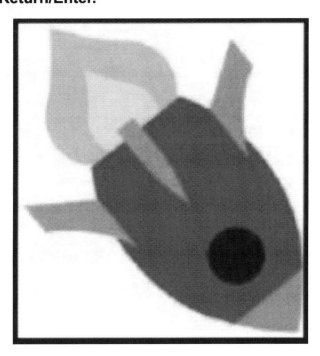

EDITING MULTIPLE FRAMES

Ensure you return to your cinematic animation in the file named "03_workingcopy.fla" to continue with this lesson. To efficiently modify multiple keyframes, you can use the Edit Multiple Frames feature located above the timeline. The provided functionality enables users to make modifications that have an impact on multiple keyframes within a single layer or even across multiple layers simultaneously. For in- stance, consider a scenario where you appreciate the movement of the primary and supporting characters as well as the presence of fore- ground bandits, but you desire to relocate all of them to a different position on the Stage. Instead of individually adjusting each instance at every keyframe of the animation, a more efficient approach is to Use the Edit Multiple Frames option. This feature allows for a single adjustment to be applied to all instances simultaneously. The animations contained within movie clip symbols will loop automatically. To prevent the occurrence of looping, it is necessary to incorporate code that instructs the movie clip timeline to cease its progression on the final frame. In subsequent lessons, you will acquire the skills to manipulate those timelines using ActionScript or JavaScript.

REPOSITIONING MULTIPLE KEYFRAMES

The animation of the characters and the bandits should be relocated to the left side of the Stage.

The steps:

1. Lock all layers except for the specific ones that require editing, such as the foreground, mark_sousa, and wendy_carter layers.

2. To perform the desired action, select the **"Edit Multiple Frames"** option located above the timeline and then proceed to choose the **"All Frames"** option. The timeline is marked with brackets that indicate the range of frames that can be edited. The **"All Frames"**

option automatically places brackets at the beginning and end of the timeline to encompass all frames. If you desire to exclusively select a specific range of frames, opt for the **"Selected Range"** option. The Selected Range option allows for the adjustment of the starting or ending bracket position.

3. To select all, navigate to the Edit menu and choose the **"Select All"** option. On a Mac, you can use the **Command+A** short - cut, while on a PC, you can use the Ctr!+A shortcut. The selection is extended to include all instances within unlocked lay-ers across all keyframes. Multiple instances of the main character and the foreground bandits are observable.

4. To select multiple instances on the Stage, simply hold down the **Shift key** and drag the selection to the left. The title will collide with the main character's head, but that can be adjusted at a later stage. The user is currently performing simulta-neous movement of multiple instances across multiple keyframes on all three layers.

5. Deselect the option to edit multiple frames.

6. Adjust the timeline to initiate the playback of the new animation. The primary protagonist and the group of criminals sustain their animated state, albeit they have been repositioned toward the left side of the Stage.

7. Unlock the title and revolver layers. Then, in the last keyframe, proceed to move the title and revolver elements towards the right on the Stage, taking advantage of the newly created space.

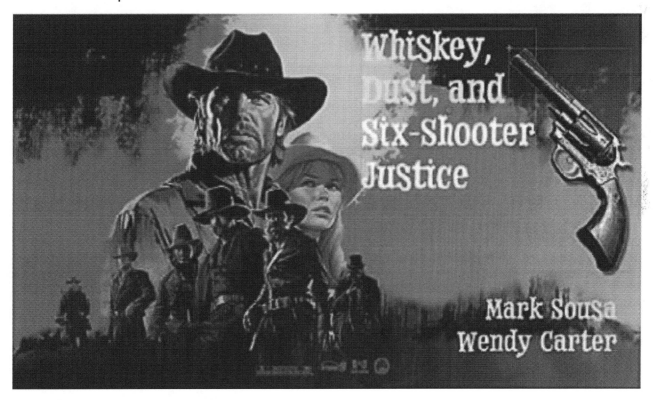

HOW TO ADD A 3D TITLE

Ultimately, the title will be strategically placed within a three-dimensional space to enhance its visual appeal. The use of the 3D Rotation tool and 3DTranslat ion tool enables the manipulation of symbol instances within a three-dimensional space, thereby enhancing the visual depth of your projects. Both tools are available in the supplementary Drag and Drop Tools panel and need to be added to your Tools panel.

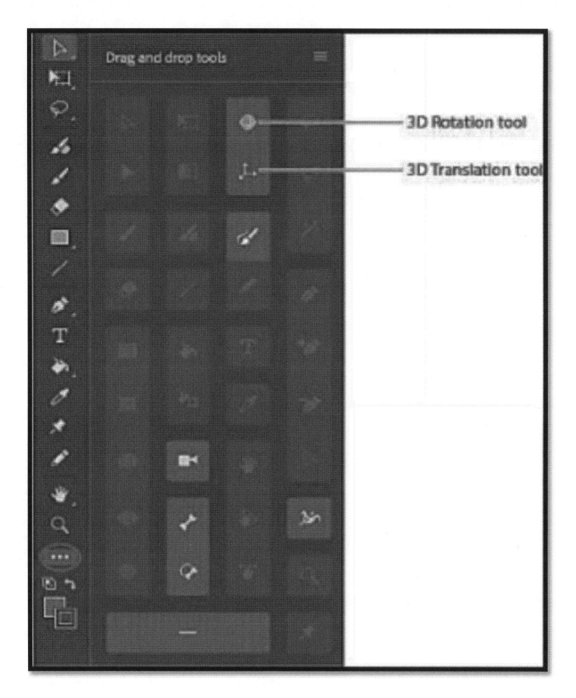

Manipulating objects in a three-dimensional space introduces the additional complexity of a third axis, commonly referred to as the z- axis. When using the 3D Rotation or 3DTranslation tool, it is important to take into consideration the Global Transform option located at the lower section of the Tools panel. The Global Transform feature allows users to switch between a Global setting (when the button is selected) and a Local setting (when the button is deselected). When an object is moved in Global mode, the transformation is performed concerning the global coordinate system. On the other hand, moving an object in Local mode means that the transformation is carried out relative to the object itself. The inclusion of a 3D title within the composition will enhance its dramatic impact, although it will not pos-sess any animation. It is not possible to animate three-dimensional objects using classic tweens. To animate symbol instances using the 3D Rot at ion tool or 3DTranslation tool, it is necessary to employ a motion tween.

COMPARISON OF GLOBAL AND LOCAL TRANSFORMATIONS

When using the 3D Rotation or 3D Translation tool, it is important to take note of the Global Transform toggle button located at the lower section of the Tools panel. This toggle button becomes visible when one of the 3D tools is selected. When the toggle button is switched on and highlighted, the Global mode is activated. In this mode, the rotation and positioning of 3Dobjects are determined by the global coordi-nate system, also known as the Stage coordinate system. The 3Ddisplay superimposed on the object being manipulated provides a visual representation of the three axes, which remain fixed in position regardless of the object's rotation or movement. Observe the image below to note the perpendicular alignment of the 3Ddisplay concerning the Stage.

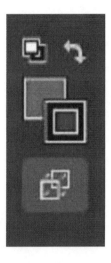

When the Global Transform option is disabled (indicated by the button not being highlighted), the Local mode is activated, causing rota-tion and positioning to be relative to the object. The 3Ddisplay exhibits the three axes aligned concerning the object, rather than the Stage. As illustrated in the provided image, it is important to observe that the3D Rotation tool displays the rotation with the object itself, rather than concerning the Stage.

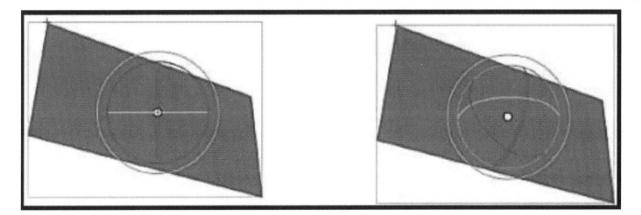

1. Firstly, lock all layers except for the title layer. Then, proceed to select the title layer.
2. Choose the 3D Rota t ion tool. The 3D Rotation tool can be found in the additional tear-off tools located at the bottom of the Toolbar. To access this tool, you will need to add it to your Toolbar. The control for 3D rotation is displayed on the movie clip that has been selected.

3. To activate Local mode for the 3D Rotation tool, ensure that you deselect the Global Transform button located at the bot- tom of the Tools panel.
4. Manipulate the left arm of the green Y control to rotate the title along the y-axis, creating an illusion of it moving away into the distance. If you encounter difficulties with the 3Dcontrols on the Stage, simply modify the 3D Rot at ion values in the Transform panel (located under **Window > Transform).** Use the subsequent 3D Rot at ion values: X=6 degrees, Y=- 2 4 degrees and Z=8 degrees.

Use the Selection tool to reposition the title to optimize its placement within the available space. The title exhibits a visual effect of reced-ing into the distance due to its tilted angle in three-dimensional space.

5. To achieve a similar effect, unlock the credits layer and Use the 3D Rotation tool to rotate the credits. One may choose to replicate the design showcased in the provided screenshot or explore alternative design options.

The current version of HTML5 Canvas documents does not support the animation of 3D rotation or translation of symbols.

HOW TO EXPORT YOUR FINAL MOVIE

One can efficiently preview their animation by manipulating the play head in a back-and-forth motion on the timeline, selecting Control > Play, or using the Time Scrub tool found in the Tools panel. An alternative option is to Use the integrated controller located at the top of the Timeline panel. To generate a final project in the form of a movie and view any nested animations within movie clip symbols, it is necessary to perform an export. Use the Quick Share and Publish feature to generate an MP4 movie file. The animation is converted using Adobe Media Encoder, which is a standalone application included in the Adobe Creative Cloud suite.

1. Select the option **"Quick Share and Publish"** followed by **"Publish"** and then choose the file format "Video (.mp4)". Click on the **"Publish"** button to complete the action.

Animate facilitates the process of exporting a video by seamlessly integrating with Adobe Media Encoder, thereby automatically initiating the export operation. The project you submitted has been successfully added to the Queue panel for processing.

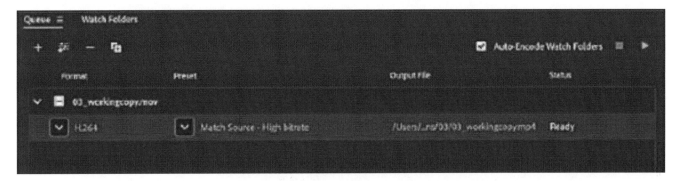

2. The encoding process will commence automatically. If it doesn't, click the **Start Queue** button (the green triangle) or press Return/Enter to begin the encoding process.

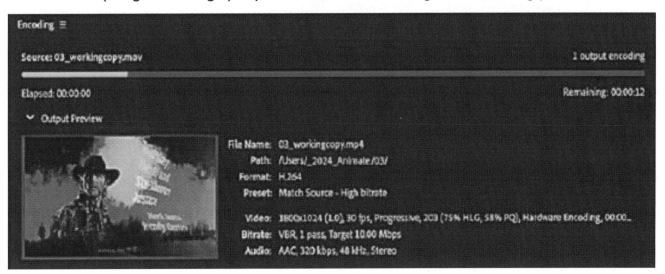

Media Encoder converts your project files into an H.264-formattedvideo with the standard .mp4 extension and notifies you when the process is finished. The completed file can be uploaded to various popular video-sharing platforms or used to showcase on a promotional website, specifically designed for the fictional cinematic release. To publish an MP4 movie, you can select the **"File"** option from the menu bar and then choose **"Export"** followed by **"Export Video/Media"**. By selecting this approach, you will be allowed to manipulate various settings within Adobe Media Encoder, allowing you to modify audio/video encodings, perform cropping and trimming operations, and ad- just other properties of your video.

FREQUENTLY ASKED QUESTIONS

1. How do you import Adobe Photoshop assets and layers?
2. How do you preview an animation in Adobe Animate 2024?
3. How do you animate multiple properties?
4. How do you animate the main character?
5. How do you understand the frame rate?
6. How do you change the pacing and timing in animation?
7. How do you create a path for motion and edit multiple frames?

CHAPTER 5: CRAFTING GRAPHICS AND TEXT

OVERVIEW

Chapter three talks about graphics and text in Adobe Animate 2024. In this chapter, you will learn and understand what strokes and fills mean, how you can create shapes for your projects, how to make selections, how to edit shapes and others.

UNDERSTANDING STROKES AND FILLS

The creation process for any graphic within Animate begins by first establishing a shape. A shape is composed of two primary elements: the fill, which represents the interior of the shape, and the stroke, which outlines the shape. By consistently considering these two fun-damental elements, you will make significant progress in producing visually stunning and intricate designs. The fill and stroke functions operate independently, allowing you to modify or remove one without impacting the other. As an illustration, it is possible to generate a rectangle with a blue fill and a red stroke, and subsequently modify the fill to purple while completely removing the red stroke. The result will be a purple rectangle devoid of any outline. Additionally, it is possible to independently adjust the position of the fill or stroke. There- fore, when intending to relocate the entire shape, it is crucial to select both the fill and stroke components.

HOW TO CREATE SHAPES

For this example, we will be focusing on the shape of an octopus.

Animate offers a variety of drawing tools that function within various drawing modes. It is crucial to have a strong grasp of drawing basic shapes like rectangles and ovals, as they often serve as the foundation for many of your designs. Being able to confidently modify their appearance, as well as apply fills and strokes, is equally important. Colors are commonly specified using hexadecimal numbers in Animate, as well as in HTML documents and the field of web design and development. The numerical values following the hash symbol denote the individual intensities of red, green, and blue components that collectively constitute the color.

USING THE OVAL TOOL

The ocular structure of the octopus consists of a sequence of elliptical shapes that overlap with each other. To create an expression of anger in the eyes, a diagonal line is used to intersect the largest oval at an inclined angle. The first step involves sketching the ovals. It is ad-vantageous to deconstruct intricate objects into their constituent elements to facilitate their depiction.

1. First of all, rename the layer named "Layer_1 " to "octopus".

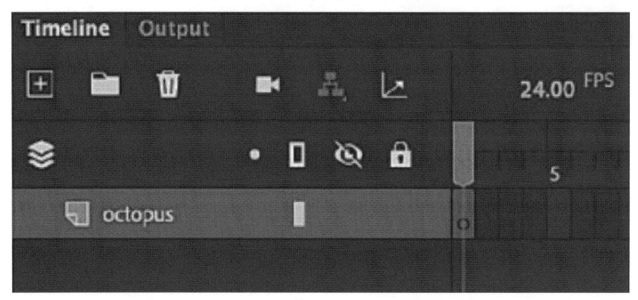

2. Within the Tools panel, locate and choose the Oval tool, which is concealed beneath the Rectangle tool. To access the Oval tool, press and hold the Rectangle tool. Ensure that the Object Drawing button located either at the bottom of the Tools panel or in the Properties panel, is not currently selected.

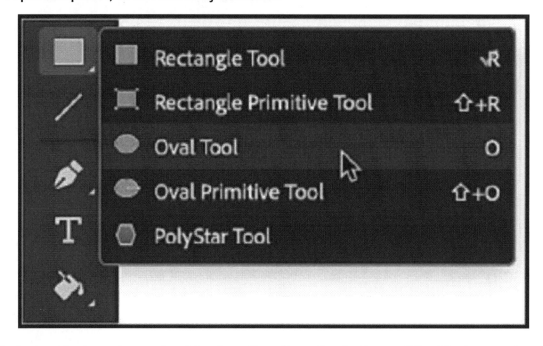

3. Select a stroke color and a fill color either from the bottom of the Tools panel or from the Properties panel. Input the hexa-decimal color code #CCCCCC (representing light gray) for the fill and #000000 (representing black) for the stroke.

4. Using the Stage, create an oval shape that has a slightly greater height than its width.

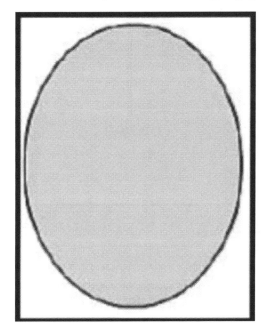

5. Choose the Selection tool.
6. Use the Selection tool to encompass the entirety of the oval to select both its stroke and fill. When a shape is selected, Adobe Animate presents it visually by displaying white dots. In addition, it is possible to activate a shape by double-click-ing on it, prompting Animate to automatically highlight both the stroke and fill of said shape.
7. Within the Properties panel, navigate to the Position And Size section. Proceed to input the value of 40 for the Width and 55 for the Height. Press the Return key on macOS or the Enter key on Windows to apply the values.

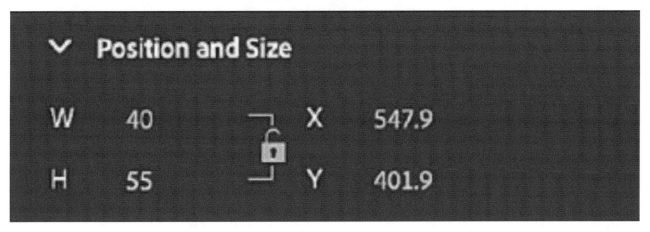

ADDING THE INSIDE OF THE EYE

Next, you will proceed to create the interior of the eye as well as the white highlight. When creating new objects, it is important to note that the fill and stroke settings from your previous action will be automatically applied, unless you manually modify these settings before drawing.

1. Within the Tools panel, proceed to select the **Oval tool.**
2. Select a stroke color and a fill color from the lower section of the Tools panel. input the hexadecimal code#000000 to spec-ify the fill color as black, and use the same code #000000 to indicate the stroke color as black.
3. Create a smaller black oval and position it inside the larger oval on the Stage.

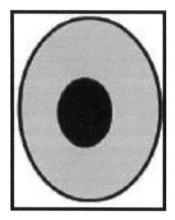

To maintain shape constraints while drawing, ensure that you hold down the Shift key. Using the Shift key while employing the Oval tool facilitates the creation of flawless circles, akin to the functionality of the Shift key when using the Rectangle tool for generating impecca-ble squares.

4. Input the hexadecimal color code #FFFFFF (white) as the fill for your Oval tool.
5. Proceed by creating an additional oval positioned above the existing black oval, serving as the designated highlight.

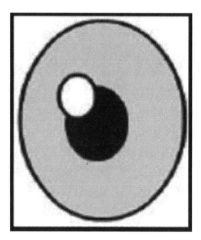

ANIMATE DRAWING MODES

Animate offers three distinct drawing modes that dictate how objects interact with each other on the Stage, as well as the methods by which they can be edited. By default, Adobe Animate uses the Merge Drawing mode. However, users have the option to enable Object Draw- ing mode or use the Rectangle Primitive or Oval Primitive tool to access the Primitive Drawing mode.

MERGE DRAWING MODE

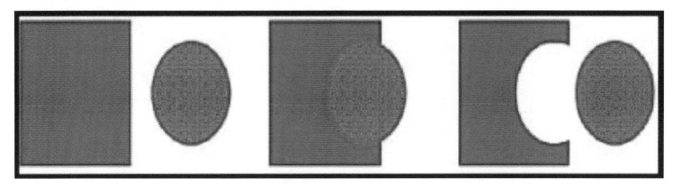

Within this particular mode, Animate skillfully combines various drawn shapes, such as rectangles and ovals, in a manner that allows for the overlapping of these shapes, resulting in the visual perception of a singular, unified shape. When relocating or removing a shape that has been merged with another shape, it is important to note that the overlapping section will be permanently eliminated.

OBJECT DRAWING MODE

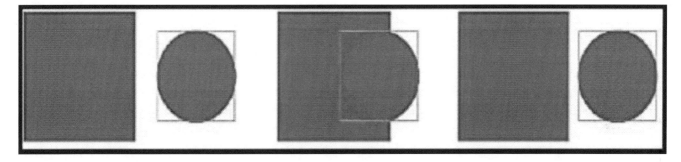

Within this particular mode, Animate does not amalgamate drawn objects; instead, they retain their individuality and remain separate entities, even in instances where they may overlap. To activate **Object Drawing mode**, proceed by selecting the desired drawing tool and subsequently clicking on the **Object Drawing button** located at the lower section of the Tools panel. To convert an object to a shape using the Merge Drawing mode, it is necessary to select the object and then navigate to the Modify menu. From there, choose the option labeled Break Apart (shortcut: Command +Bon Mac or Ctrl +Bon Windows). To convert a shape into an object using the Object Drawing mode, the user should first select the desired shape. Then, they should navigate to the Modify menu and choose the option labeled Combine Objects.

From the subsequent dropdown menu, the user should select the Union option. The current shape is transformed into an object, although it is important to note that this transformation does not revert the shape to its original drawn state.

PRIMITIVE DRAWING MODE

When Using the Rectangle Primitive tool or the Oval Primitive tool in Animate, the software will create rectangles or ovals as separate objects that retain certain editable attributes. When working with rectangle primitives, it is possible to modify the comer radius, as well as the start and end angles. Additionally, the inner radius of oval primitives can be adjusted using the Proper ties panel.

MAKING SELECTIONS

To make modifications to an object, it is imperative to possess the capability of selecting various components of said object. Within the Animate software, users can create selections by Using the Selection, Sub selection, and Lasso tools. The Selection tool is commonly used to choose either an entire object or a specific portion of an object. The Sub selection tool allows users to precisely select individual points or lines within an object. The Lasso tool enables users to create a selection in a free-form manner.

SELECTING STROKES AND FILLS

When it comes to the task of selecting strokes and fills, there are a few key considerations to keep in mind. It is important to carefully assess the various options available and make informed decisions based on the desired outcome. By taking a systematic approach to. Now, it is time to further refine the ovals to achieve a more accurate representation of an eye. The Selection tool is used to remove undesired strokes and fills.

1. Within the Tools panel, choose the **Selection tool.**
2. Perform a double-click action on the stroke surrounding the white oval. Both the white oval and the black oval strokes are selected.

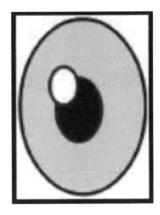

3. Use the **Delete / Backspace key** to proceed. The brushstrokes have been removed, resulting in a white oval shape that serves as the highlight.

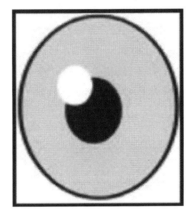

4. Use the Line tool and input #000000 (black) as the stroke color.
5. Create a diagonal line that intersects the upper portion of the eyeball. The straight line generates intersecting shapes within the eyeball, allowing for individual selection of these shapes.

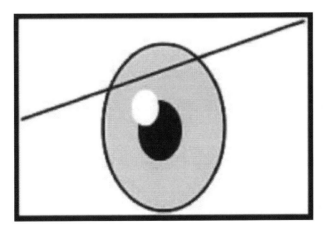

6. Use the Selection tool to precisely target and select the half-dome gray shape located at the tip of the eye.
7. Use the Delete/Backspace key to proceed. The gray fill has been removed.
8. Select the curved stroke located above the straight line and proceed with its deletion.
   The completion of one eye has been achieved.

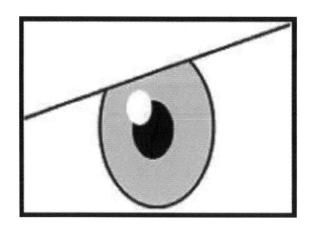

HOW TO EDIT SHAPES

When Using the Animate software, it is common practice to commence the drawing process by employing basic geometric forms such as rectangles, ovals, and lines. However, to generate more intricate graphics, it is necessary to employ additional tools to modify the afore- mentioned fundamental shapes. The utilization of the Free Transform tool, the Copy and Paste commands, and the Selection tool an sig-nificantly enhance the efficiency of your workflow.

USING COPY AND PASTE

Use the Copy and Paste commands to effortlessly replicate shapes on the Stage. Your octopus needs to possess a pair of eyes, making the use of copying and pasting a valuable tool. To paste a copied graphic in the precise location from which it was copied, use the Paste in Place function **(Shift + Command +V/Shift + Ctrl+ V).**

1. Use the Selection tool to encompass the entirety of the eye drawing by dragging it.
2. To copy, navigate to the **Edit menu** and select the **Copy option**. Alternatively, you can use the keyboard shortcut **Com-mand + C** on a Mac or **Ctrl + C** on a Windows computer.
3. To perform the paste operation, navigate to the **Edit menu** and select the **Paste option.** Alternatively, you can use the keyboard shortcut Command +Von a Mac or Ctrl + V on a Windows computer. An additional eye emerges on the Stage. The duplicated item remains selected.

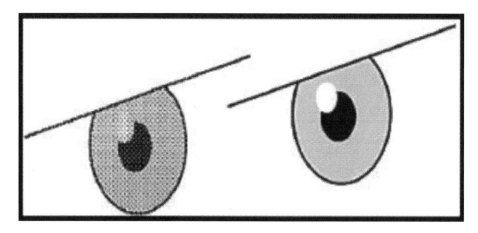

4. Position the duplicate eye close to your original eye.

USING THE FREE TRANSFORM TOOL

The duplicated eye should be mirrored to achieve a visually correct appearance. The Free Transform tool will be used to create a mirror image of the given object. The Free Transform tool can be used to modify an object's scale, rotation, or skew, as well as to distort an object by manipulating control points within a bounding box.

1. Click on the Modify menu, then select **Transform,** and finally choose Flip Horizontal. The object undergoes a rotational movement, resulting in the acquisition of distinct ocular perspectives for both the right and left eyes.
2. Access the Free Transform tool by selecting it from the Tools panel. The eye is adorned with transformation handles.
3. Adjust the size of the left eye by dragging one of its corner points inward. To maintain the same aspect ratio of the eye, it is recommended to hold down the Shift key while dragging.

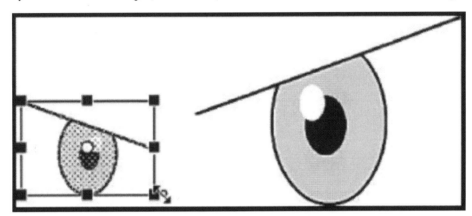

When the Option or Alt key is pressed while manipulating a control point, Animate will proportionally scale the chosen object based on its transformation point, which is indicated by the circle icon. The transformation point has the flexibility to be relocated to any position, including outside the object. Depress the Shift key to maintain the object's proportions. To distort the object from a single control point, hold down the Command/Ctrl key.

4. Enjoy the process of creating a slightly eccentric second eye. Manipulating an object can be achieved by dragging the corner points. This action allows for the adjustment of the object's proportions by either squashing or stretching it, as well as rotating it. Additionally, it is possible to manipulate the object's appearance by dragging the sides of the bounding box to create a slanted effect.

HOW TO CHANGE SHAPE CONTOURS

The Selection tool allows users to manipulate lines and corners to modify the overall contours of any given shape. The software provides a rapid and user-friendly approach to manipulating geometric figures. The technique described will be employed to generate the organic form of the octopus head and body.

Follow the steps below:

1. Create a new layer on the timeline and assign it the name **"body"**. Move the layer below the octopus layer, which presently houses the eyes.

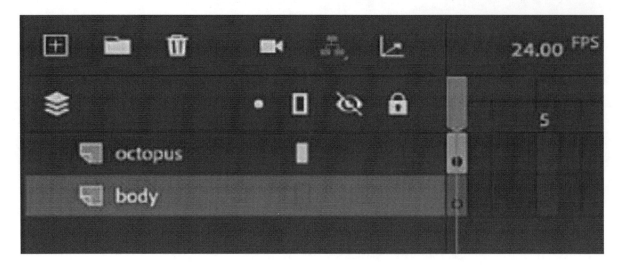

2. Within the Tools panel, proceed to choose the Oval tool. Select a green color (#33CCCC) for the fill and black for the stroke.
3. Generate three elliptical shapes that intersect with each other, resembling the provided illustration, positioned adjacent to the eyes. It is not necessary to be precise at this stage, as you will have the opportunity to make adjustments to these shapes later on.

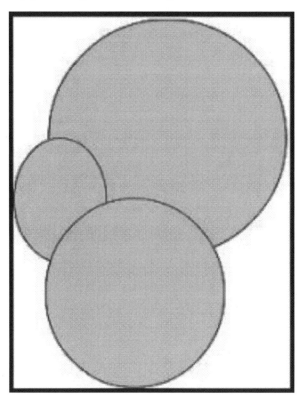

4. Select the black outlines and proceed to press the Delete key. The black strokes have been removed.
5. Position your mouse cursor near one of the ovals. An arc-shaped line is displayed near the cursor, signifying the ability to modify the curvature of the stroke.
6. Extend the stroke in an outward direction. The curvature of the oval shape causes a gentle protrusion in the region of the octopus's head. Apply gentle pressure and manipulation to the outlines of the three ovals to achieve a more fluid and rounded shape for the head of your octopus, as well as a brow ridge that appears more authentic and in harmony with nature.

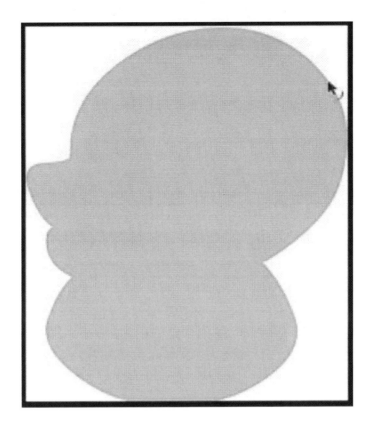

To create a new corner point and modify the direction of a curve, simply hold down the **Option/Alt** key while dragging along the curve.

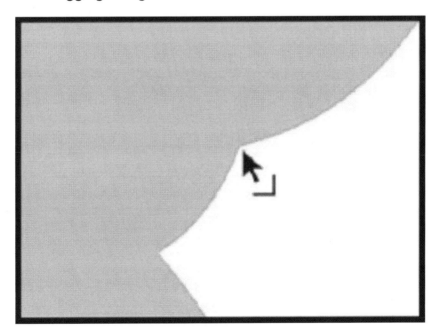

MODIFYING STROKE AND FILL PROPERTIES

To modify the attributes of a stroke or fill, you have the option to use either the Ink Bottle tool or the Paint Bucket tool. The Ink Bottle tool is used to modify stroke colors, while the Paint Bucket tool is used to alter fill colors. The presence of a check mark adjacent to the quick key serves as an indication of the presently chosen tool, which is being showcased in the Tool panel.

If the Paint Bucket tool alters the fill in adjacent areas, there may exist a minor discontinuity in the outline of the shape, thereby permit- ting the fill to overflow. To close the gap, you have two options: you can manually close it yourself, or you can use the Gap Size menu lo-cated at the bottom of the Tools panel to select the desired gap size, which will then be automatically closed by Animate.

- First, locate and click on the Paint Bucket tool in the toolbar. Then, access the Properties panel and select a new fill color for the tool. Select a fill to modify its color.
- Locate the Ink Bottle tool, which can be found hidden under the Paint Bucket tool. Once you have selected the Ink Bottle tool, proceed to the Properties panel to choose a new stroke color. Additionally, users have the option to select the desired thickness and style of the stroke. Select a stroke to modify its properties.
- Additionally, it is possible to conveniently modify the properties of a stroke or fill on the Stage by selecting it and using the Proper - ties panel.

USING VARIABLE-WIDTH STROKES

There are various techniques available to create a wide range of stroke styles. Furthermore, apart from the standard solid line, users have the option to select a dotted, dashed, or ragged line, or they can personalize their line style. Additionally, it is possible to generate lines with varying widths and modify these variations using the Width tool.

APPLYING BOTH THICK AND THIN OUTLINES

The use of variable stroke widths can significantly enhance the expressive quality of your drawings.

1. Use the Ink Bottle tool and navigate to the Properties panel. Proceed to designate a Stroke Size of 6 and select Width Profile 1 for the Width.

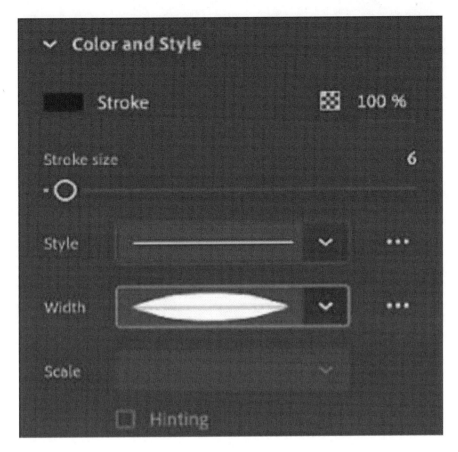

2. Secondly, select the prominent green octopus head. The Animate function applies the thick-thin width profile to the out- line of the green fill.

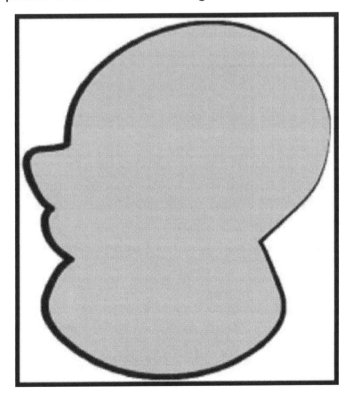

3. Use the Selection tool to carefully select a singular stroke segment encompassing the green head. Proceed to adjust the Stroke Size to a value of 4. Presently, two distinct stroke widths encompass your shape.

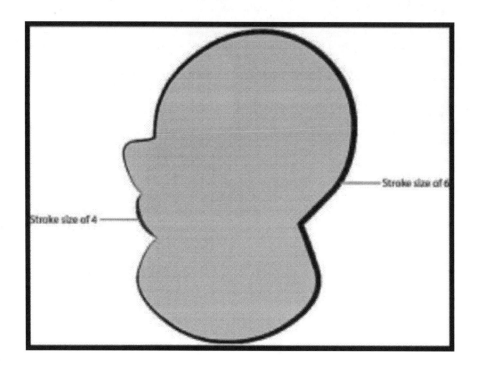

4. Remove the stroke surrounding the lower oval shape. Connect the octopus tentacles at that location, eliminating the ne-cessity for the black outline.

REFINING VARIABLE-WIDTH LINES

The Width tool allows for the customization of bulge placement and width in addition to applying various width profiles to a stroke.

The steps:

1. Press and hold the Shift key while selecting the three-line segments that makeup one of the eyebrows.
2. Within the Properties panel, proceed to modify the Stroke Size to a value of 10.
3. Modify the width parameter to Width Profile 1. When dealing with variable-width lines, it is important to approach them in the same manner as any other stroke. Use either the Selection or Sub selection tool to manipulate the curves or relocate the anchor points. The straight line transforms, becoming a line with increased thickness that tapers at the ends and widens in the middle, thereby imbuing it with a touch of individuality.

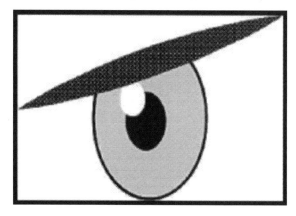

4. To edit the Toolbar, locate and click on the three dots located at the bottom of the Tools panel.

5. Transfer the Width tool from the Drag and Drop Tools panel to your Tools panel to enable its usage. To collapse the Tools panel, either click outside of it or press the Esc key. To remove an anchor point from a variable-width line, you must first click on the anchor point to select it. Once selected, you can then press the Delete or Backspace key to delete the anchor point.

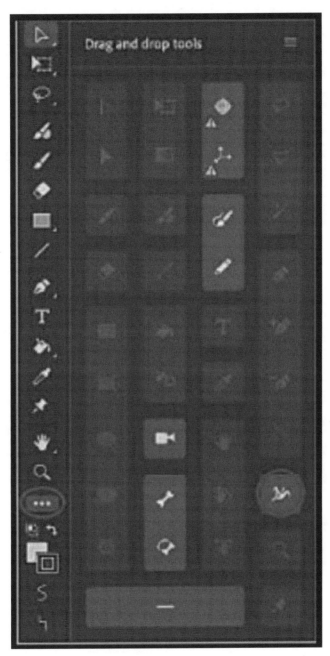

6. Position your mouse pointer over one of your variable-width strokes. Anchor points are strategically placed along the line to indicate the precise locations of the thicker and thinner sections of the line.
7. Manipulate the anchor points by dragging the handles to adjust the line's width. Emphasize certain limitations and ex-pansions. Press and hold the Option/Alt key to selectively modify one side of a variable-width line.
8. Manipulate an anchor point by dragging it along the stroke to adjust its position.

9. anywhere along the stroke. The Animate software application features a visual indicator in the form of a small plus (+) symbol that is displayed adjacent to the user's pointer. This symbol serves to signify the user's ability to add an anchor point within the application.
10. Make adjustments to both eyebrows of your octopus according to your preferences. Additionally, consider applying a dis-tinct width profile to the outline surrounding the eyes.

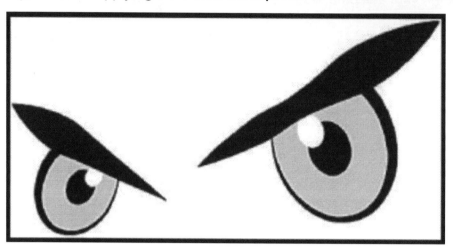

HOW TO ORGANIZE YOUR DRAWING

After completing the creation of the eyes and the head, it is advisable to commence the process of organizing the various components of the drawing. One method of organizing various shapes is by placing them in distinct layers. However, an alternative approach is to use groups to maintain separation between them.

ORGANIZING OBJECTS INTO GROUPS

A group is a mechanism that consolidates a variety of shapes and graphics to maintain their structural integrity. When the constituent elements of the eyes are grouped, they can be manipulated collectively, alleviating concerns of potential merging and intersection with underlying shapes within the same layer.

1. Choose the Selection tool.
2. Identify and select all the geometric forms that constitute one of the ocular structures, encompassing the eyebrows as well.

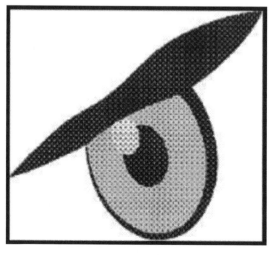

3. Select the option **"Group"** from the **"Modify"** menu. The eye undergoes a process of consolidation, resulting in the forma-tion of a unified group. Upon selection, the object is visually highlighted with a blue-green outline, indicating the bound-aries of its bounding box.

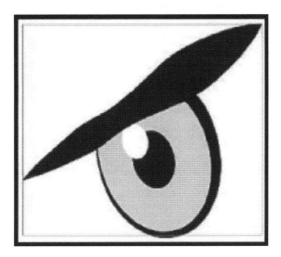

4. To modify any element of the eye, simply double-click on the group to access the editing options. It is important to observe that the remaining elements on the Stage are dimmed, and the Edit bar located above the Stage indicates **"Scene 1 > Group"**. The statement suggests that you have successfully joined a specific group and have been granted the ability to make changes to its contents.

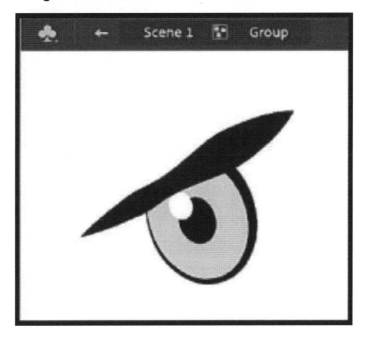

5. To access Scene 1, click on the corresponding icon located in the Edit bar at the top of the Stage. Alternatively, you can dou-ble-click on an empty area of the Stage to return to the main scene.
6. Align the second eye with the first eye and position both eyes on the top of the head. It is important to note that the Free Transform tool can be used to resize the head or eyes to achieve optimal graphic fitting.

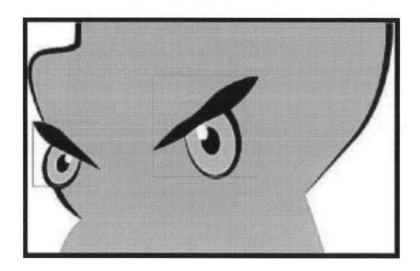

USING BRUSHES

While the Oval and Line tools, along with their counterparts like the Rectangle tool, serve as valuable resources for constructing intricate shapes from basic elements, they may not be as effective when it comes to generating impromptu and expressive marks. To achieve a more painterly aesthetic, it is recommended to use the brush tools. The available brush tools include the Fluid Brush tool, the Classic Brush tool, and the Paint Brush tool.

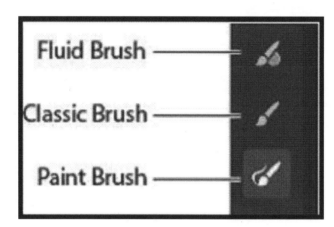

- The Fluid Brush tool has been specifically developed to accurately detect and respond to the pressure applied by a graphics tablet or the speed at which the user draws. As one engages in the act of drawing, the brush size can undergo alterations, thereby facili-tating the creation of both broad and narrow strokes.
- The Paint Brush tool provides the option to use a brush shape that can either stretch or repeat in a regular pattern, enabling the creation of borders and decorations. Users have the option to select from a wide array of brush options, offering a diverse range of choices. If a suitable brush is not readily available, users can personalize existing brushes or even generate their unique brushes.
- The Classic Brush tool is considered the most fundamental among the three brushes, offering a limited range of options for adjusting its size and shape.

The Fluid Brush and the Classic Brush are designed to generate fills rather than strokes. The Paint Brush tool, by default, generates strokes. However, it is possible to activate the Draw As Fill option in the Properties panel for the Paint Brush, which will result in the production of fills instead.

USING THE FLUID BRUSH

The Fluid Brush will be used to generate the diverse furrows and wrinkles on the face of the octopus.

1. Firstly, choose the Fluid Brush tool.
2. Within the Properties panel, navigate to the Tool tab and select the Velocity option. Proceed to designate black as the Fill color, and proceed to configure the desired parameters about the size and shape of the mark you intend to create.

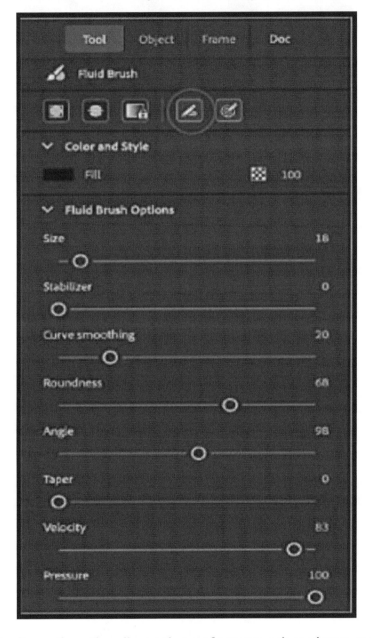

When Using the Velocity option, the dimensions of your mark undergo modifications following the velocity of your pointer as you move your brush across the Stage. When selecting the Pressure option, the size of the mark you make is determined by the level of pressure applied by your pointer, which is measured by a pressure-sensitive stylus and tablet. Perform a trial run by applying several marks on the Stage and make necessary adjustments to the Velocity influence or other relevant parameters until you are satisfied with the desired be-havior of your brush.

3. Choose the octopus layer.

4. Use the Fluid Brush tool to carefully apply a few strokes on the octopus head. Embrace a courageous approach! Create a facial expression that conveys anger by furrowing the brows and creating bulges in the appropriate areas. One may use this example as a reference; however, it is not necessary to replicate all of the marks precisely. Design a customized octopus face that accurately represents and embodies your unique personality.

SMOOTHING SHAPES

At this juncture, it is possible to observe that certain lines that have been generated exhibit a degree of instability. Fortunately, there is a quick and easy method to achieve smooth curves.

1. Firstly, identify and select all of the fills that were created using the Fluid Brush tool.

2. Locate the Smoothen option in the Tools panel and click on it. The selected shapes exhibit simplified and more stream- lined curves, resulting in a smoother appearance.

For a more precise manipulation of smoothing curves, you can access enhanced options by navigating to the Modify menu, then selecting Shape, and finally choosing either Advanced Smooth or Optimize. The advanced options provided enable users to fine-tune the number of curves and points that define their shapes.

3. Continuously click the **Smoothen button** until you have achieved the desired level of smoothness.

CREATING CURVES

The Selection tool has been used to manipulate the boundaries of shapes to create smooth curves intuitively. To achieve a higher level of precision, the Pen tool can be employed.

USING THE PEN TOOL

Without its arms, an octopus would lose a significant aspect of its anatomical structure. Next, you will proceed to craft the elegantly curved and sinuous tentacles that will comprise the anatomy of your octopus.

1. Create a new layer named **"tentacles"**.
2. To begin, navigate to the Tools panel and locate the Pen tool. Once found, proceed to select it. If the desired tool is not currently displayed in the Tools panel, it can be added by selecting **"Edit Toolbar"** located at the bottom of the panel. From there, the tool can be dragged and dropped from the drag-and-drop panel to the desired location.
3. Configure the stroke color to black. Select the Hairline option from the Style menu and the Uniform option from the Width menu.
4. Commence the creation of your shape by initiating a mouse click on the Stage, specifically in a location that is not in prox-imity to the octopus head. This action will establish the initial anchor point of the shape.
5. Relocate the mouse pointer to a different position and proceed to press the designated button, ensuring that you do not release it immediately. Click the mouse button to position the subsequent anchor point. Maintain continuous pressure on the mouse button while dragging it in the desired direction to extend the line further. One should extend a direction line from the newly created anchor point. Upon releasing the mouse button, a seamlessly curved line will be generated, con-necting the two designated anchor points.

6. Proceed with the addition of curved lines to fashion a tentacle that exhibits a shape resembling the letter J. Use the action of pressing and dragging the direction lines to construct the contour of the tentacle. It is not necessary to be concerned if the curves are not perfectly smooth. It is always possible to make edits at a later time.

7. Once you reach the tip of the tentacle, proceed to click on the anchor point directly. When one-half of each pair of anchor- point handles is removed, a corner point is created, enabling the ability to alter the direction.
8. Proceed by sketching additional undulating lines that run parallel to the initial curved line.

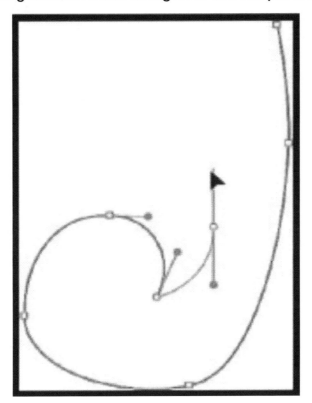

9. Finalize the shape by selecting the initial anchor point.

10. Choose the Paint Bucket tool.
11. Adjust the fill color to match the color of the octopus head. Use the Eyedropper tool to sample the fill color from the octopus head and apply it to the tentacle.
12. Click within the outline that you have recently created to apply a color fill to it.
13. Use the Selection tool and proceed to double-click on the outline to select its entirety.

14. Use the Delete key to eliminate the stroke.

There is no need to be overly concerned with achieving perfect curves. Acquiring proficiency with the Pen tool requires consistent practice and dedication. In the subsequent portion of the lesson, you will also be provided with an opportunity to enhance and perfect your curves.

EDITING CURVES USING THE SELECTION AND SUBSELECTION TOOLS

Likely, your initial attempt at creating smooth waves may not yield satisfactory results. Use either the Selection tool or the Subselection tool to enhance the precision of your curves.

1. Firstly, choose the Selection tool.
2. Place your cursor over a line segment and observe the curved line segment that appears near your pointer. The statement suggests that the curve is editable. When a right-angle segment is displayed near your cursor, it signifies that you can modify the corner point.

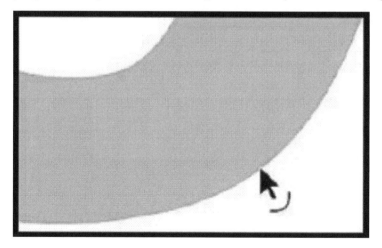

3. Manipulate the curve to modify its shape.
4. Within the Tools panel, locate and choose the Subselection tool, which is concealed beneath the Selection tool.
5. Select the outline of the shape.

6. Manipulate the anchor points by dragging them to different positions, or adjust the handles to enhance the overall shape. Increasing the length of the handles results in a more pronounced flattening of the curve. Adjusting the position of the handles allows for modification of the curve's trajectory.

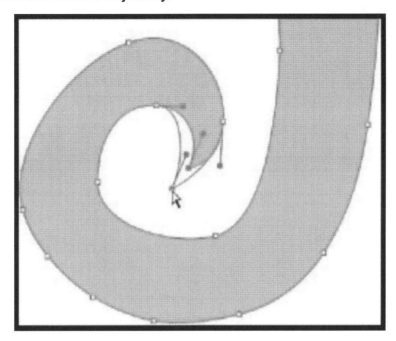

DELETING OR ADDING ANCHOR POINTS

Use the concealed tools located beneath the Pen tool to selectively remove or insert anchor points as required.

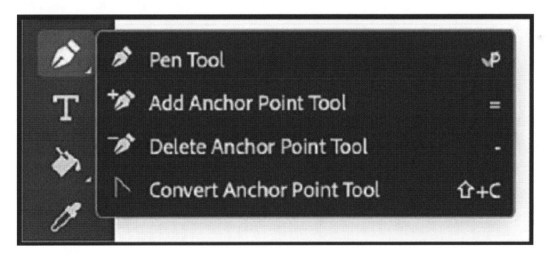

- By clicking and holding the Pen tool, users can access a range of hidden tools that are located beneath it.
- Use the Delete Anchor Point tool to remove an anchor point that already exists.
- Use the Add Anchor Point tool to incorporate an anchor point into a curve.
- Use the Convert Anchor Point tool to manipulate the handlebars and extend them from an anchor point.

USING THE PEN TOOL TO CREATE PATHS

The Pen tool can be used to generate paths with straight or curved segments, which can either be open or closed. For individuals who lack familiarity with the Pen tool, its initial usage can be perplexing. Gaining a comprehensive comprehension of the constituent components of a path and acquiring the skill to construct said components using the Pen tool significantly facilitates the process of drawing paths. To generate a linear trajectory, proceed by clicking the designated mouse button. Upon initial activation, the user establishes the designated starting point by executing a single click. Upon each subsequent click, a linear segment is generated connecting the preceding point to the current point. When Using the Pen tool, it is possible to create intricate straight-segment paths by consistently adding points.

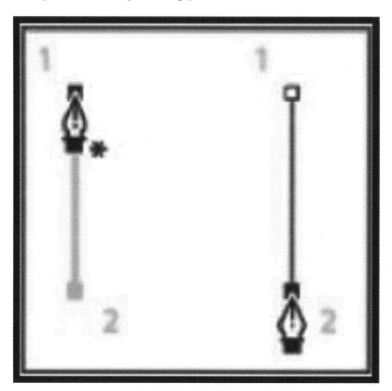

CREATING A STRAIGHT LINE

To gene rate a curved trajectory, initiate the process by exerting pressure on the mouse button to establish an anchor point. Subsequently, proceed to drag the cursor to form a direction line for the aforementioned point. Finally, release the mouse button to complete the op-eration. Position the cursor to determine the desired location for the subsequent anchor point, and proceed to extend another pair of direction lines. The curved segment's size and shape are determined by the positions of the direction lines and points, which are located at the end of each direction line. Manipulating the direction lines and points results in the alteration of the curvature of the path. The smooth curves are formed by connecting anchor points known as smooth points. The corner points serve as connections between sharply curved paths. When manipulating a direction line on a smooth point, the curved segments on both sides of the point will adjust in unison. How- ever, when adjusting a direction line on a corner point, only the curve on the same side as the direction line will be modified.

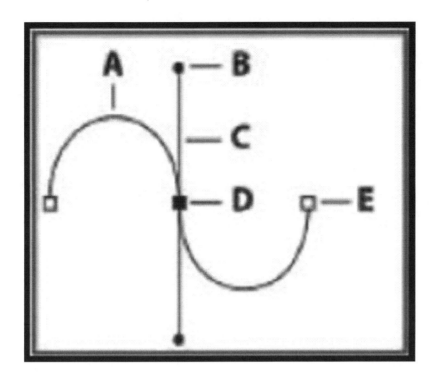

CREATING A CLOSED PATH

Closed paths and open paths differ in their respective methods of termination. To conclude an open path, the user should either choose the Selection tool or use the Escape key. To create a closed path, it is necessary to position the Pen tool pointer precisely over the starting point. This can be identified by a small 2 symbol that will appear adjacent to the pointer. Once the starting point has been identified, a click should be executed. The closure of a path is automatically executed, resulting in the termination of the path. Once the path has been closed, the Pen tool pointer will be displayed with a small asterisk (*), indicating that the subsequent click will initiate a new path.

USING THE BRUSH MODE OPTIONS

Optimizing brush mode selection for the brush tool can significantly enhance the efficiency of drawing in Animate. Typically, one would anticipate the presence of color when applying brush strokes. However, it is possible to modify and alter that particular behavior.

USING PAINT FILLS ONLY

If you wish for your brush to exclusively impact the current fills on the Stage, opt for the Paint Fills Only brush mode.

The steps:

1. Firstly, choose the **Classic Brush tool**
2. Within the Properties panel, select a visually appealing orange fill color. Within the Classic Brush options section, adjust the Size parameter to approximately 20 units (or any other suitable value that corresponds to the desired size, taking into consideration the dimensions of the tentacle you have previously drawn).

141

3. Within the Properties panel, locate the option for Brush Mode and proceed to select the setting that restricts the applica-tion of color exclusively to fills. When this option is enabled, the brush will exclusively impact the fills of your shapes.

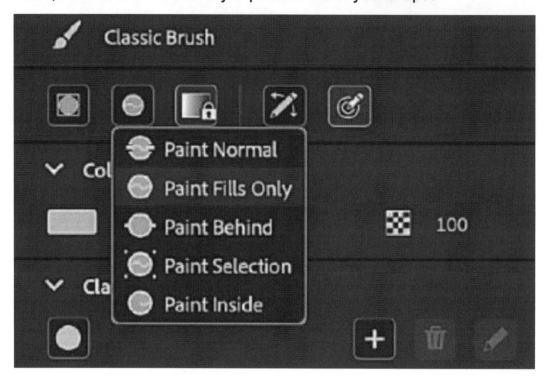

4. Commence the process of painting a small circular shape at the lower edge of the tentacle, serving as a visual represen-tation of a sucker. There is no need to be concerned about meticulously tracing the contour of the tentacle. Release the mouse button. The paint applied by the Fluid Brush tool exclusively impacts the interior fill of the tentacle.

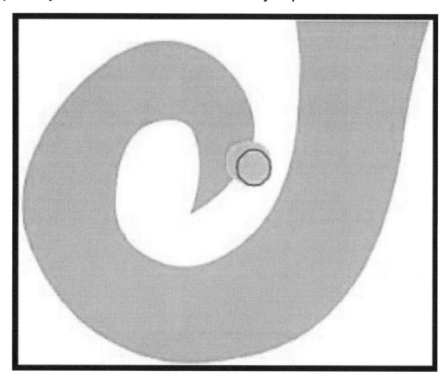

5. Proceed with the addition of appendages along the lower perimeter of your tentacle. The construction of your tentacle has been completed.

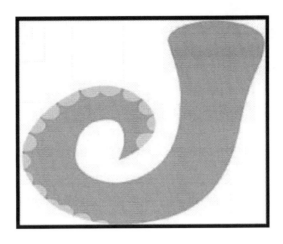

BRUSH MODES

Brush modes refer to the different settings and options available when using a brush tool in digital art or design software. These modes allow users to control how the brush interacts. The paint brushes offer five distinct brush modes: Paint Normal, Paint Fills Only, Paint Behind, Paint Selection, and Paint Inside. Each of these techniques operates with slight variations, and acquiring proficiency in each can greatly enhance one's efficiency when drawing in Animate.

- The **Paint Normal function** is designed to apply color to all elements on the Stage within the active layer, effectively covering strokes and fills.
- The **Paint Fills Only** feature exclusively applies color to areas that require filling.
- The **Paint Behind feature** exclusively applies to vacant regions of the Stage, preserving the current strokes and fills on the active layer.
- The **Paint Selection feature** allows for the application of color exclusively to chosen fills or strokes.
- The **Paint Inside function** selectively applies color exclusively to the fill of the initial shape.

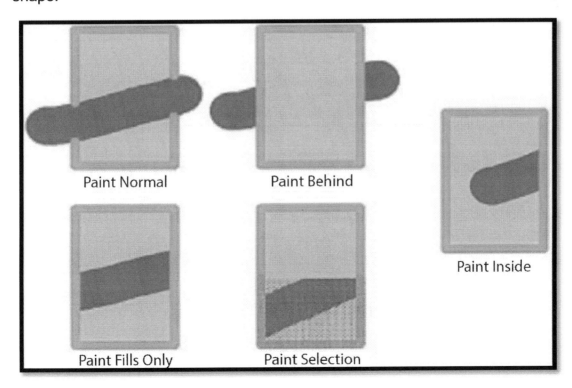

THE PAINT BRUSH TOOL AND CUSTOM BRUSHES

Animate offers three distinct brush tools: the Fluid Brush, which enables the creation of expressive marks with varying thickness for the octopus face; the Classic Brush, a straightforward and uncomplicated brush option; and the Paint Brush, which can be added to the workspace from the Drag and Drop Tools panel. The Paint Brush tool offers a variety of brushes within the Brush Library, which can be ac-cessed through the Style options.

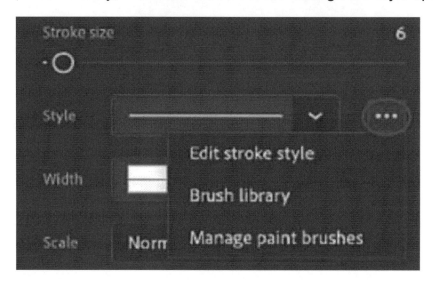

The available options for selection include arrows, decorative borders, as well as calligraphic and artistic brushes.

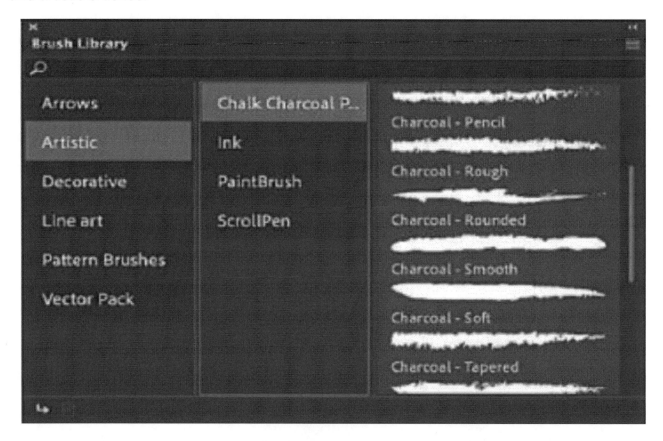

If you are unable to locate a brush that meets your preferences within the Brush Library, or if you require a highly specific brush for your project, it may be necessary to explore alternative options. Regardless of the scenario, it is possible to modify an existing brush or generate a completely novel one. Pattern brushes are designed to repeat a specific shape along the entire length of a stroke. On the other hand, Art brushes are intended to stretch the underlying artwork along the length of the stroke. To modify a brush, locate and select the **"Edit Stroke Style"** button that is situated adjacent to the Style menu within the Properties panel. The Paint Brush Options dialog box is displayed, presenting various controls that are specific to the currently selected brush type. Art brushes and pattern brushes offer distinct sets of options. Conduct experiments to explore various spacing options, observe how shapes repeat or stretch to accommodate different layouts and analyze the handling of corners and overlaps. Once you have reached a level of satisfaction with your newly created brush, proceed to click on the **" Add"** button. This action will enable you to include your customized brush in the Style menu.

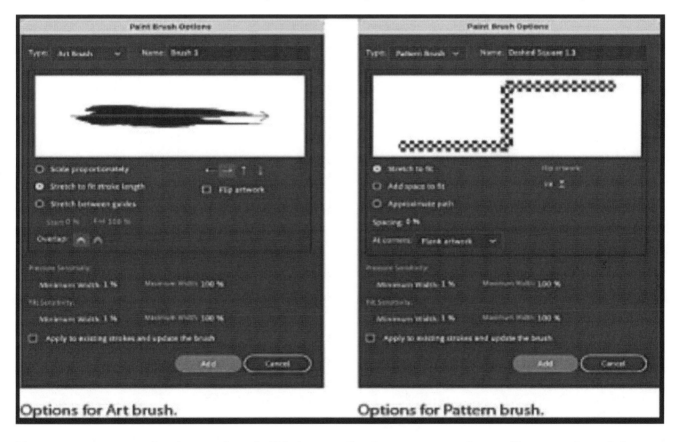

Options for Art brush.   Options for Pattern brush.

To generate a completely new brush, it is imperative to commence by crafting a series of shapes on the Stage that shall serve as the founda-tion for said brush. For instance, if you desire to construct a train track, it is recommended to generate the foundational artwork that can be repeated to form a Pattern brush. To proceed, choose the artwork located on the Stage and subsequently click on the icon labeled **"Create New Paint Brush"** situated at the uppermost section of the Properties panel.

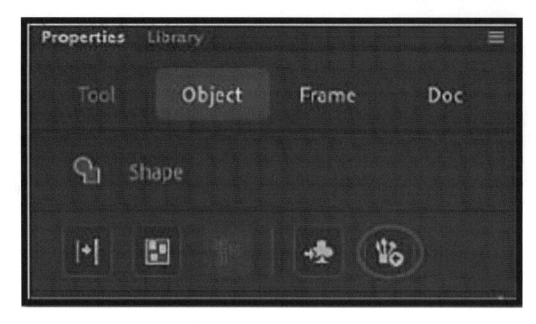

The dialog box for Paint Brush Options is displayed. Within the Type menu, users have the option to select either an Art Brush or a Pattern Brush, followed by the ability to further customize the brush settings. The preview window displays the outcomes of the selected options. Provide a name for the new brush and then proceed by clicking the Add button. The newly acquired brush will be seamlessly integrated into your Style menu, granting you immediate access to its functionality.

ROTATING THE STAGE FOR EASIER DRAWING

When using standard paper for drawing purposes, it is frequently advantageous to rotate the page to achieve a more favorable angle for drawing or writing. Within the Animate software, it is possible to achieve a similar effect on the Stage by Using the Rotation tool.

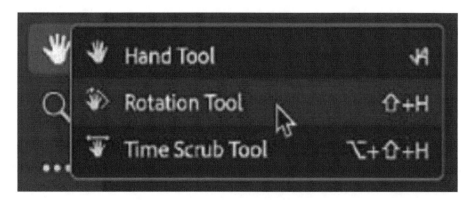

The Rotation tool is located within the Hand tool group in the Tools panel and can also be accessed from the toolbar above the Stage. Use the Rotation tool and proceed to click on the Stage to designate the pivot point, which will be visually represented by a crosshair. After de-termining the pivot point, proceed to manipulate the Stage by dragging it to achieve the desired rotation angle.

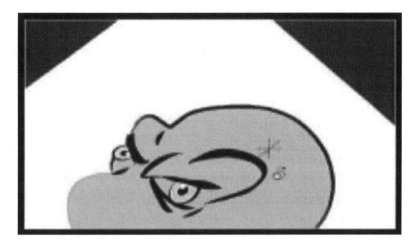

To reset the Stage to its normal orientation, simply click on the Center Stage button located at the top of the Stage.

ABOUT AND UNDERSTANDING SYMBOLS

One may inquire as to the reason behind the presence of a solitary tentacle on your octopus. It is possible to create an additional seven; however, there exists a more efficient method by Using symbols. Symbols are a collection of reusable assets that can be created and stored in the Library panel. In addition to their conventional usage, symbols are employed to enhance special effects, facilitate animation, and enable interactivity. The Animate software uses three distinct types of symbols, namely graphic symbols, button symbols, and movie clip symbols. The symbol can be used multiple times within a project; however, Animate incorporates its data only once. In addition, the use of symbols can greatly facilitate the process of editing.

By using a single symbol as the basis for all eight tentacles on the Stage, any edits or modifications only need to be made once. The symbols are stored within the Library panel. When a symbol is dragged onto the Stage in Animate, the software generates an instance of the symbol while retaining the original in the library. An instance refers to a replicated representation of a symbol that has been strategically positioned on the Stage. The symbol can be conceptualized as an authentic photographic negative, while the instances on the Stage can be likened to prints derived from the negative. It is possible to produce multiple prints from a single negative. Contrary to its nomenclature, a movie clip symbol does not necessarily possess animation. Addition ally, it is beneficial to conceptualize symbols as vessels for containing content. A symbol can include a JPEG image, an imported Illustrator drawing, or a drawing that has been created within Animate. Users can access and modify the contents of a symbol at their convenience. Modifying the contents of a symbol will result in the corresponding modifications being applied to all instances of that symbol.

THERE ARE THREE DISTINCT CATEGORIES OF SYMBOLS:

The three types of symbols in Animate serve distinct purposes. One can discern the nature of a symbol, whether it is a graphic, button, or movie clip, by observing the corresponding icon displayed adjacent to it in the Library panel.

MOVIE CLIP SYMBOLS

The movie clip is widely regarded as one of the most versatile types of symbol in the field. When creating animation, it is common practice to use movie clip symbols. One can apply various filters, color settings, and blending modes to a movie clip instance to enhance its appear-ance by incorporating special effects. The movie clip symbol possesses its autonomous timeline. It is equally feasible to incorporate an animation within a movie clip symbol as it is to include an animation on the main timeline. This feature enables the creation of intricate animations, such as a butterfly gracefully traversing the Stage with the ability to move horizontally and vertically while also animating its wings in a separate motion. Movie clips can be controlled using code to create interactive responses to user input. As an illustration, it is possible to manipulate the position or rotation of a movie clip to develop arcade-style games. Alternatively, a movie clip can possess drag- and-drop functionality, which proves useful when constructing a jigsaw puzzle.

BUTTON SYMBOLS

The use of button symbols is employed to enhance interactivity. The elements encompass four distinct keyframes that delineate their appearance during mouse pointer interaction. Nevertheless, buttons require code to execute specific actions. In addition, it is possible to apply various filters, blending modes, and color settings to buttons.

GRAPHIC SYMBOLS

Frequently, graphic symbols are used to construct movie clip symbols of greater complexity. Interactivity is not supported by the system, and the application of filters or blending modes to a graphic symbol is not possible. Graphic symbols serve as a valuable tool for efficiently switching between multiple versions of a drawing. This is particularly beneficial when synchronizing lips with sound, as storing various mouth positions in separate keyframes of a graphic symbol greatly simplifies the process of voice syncing. Graphic symbols are commonly used to achieve synchronization between an animation within a symbol and the main timeline.

HOW TO CREATE SYMBOLS

There are two primary methods for creating a symbol. Both methods are considered valid, and the choice of which one to use depends on your preferred approach to work. One approach is to begin by ensuring that no elements are currently selected on the Stage. Next, navigate to the menu and select Insert > New Symbol. The Animate software will transition you into symbol editing mode, providing you with the ability to commence the process of drawing or importing graphics for your symbol. A not her approach involves choosing pre-existing artwork on the Stage and subsequently transforming it into symbols. The selected item will be automatically inserted into the newly cre-ated symbol. When Using the Convert to Symbol command, it is important to note that the action does not involve an actual conversion process. Instead, it involves the placement of the selected elements within a symbol container. The second method is often favored by designers due to its ability to allow them to create all of their graphics on the Stage and view them collectively before converting the indi-vidual components into symbols.

CONVERTING ARTWORK ON THE STAGE INTO A SYMBOL

To complete this task, you will need to first select your tentacle and then proceed to convert it into a movie clip symbol.

1. When on the Stage, ensure that only the tentacle is selected.
2. Click on the Modify menu and select **Convert To Symbol (F8)**. The dialog box for converting to a symbol is opened.
3. Assign the name **"tentacle "** to t h e symbol and select **"Movie Clip"** from the Type menu.

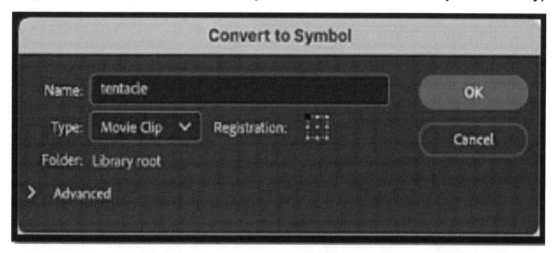

4. Maintain the current configuration for all other settings. The Registration grid displays the coordinates of the registration point (x=O, y=O) for your symbol. The center point is the focal point for all transformations, such as rotations and scalings. It is also the reference point that Animate uses to determine its position on the Stage. Position the registration at the upper-left corner.
5. Click the OK button to proceed. As a result, the tentacle symbol will be displayed in the Library panel.

At present, you possess a symbol within your library, and a specific instance of said symbol has been placed on the Stage.

MANAGING SYMBOL INSTANCES

By saving a symbol in your library, you can use multiple copies, or instances, of that asset in your project without any impact on the file size. Furthermore, it is worth noting that each occurrence does not necessarily need to be a replica of every other occurrence. Instances may exhibit slight variations from their original master symbol, including differences in position on the Stage, size, rotation, color, trans-parency, and applied filters. Subsequently, it is recommended to incorporate an additional seven iterations of your tentacle symbol, while making slight modifications to each, to introduce some variation to the overall octopus pose.

CREATING AN ADDITIONAL SYMBOL INSTANCE

The Stage can be enhanced with additional symbol instances by simply dragging them from the Library panel.

1. Firstly, choose the layer labeled **"tentacles"**.
2. The   second point is as follows: proceed to drag the tentacle movie clip symbol from the Library panel and place it onto the Stage. An instance of the tentacle graphic has been replicated and is now visible on the Stage. There are now two instances of the tentacle symbol present on the Stage.

3. Add six tentacle symbols to the Stage.

CHANGING THE SIZE, POSITION, AND OVERLAPPING OF INSTANCES

The Free Transform tool will now be used to create slight variations among the tentacles.

1. Position four tentacles on a single side of the octopus.
2. Use the Free Transform tool to manipulate the instances by rotating, skewing, and scaling them accordingly to align them with the octopus body and introduce subtle variations between each instance.

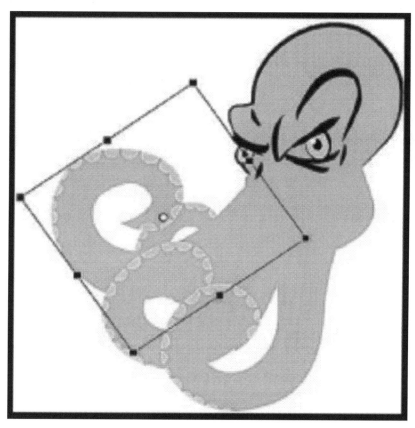

3. Position the remaining four tentacles symmetrically on the opposing side of the octopus's body and execute a horizontal flip.

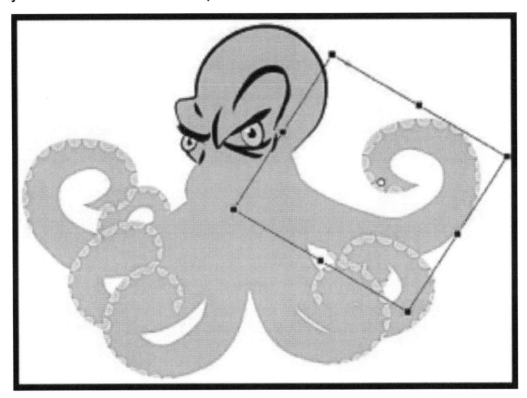

4. To modify the stacking order of your tentacle instances, it is recommended to right-click on a specific instance. From the context menu, select the **"Arrange"** option. Then, choose the **"Bring to Front** option to position the instance at the top-most layer, ensuring that it overlaps all other instances. Alternatively, you can select the **"Bring Forward"** option to move the instance one step higher in the stacking order. Choose the **" Send to Back"** option to relocate the instance to the bottom, causing it to be overlapped by all other instances. Alternatively, select **"Send Backward"** to move it one position lower in the stacking order.

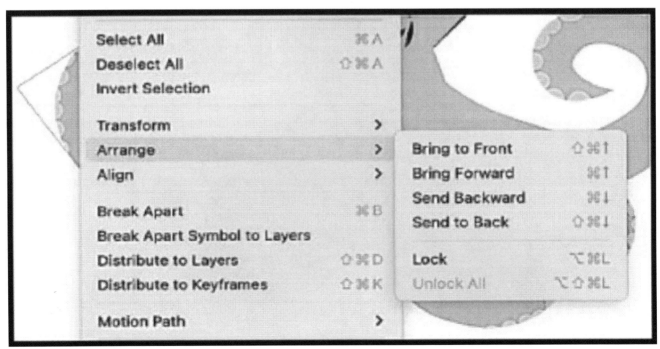

EDITING A SYMBOL FROM THE LIBRARY

It is also possible to modify any symbol at any given moment. If the user desires to modify the shape of the tentacle, they can conveniently enter symbol editing mode to implement the desired alteration. It is possible to directly edit symbols from the Library panel, regardless of whether or not they have been used on the Stage. It is crucial to bear in mind that when you modify a symbol, you are essentially altering the **master** version, resulting in the changes being applied to all the individual instances of that symbol present on the Stage.

1. Locate and double-click on the tentacle movie clip symbol icon within the Library panel.

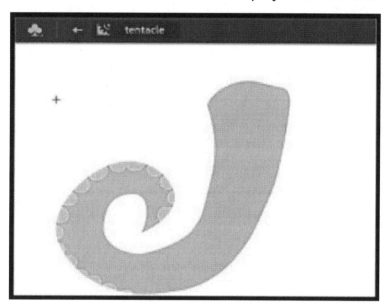

The Animate feature enables the user to enter symbol editing mode. Within this mode, you can observe the contents of your symbol, specifically the tentacle located on the St age. It is important to observe that the Edit bar located at the top of the Stage provides informa-tion indicating that the current location is no longer Scene 1, but rather within the symbol referred to as **"tentacle "**.

2. Use the Selection or Subselection tool to create bulges for each orange sucker located on the tentacle. It is important to re- member that the Selection tool can be used to manipulate lines by dragging them to modify their curvature. Alternatively, the Subselection tool can be employed to relocate anchor points and adjust curvatures by dragging their handlebars.

One can efficiently and effortlessly replicate symbols within the Library panel. To duplicate the symbol, select it, right-click, and then se-lect the **"Duplicate"** option. Alternatively, you may opt to select the **"Duplicate"** option from the Library panel menu, located in the upper- right corner of the panel. The Animate software will initiate a dialog box, providing you with the opportunity to generate an accurate du-plicate of the symbol you have selected within your library.

3. To exit symbol editing mode and return to the main timeline, click the left-facing arrow on the Edit bar located above the Stage.

The visual representation of the movie clip symbol in the Library panel accurately reflects any modifications that have been applied. Similarly, this principle applies to all occurrences on the Stage. Whenever the symbol is edited, all occurrences of that symbol will be mod-ified accordingly.

HOW TO EDIT A SYMBOL IN PLACE

It may be advisable to make adjustments to a symbol within the context of the other objects present on the Stage. The desired action can be achieved by performing a double-click on an instance located on the Stage. Upon entering symbol editing mode, users will have the ability to observe the symbol's immediate surroundings. The editing mode being referred to is commonly known as **"editing in place."** When Using the Fluid Brush tool or the Classic Brush tool to make modifications to a symbol directly, it is important to take note of the presence of an option labeled **"Scale Size With Symbol Instance"** within the Properties panel. It is worth mentioning that this option is enabled by default. The functionality in question enables the automatic adjustment of the brush size, ensuring that any edits made are proportionate to the objects on the Stage that may have been resized.

The steps:

1. Use the Selection tool to perform a double-click action on a specific tentacle movie clip instance located on the Stage. Upon entering symbol editing mode, all other objects on the Stage are visually subdued. It is important to observe that the Edit bar indicates a transition from Scene 1 to the interior of the symbol referred to as the **"tentacle "**.

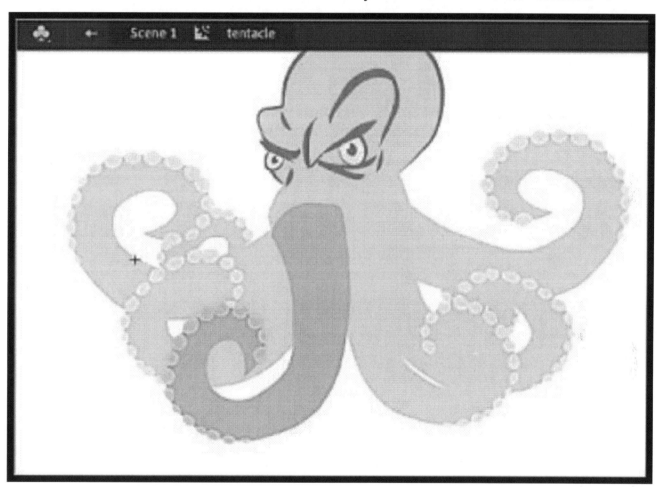

2. Apply a variable-width stroke to both the sides of the tentacle and the suckers. To remove solely the upper contour of the tentacle, it is imperative to ensure the presence of corner points on both sides. When making edits to the symbol, it is im-portant to observe that these modifications will have a cascading effect on all instances of the symbol present on the Stage.

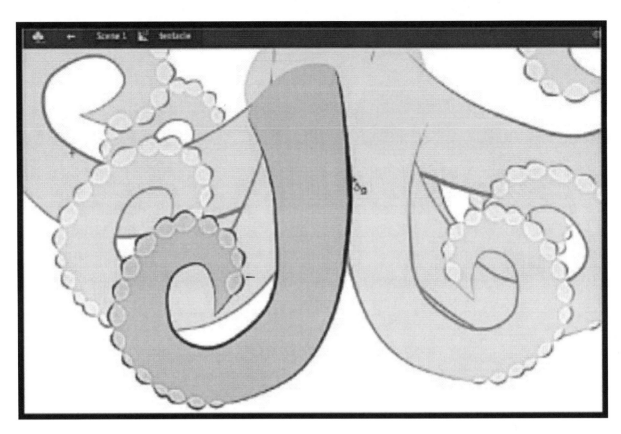

3. To navigate back to the main timeline, click on "**Scene 1** "located on the Edit bar above the Stage. To return to the next- highest group level, you have the option to simply double-click any part of the Stage outside the graphic using the Selec-tion tool.

HOW TO BREAK APART A SYMBOL INSTANCE

If the user desires to remove the symbol instance status of an object on the Stage, they can use the Break Apart command to restore it to its original form. First, locate the symbol instance that you wish to modify. Once you have identified it, proceed to the menu and select the **"Modify"** option. From the dropdown menu that appears, choose the **"Break Apart"** command. The Animate software application is capa-ble of breaking apart a movie clip instance. The remaining elements on the Stage consist of the contents of the movie clip symbol, specifi-cally the shape.

USING GRADIENT FILLS

Up until this point, you have used solid colors as fills. However, it is worth noting that you also have the option to use gradients as fills, which can result in a more captivating and visually appealing effect. A gradient is a visual effect where one color transitions smoothly into another. Animate can generate linear gradients, which allow for color transitions in a horizontal, vertical, or diagonal direction. Addition- ally, it can also produce radial gradients, which involve color transformations that radiate outward from a central focal point.

HOW TO CREATE GRA DIENT TRANSITIONS

The Color panel is used to establish the colors that will be used in your gradient. By default, a linear gradient transitions smoothly between two colors. However, in Animate, it is possible to incorporate up to 15 color transitions within a gradient. The color pointer serves to establish the location of each color definition, facilitating smooth transitions between adjacent pointers. It is suggested to incorporate color pointers beneath the gradient definition bar in the Color panel to expand the range of available colors and subsequently increase the vari-ety of gradients that can be created. The task at hand involves the creation of a gradient that transitions from a lighter shade of blue to a darker shade of blue, to simulate the visual impression of the deep ocean.

1. Proceed by creating a new layer and assigning it the name **"background"**. Relocate the layer to the lowest position among the layers.

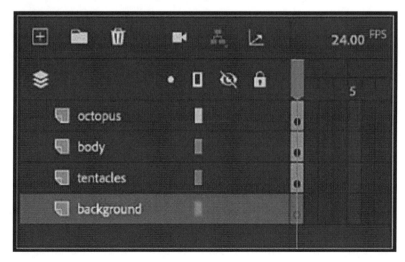

2. Access the Color panel by navigating to the Window menu and selecting Color. Within the Color panel, locate the Fill Color icon and proceed to select Linear Gradient from the Color Type menu.

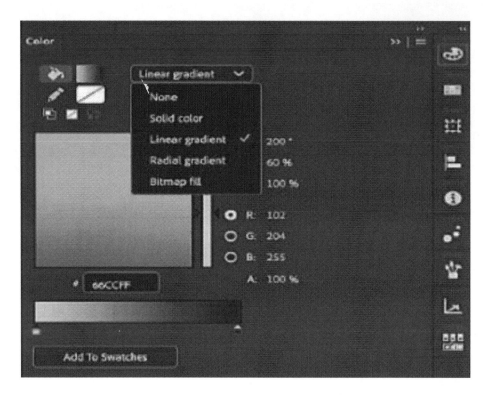

3. Within the Color panel, locate and choose the color pointer situated at the leftmost position of the color gradient defini-tion bar. Confirm that the triangle above the selected color pointer has turned black, indicating its selection. Proceed to input the hexadecimal value 66CCFF into the designated field for specifying a light blue color. Press the Return/Enter key to apply the selected color. Alternatively, users have the option to choose a color from the Color Picker or sim ply double- click the color pointer to select a color from the available color swatches.

4. Choose the color pointer located on the far-right side. Next, input the hexadecimal code 000066 to achieve a dark blue color. Press the **Return/Enter key** to apply the selected color. To remove a color pointer from the gradient definition bar, one can easily accomplish this by dragging the pointer off the bar.

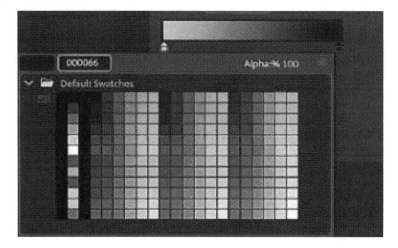

5. Select the Rectangle tool.
6. Ensure that the gradient defined in the Color panel is applied to the Fill in the Properties panel. Select the stroke color chip with the red diagonal line through it to indicate no color.
7. Create a large rectangle that spans the entire Stage. The expansive square is adorned with a hue that seamlessly transitions from a pale shade of blue to a deep, rich blue.

USING THE GRADIENT TRANSFORM TOOL

Furthermore, apart from the selection of colors and the arrangement of color pointers for a gradient, it is possible to modify the dimen-sions, orientation, and focal point of a gradient fill. The Gradient Transform tool is used to modify the location at which the color transi-tion occurs within the gradient of your ocean background.

1. Firstly, proceed to select the Gradient Transform tool. The Gradient Transform tool is categorized alongside the Free Trans- form tool.
2. Select the rectangle tool and apply it to your background layer to fill it. The transformation handles are now visible. Manipulate the position of the center circle to alter the focal point of the gradient. Adjust the round handle to rotate the gradient, and modify the square handle to expand or contract the gradient.

3. Adjust the square handle located on the right side of the bounding box by dragging it inward to compress the gradient and make it narrower. Manipulate the circular control located in the corner to adjust the rotation of the gradient, ensuring that the lighter shade of blue is positioned in the upper-left corner and the darker shade of blue is positioned in the lower-right corner.

USING TRANSPARENCY TO CREATE DEPTH

The measurement of transparency is typically expressed as a percentage and is commonly referred to as alpha. The alpha value of 100% signifies complete opacity for a color, while an alpha value of 0% signifies complete transparency.

ADJUSTING THE ALPHA VALUE OF A FILL

The addition of small transparent bubbles to your scene will serve to enhance the overall visual appeal by introducing captivating details. It is widely acknowledged that octopuses do not produce bubbles. **However, it is also important to note that they do not possess angry eyes, correct?**

1. Create a new layer and label it as **"bubbles"**. Proceed to reposition this layer to the highest position among all the existing layers.
2. Select the Oval tool from the available options.
3. Within the Properties panel, select the color white for the Fill option and opt for None for the Stroke option.
4. Modify the Alpha value of the Fill to 60%. One can also modify the transparency of a shape by accessing the Properties panel and selecting the Fill Color icon. From there, the Alpha value in the color picker can be adjusted accordingly. The color swatch located in the Properties panel provides a preview of the color that you have recently selected. The level of transparency is visually represented by the presence of a gray grid, which becomes visible when observing the transparent color swatch.

5. Press and hold the **Shift key** while using the mouse to create circles of different sizes on your octopus. The bubbles exhibit a degree of transparency, facilitating the visualization of the underlying graphics in the layers.

USING SWATCHES AND IMPLEMENTING TAGGED SWATCHES

Swatches refer to preselected samples of color. To access them, navigate to the Swatches panel by selecting **Window > Swatches** or using the keyboard shortcut **Command+F9 (Ctrl+F9).** One can save colors that have been used in graphics as new swatches, ensuring their avail- ability for future reference. Tagged swatches refer to specifically designated swatches that are associated with the graphics on your Stage that use them. To create a tagged swatch, select **"Convert To A Tagged Swatch"** located at the bottom of the Swatches panel. You will then have the option to provide a name for your tagged swatch. A tagged swatch can be identified by the presence of a white triangle located in the lower-right corner of the color.

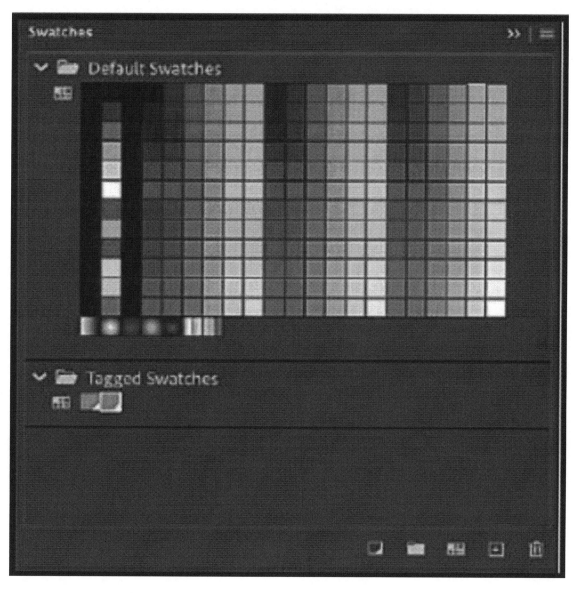

The true potential of tagged swatches becomes evident when you are required to make revisions to your project. Assume that the art director or your client expresses dissatisfaction with the color of the white transparent bubbles. By using a tagged swatch for the bubbles, it becomes possible to effortlessly modify the color of the tagged swatch, resulting in automatic updates to all graphics that make use of said tagged swatch.

USING VARIOUS FILTERS AND APPLYING COLOR EFFECTS

Use filters to gene rate unique visual effects, such as blurs, glows, and drop shadows. Use color effects to enhance the brightness, darkness, colorization, and other modifications of your transparencies.

MODIFYING THE COLOR EFFECT OF AN INSTANCE

Each instance can possess its distinct value for attributes such as transparency, color, tint, or brightness. The controls for adjusting these settings can be found in the Color Effects section of the Properties panel.

1. Use the Selection tool to choose a subset of the tentacles that are positioned behind the remaining ones.
2. Within the Color Effects section located in the Properties panel, select the option labeled Brightness from the Style menu.
3. Adjust the Bright slider to a valueof-20%. By selecting the Advanced option from the Style menu, users can simultane-ously modify the tint, transparency, and brightness of an instance. This can be achieved by making adjustments to the in-dividual color components (RGB) in conjunction with the Alpha percentage.

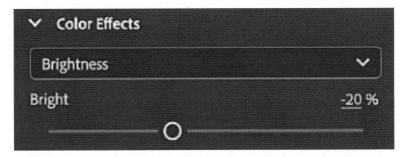

The tentacle instances that have been selected on the Stage undergo a visual transformation, becoming darker in color and creating the illusion of receding into the distance.

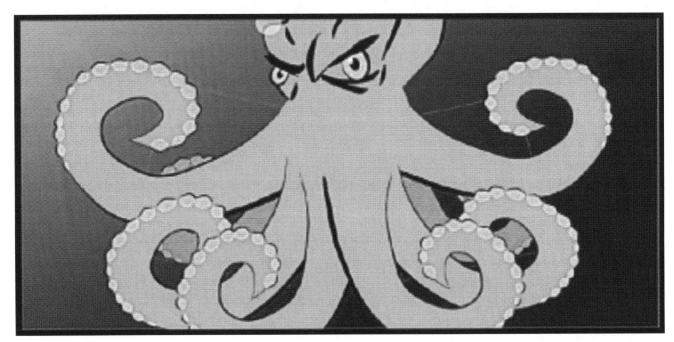

To reset the color effect of any instance, select the **"None"** option from the Style menu.

USING AND APPLYING THE BLUR FILTER

Additionally, it is possible to apply a Blur filter to the instances of the farthest tentacles to enhance the perception of depth within the scene.

1. Firstly, identify the instances of the tentacles that have already been dimmed.
2. Expand the Filters sect ion in the Properties panel.
3. Locate the **"Add Filter"** button and click on it. Then, select the **"Blur"** option from the menu that appears. The properties and values of the Blur filter are presented.
4. To ensure the blur effect is applied uniformly in both directions, click on one of the link icons adjacent to the Blur X and Blur Y values if they are not already selected.
5. It is recommended to keep the values of Blur X and Blur Y at their default settings of 4 pixels.

The object on the stage appears blurred, contributing to the creation of an atmospheric perspective within the scene.

ADDITIONAL FILTER OPTIONS

The Options menu, located in the upper-right comer of the Filter s section, provides a range of commands that facilitate the manage-ment and application of multiple filters.

- The **"Save as Preset"** feature allows users to save a specific filter along with its corresponding settings, enabling them to easily apply it to other instances as needed.
- The functions **"Copy Selected Filter"** and **"Copy All Filters"** allow users to duplicate one or multiple filters.
- The Paste Filters feature allows users to easily copy and apply selected filters to multiple instances.
- The **Reset Filter command** restores the selected filter to its default values.
- The **"Enable or Disable Filter"** button, represented by the eyeball icon located at the head of the Value column, provides the option to view your instance with or without the filter applied.

HOW TO CREATE AND EDIT TEXT IN ADOBE ANIMATE 2024

Let us proceed to incorporate textual elements into this illustration. There are several options available for text, depending on the type of document you are working on. When working with an HTMLS Canvas document, such as the one demonstrated in this lesson, you have the option to incorporate either static text or dynamic text. Use static text to present straightforward display text that relies on the fonts accessible on the designer's computer. When static text is created on the Stage and published to an HTMLS project, Animate automatically converts the fonts into outlines. This implies that there is no need for concern regarding whether your audience possesses the necessary fonts to perceive the text in the manner you intended. One potential drawback is that an excessive amount of text has the potential to in- crease the file size, resulting in bloating. Use dynamic text to harness the capabilities of web fonts offered by either Adobe Fonts or Google Fonts. There is a vast selection of top-notch fonts at your disposal as part of your Creative Cloud subscription. These fonts are conveniently hosted by Adobe and can be easily accessed through the Properties panel within Animate. Google Fonts provides access to a wide range of high-quality open-source fonts that are conveniently hosted on Google servers.

USING THE TEXT TOOL TO INCORPORATE DYNAMIC TEXT

The text can be generated using the Text tool.

1. Firstly, choose the top layer.
2. Proceed to the Insert menu, then select **Timeline,** and finally choose **Layer.** Assign the newly created layer the name **'text".**

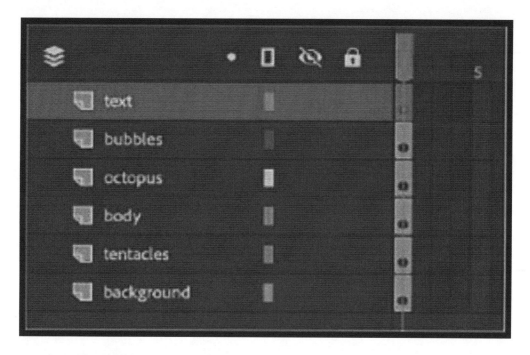

3. Choose the **Text tool.**
4. Select the option for Dynamic Text from the Text Type menu located in the Properties panel.

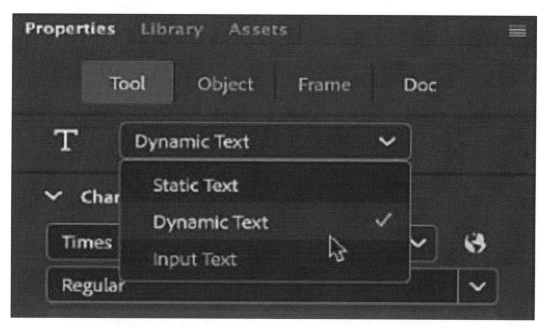

5. Choose a font, keeping in mind that you will eventually replace it with an Adobe font sourced from the web. The selected fonts may not align with the ones used in this publication.
6. Select the **"Align Center "**option to align the paragraph in the center.
7. Position a text box adjacent to your octopus.
8. **Provide the following text:** Why do octopuses make the best criminals? There is a possibility that the text may not align properly or it may not meet your desired specifications in terms of size or font. Rest assured, you will have the opportunity to choose a suitable web font for your text box in the upcoming task.

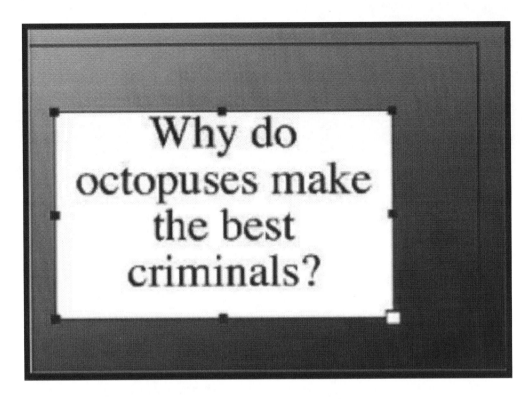

9. To exit the Text tool, simply select the Selection tool.

10. Place the punchline on the Stage in the same layer below the first piece of text: **"Because we are well armed."**

IMPLEMENTING A WEB FONT

Next, you will need to establish a connection between a web font and your project. It is important to ensure that you have a stable internet connection as Animate relies on retrieving the list of available fonts from the web. The procedures for incorporating an Adobe font and a Google font exhibit notable similarities. For this particular exercise, you will be incorporating an Adobe font.

1. To begin, choose the initial block of text. Then, navigate to the Character section within the Properties panel. Locate the option labeled **"Add Web Fonts,"** which is identifiable by its globe icon. Proceed to click on this icon. Select **Adobe Fonts** from the dropdown menu that is displayed.

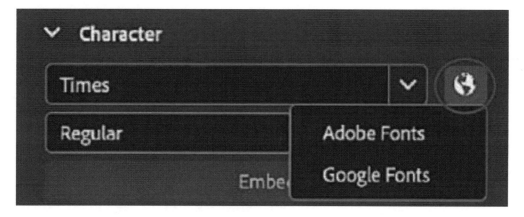

The Animate software application presents the user with the Add Adobe Fonts dialog box. The loading time for the list of fonts can be quite slow.

2. Select Name from the Sort by menu.

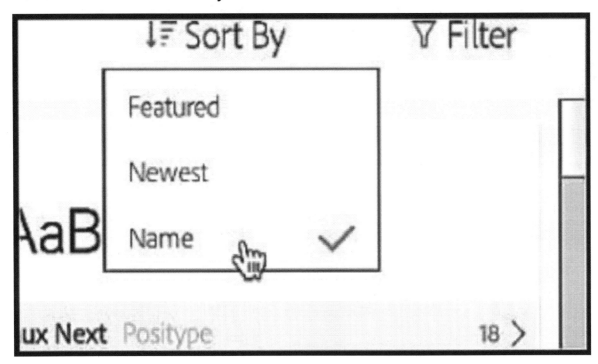

The alphabetical display of Adobe fonts can be found on the right side of the screen. Users have the option to select from various sorting options in the Filter, including sorting by featured, newest, or other criteria. The Adobe fonts are presented alongside a sample string of characters, showcasing the letters AaBbCcDd. Users can navigate through the available font families by using the scroll bar located on the right-hand side of the screen. Additionally, users have the option to conduct targeted searches for specific fonts or use the Category menu to refine their search parameters.

3. Take a moment to review the selection of typefaces and choose one that you believe would be suitable for this illustration.

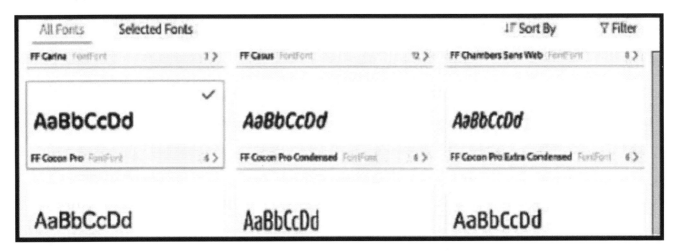

To obtain further information regarding the font, click on the font name located beneath the sample text. Adobe Fonts showcases the di- verse range of style variations available for a particular font.

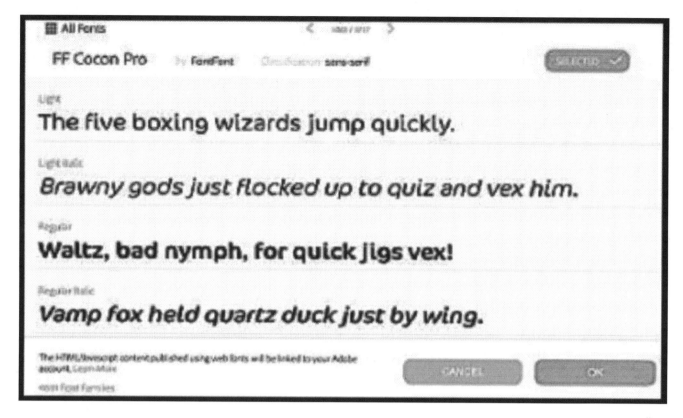

The Adobe font you have chosen has been successfully added to the list of available fonts. The web fonts are displayed at the top of the menu.

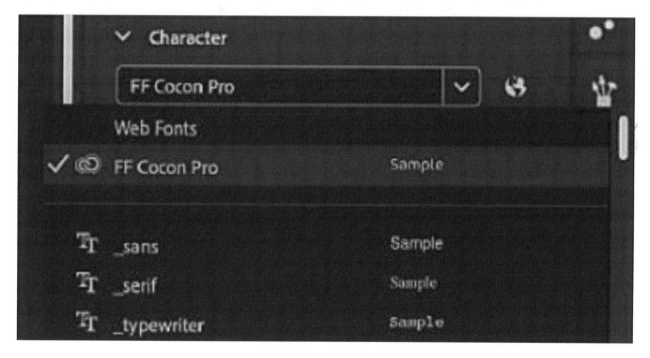

4. Proceed by selecting the desired text and subsequently applying the newly available Adobe font. Select the color black for the text. To ensure that all the text fits comfortably within the designated space, it is recommended to make adjustments to the font size and/or line spacing. These adjustments can be made in the Properties panel, specifically in the Paragraph section where the line spacing option is available.
5. Select the additional piece of text and proceed to apply the identical font.

HOW TO REMOVE A WEB FONT

If you decide to alter your preference, it is a straightforward process to remove an Adobe web font and subsequently select an alternative font of your choosing.

1. Identify and highlight all the text content that is currently using the web font that you intend to eliminate.
2. To deselect the font, select a different one.
3. Click on the **"Add Web Fonts"** button and select **"Adobe Fonts"** to access the **"Add Adobe Fonts"** dialog box.
4. Navigate to the **"Selected Fonts"** tab. The Animate software showcases all the fonts that have been chosen for your project, which are denoted by a blue check mark.

If the font displays a gray check mark, it indicates that it is currently being used in some text on the Stage. Before removing a font from your project, it is necessary to deselect it from every instance of text.

5. To deselect the font, simply click on it. Currently, there is an issue where the Selected Fonts area does not display any fonts.
6. Proceed by clicking the OK button. The dialog box for adding Adobe Fonts is closed. The web font has been removed from the Family menu in the Properties panel.

IMPLEMENTING SPEECH BALLOONS

Lastly, incorporate speech balloons to enclose both the setup and punchline text.

1. Use the Oval tool and opt for a white color for the Fill and a black color for the Stroke.
2. Within the Properties panel, select a solid line as the Style for the Stroke, and opt for a uniform thickness as the Width.
3. Create an oval shape that encompasses the first text box and another oval shape that encompasses the second text box.

4. Select the Selection tool. While holding down the **Option/Alt key**, proceed to dragon one side of each oval to extend a point for the tail of the speech balloon, directing it towards the octopus. By holding down the Option/Alt key, you can gen-erate a new anchor point on your shape.

5. Ensure that the text is properly aligned with each speech balloon, if necessary. Afterward, proceed to group the text with its corresponding speech balloon to enable the movement of the speech balloons as a cohesive entity.

ALIGNING AND SHARING OBJECTS

Using the functionality of rulers (located under the **View menu > Rulers**) and grids(located under the **View menu> Grid > Show Grid**) can assist in accurately positioning objects However, for scenarios involving multiple objects, it   is recommended to employ the Align panel, as it offers a more efficient approach. Additionally, one will depend on the   use of the intelligent guides that become visible when manipulat-ing objects on the Stage.

ALIGNING OBJECTS

The Align panel is designed to align multiple selected objects either horizontally or vertically. Addition ally, it can evenly distribute objects.

1. Firstly, choose the **Selection tool.**
2. To select both pieces of text, use the shift-click function.
3. To access the Align panel, navigate to the Window menu and select Align.
4. Ensure that the Align to Stage option is deselected, if it is currently selected. Click on the **"Align Left Edge"** button.

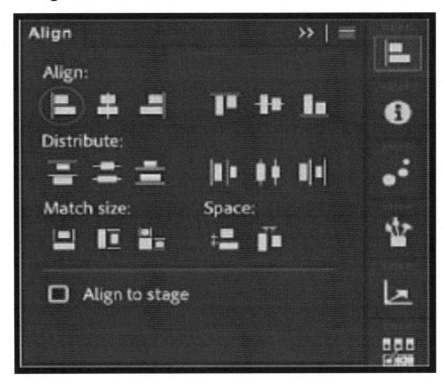

The Animate software aligns the speech balloons in a manner where they are positioned along the left edge of their respective bounding boxes. If desired, one may attempt to align them along their central axis.

It may be necessary to secure the lower layers to prevent inadvertent selection of the shapes within those layers.

USING RULERS AND GUIDES

It is advisable to ensure greater precision in the placement of your graphics. One alternative method for positioning objects on the Stage involves Using rulers and guides. The rulers are positioned along the top and left edges of the pasteboard, serving the purpose of providing measurements along the horizontal and vertical axes. Guides are lines that can be either vertical or horizontal and are visible on the Stage during the editing process. However, they are not visible in the final published movie. To use rulers, navigate to the View menu and select Rulers. Alternatively, you can use the keyboard shortcut **Option+Shift+Command+R** on a Mac or **Alt+Shift+Ctrl+R** on a Windows system. The pasteboard is equipped with horizontal and vertical rulers that are measured in pixels. These rulers can be found along the top and left edges of the pasteboard. When manipulating objects on the Stage, tick marks are displayed to indicate the positions of their bounding boxes on the rulers. The coordinates (x=O, y=O) represent the starting point located at the upper-left corner of the Stage. The x-values in- crease towards the right, while they-values increase in the downward direction. Position your mouse pointer over the top horizontal ruler or the left vertical ruler, then click and drag a guide onto the Stage. A visual indicator in the form of a colored line is displayed on the Stage, serving as a useful tool for aligning elements.

To access the Move Guide dialog box and enter pixel values for accurate guide positioning, simply double-click on any guide using the Selection tool. Access the **View menu** and navigate to the **Snapping option**. Ensure that the Snap to Guides feature is enabled. The new feature allows objects to automatically align with any guides present on the Stage. To lock your guides, navigate to the View menu, then select **Guides,** and finally choose **Lock Guides**. This feature serves to prevent any inadvertent movement of the objects. To remove all guides, navigate to the **View menu** and select **Guides**, then choose **Clear Guides**. To modify the color of the guides and adjust the snapping accuracy, navigate to the View menu and select Guides, followed by Edit Guides.

SHARING YOUR FINAL PROJECT

There are numerous methods available for disseminating your completed illustration. The Animate software provides the capability to export projects to a variety of formats and platforms.

EXPORTING ARTWORK AS PNG, JPEG, OR GIF

To obtain a basic image file in formats such as PNG, JPEG, or GIF, it is recommended to use the Export Image panel. This panel allows you to select your desired format and adjust the compression settings to optimize web download performance.

1. Click on the **"File"** menu, then select **"Export"** and choose **"Export Image"**. The dialog box for exporting images is displayed.

Vector art, particularly art that features intricate curves and a variety of shapes and line styles, can place significant strain on CPU resources. This issue can pose a challenge on mobile devices, as their less robust processors may encounter difficulties when attempting to display intricate artwork. Use the Modify > Convert to Bitmap command to transform the chosen artwork on the Stage into a singular bit-map, thereby reducing the strain on the processor. After the conversion of the object to a bitmap, it becomes possible to relocate it without any concerns about it blending with the shapes underneath. Unfortunately, the graphics can no longer be modified using Animate's edit-ing tools.

2. One should carefully consider the suitable file format, determine the desired level of compression, choose an appropriate color palette, and even conduct comparisons of various settings to evaluate the trade-off between image qualities and file size. Additionally, the image can be resized.

EXPORTING AS HTML CANVAS

The process of exporting as HTML Canvas involves converting a digital file or design into a format that is compatible with the HTML5 Canvas element. This allows the file or design to be displayed and interacted with on a webpage. If desired, it is also possible to export the project as an HTML Canvas document. However, it is worth noting that simpler graphic file formats such as JPEG, GIF, PNG, and SVG are generally more suitable for illustrations. To accomplish this, select the **"Publish"** option under the **"File"** menu, or choose **"Test Movie"** fol-lowed by **"In Browser"** under the **"Control"** menu. Another option is to click on the "Test Movie" button located at the top corner of the Ani- mate application. If your Animate document comprises multiple frames, there is also an option to export it as an animated GIF. Animate is responsible for publishing the necessary files that are required to properly display your project within a web browser. The files consist of a mixture of HTML, JavaScript, and asset support files.

COLLABORATING VIA THE ASSETS PANEL

Collaboration is a crucial aspect of working on large projects, especially when you are part of a team of designers and animators. In such scenarios, the sharing of art and other assets becomes imperative to ensure smooth workflow and effective collaboration. The Assets panel in Animate facilitates seamless collaborations. Use the capability to store both static and animated assets, employ relevant keywords to enhance search efficiency, and subsequently export the assets as an ANA file format to facilitate their utilization by others.

SAVING ART TO THE ASSETS PAN EL

The Assets panel consists of two distinct tabs: the Default tab, which contains a curated collection of animated and static assets provided by Adobe for your perusal and utilization in your projects, and the Custom tab, which serves as a dedicated space for you to store and orga-nize your assets.

1. Within the Library panel, proceed to right-click on your tentacle movie clip symbol and select the option to Save as Asset. The Save As dialog box is opened.

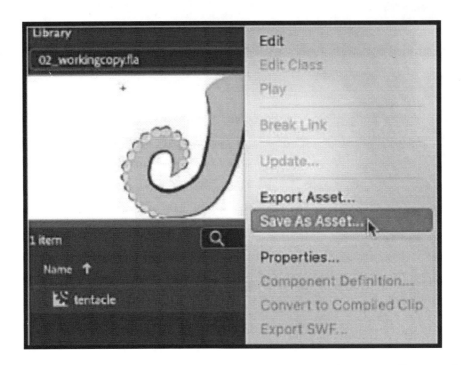

2. Provide a name for the asset. Regarding this matter, the term **"tentacle"** would be a suitable descriptor.
3. Input keywords separated by commas in the Tags field. The use of keywords will facilitate the process of locating the desired asset within the Assets panel. Descriptive terms, project names, author names, or any other identifiers can be used for this purpose.
4. Click on the **"Save"** button.

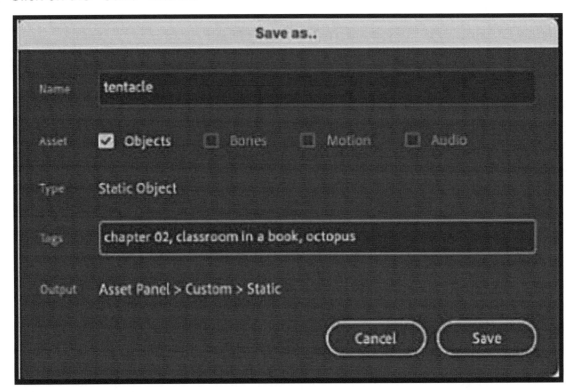

The asset has been successfully saved to the designated Custom tab within the Assets panel. Dick on the arrow located to the left of the term "Static" to expand the category and gain access to the asset. The assets will be accessible to you across various Animate files.

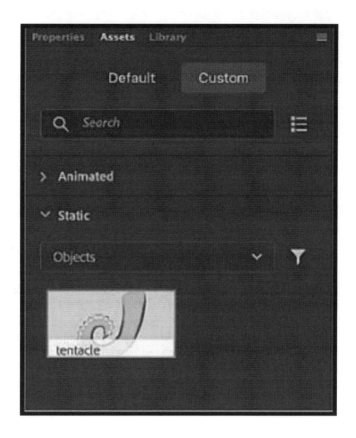

EXPORTING AND IMPORTING ASSETS

To facilitate the sharing of an asset with another user, it is recommended to export an ANA file.

1. Within the Library panel, proceed to right-click on the tentacle movie clip symbol and select the option to Export Asset.

2. In the Tags field, enter any optional keywords that you would like to include, ensuring that they are separated by commas.

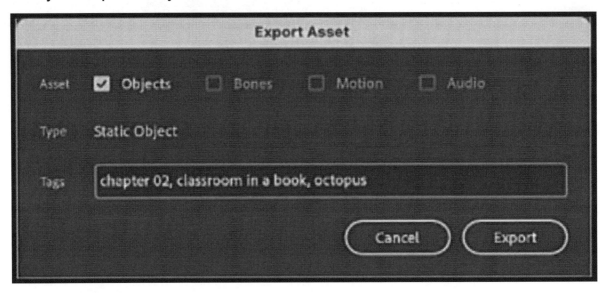

3. Select the **"Export"** option. Animate prompts the user to specify the desired location for saving the ANA file. Save the file to your computer.
4. To import an asset, locate the options menu located in the upper-right corner of the Assets panel. From the dropdown menu, select the **"Import"** option.
5. Locate the desired ANA file for import and select the **"Open"** option.

The asset has been imported into the Custom tab of your Assets panel. To incorporate the asset into your Animate file, simply drag and drop it onto your Stage. This action will automatically generate a symbol in your Library panel.

FREQUENTLY ASKED QUESTIONS

1. How do you create graphics and text in Adobe Animate?
2. How do you make selections?
3. How do you create shapes?
4. How do you edit shapes?
5. How do you use the free trans from tool?
6. How do you change shape contours?
7. How do you modify stroke and fill properties?
8. How do you use brushes?
9. What are the different brush modes?
10. How do you add or delete anchor points?

CHAPTER 6: MOTION TWEENS UNLEASHED

OVERVIEW

In this chapter, you will learn about motion tweens, how to edit the motion path, understand what the motion editor presents, as well as get to view options for the motion editor. If you are ready, check below for the information.

ABOUT MOTION TWEENS

Motion tweens provide an alternative method for generating animation using symbol instances. Motion tweens, similar to classic tweens, facilitate the animation of modifications in an instance's position, transformation, color effects, or filters. Furthermore, motion tweens can animate the 3D position or translation. Motion tweens offer a wider range of options for effectively managing and manipulating property alterations. Nevertheless, the increase in available options inevitably leads to a corresponding increase in complexity. They are generally found to have lower compatibility with other Animation techniques. It is advisable to primarily rely on classic tweens for your work, as they offer several advantages. However, acquiring the skill to create animation using both techniques is highly beneficial as it allows you to gain a comprehensive understanding of the animator's toolkit. Gaining a comprehensive understanding of both motion and classic tweens will greatly enhance your ability to select the most suitable approach for any given project.

UNDERSTANDING THE DISTINCTIONS BETWEEN MOTION TWEENS AND CLASSIC TWEENS

The fundamental distinctions between motion and classic tweens can be summarized as follows:

- Only motion tweens provide access to the Motion Editor, which is an advanced tool for adjusting properties and easing.
- The motion tweens are segregated into a dedicated tween layer. Nevertheless, both classic and motion tweens possess the common limitation that prohibits the presence of any other object within the same layer as the tween.
- The motion tweens feature provides support for 3D rotations or translations. Classic tweens do not possess such attributes.
- It is possible to modify the path of motion in a motion tween without the need to create a distinct Motion Guide layer.
- The use of motion tweens is not compatible with the animation of contemporary rigs employing the Asset Warp tool.

CREATING HAND ANIMATIONS

The project will commence with the animation of the hand, which will transition from its initial position on the Stage to forcefully push the three blocks.

1. Firstly, it is necessary to allocate a specific duration on the timeline to allow the animation to progress. Select frame 60 in all five layers by either holding down the Shift key or clicking on each layer or by dragging the selection through all layers.

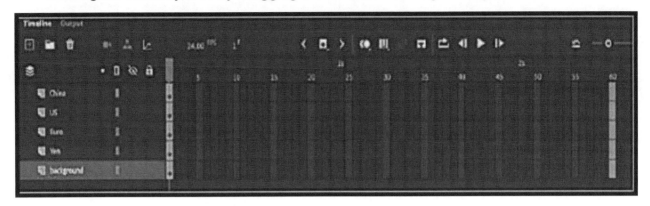

2. Select the **"Insert Frame"** option by pressing the F5 key. The animation software, Animate, includes the functionality to add frames across all five layers, extending up to frame 60.

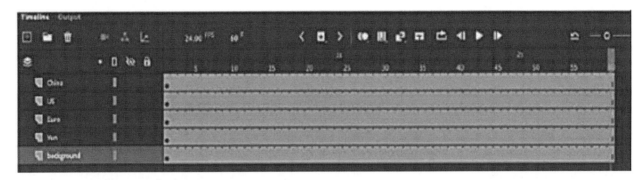

3. Proceed with the action of deselecting the five layers. To isolate the graphic of the hand on the Stage, proceed by selecting it. Subsequently, navigate to the top of the Timeline panel and opt for the option labeled **"Create Motion Tween"** (alterna-tively, you can right-click and select **"Create Motion Tween"** from the context menu).

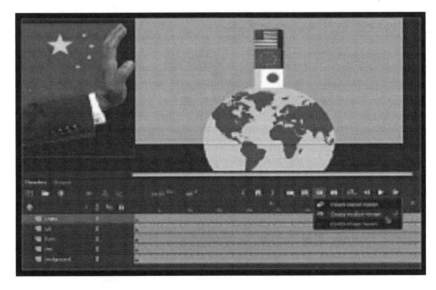

The Animate software facilitates the creation of a motion tween, which is visually represented by a frame span highlighted in a distinctive gold color. The China layer is transformed into a tween layer, which is denoted by a distinctive icon adjacent to the China layer's name.

4. Adjust the position of the play head to frame 20.

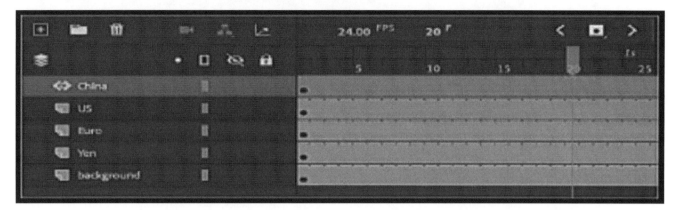

5. Manipulate the hand graphic by dragging it in such a manner that it makes contact with the blocks that are in a state of equilibrium atop the globe. The X-coordinate should be set to approximately 96.

Automatically, a new keyframe is generated at frame 20to signify the updated position of the graphic. The keyframe is visually repre-sented by a small black diamond shape. Within the Stage, a sequence of dots arranged linearly serves to represent the trajectory of move-ment for the graphic, starting from its initial position at the first keyframe and concluding at the subsequent keyframe. Despite the Auto Keyframe option being disabled, Animate will automatically insert newkeyframes when the instance is moved to the Stage. The process of motion tweening involves the manipulation of objects or elements to create smooth and seamless animation. If desired, an alternative option is to manually insert a keyframe by pressing the F6 key before relocating your graphic. Similar to the ability to adjust the timing of animation by moving the keyframes of a classic tween, the keyframes of a motion tween can be moved by simply dragging them within the tween span.

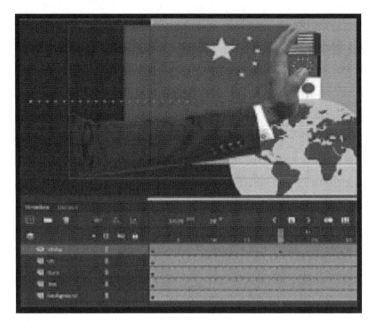

6. To preview your animation, simply press the Return key on macOS or the Enter key on Windows.

The hand undergoes a positional animation starting from the initial keyframe in frame 1 and ending at the subsequent keyframe in frame 20, exhibiting a seamless sliding motion across the Stage.

SPAN-BASED VS. FRAME-BASED SELECTION

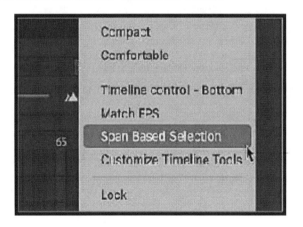

By default, Adobe Animate uses a frame-based selection method, allowing users to individually select frames within a motion tween. Alternatively, if you have a preference for selecting a motion tween by clicking and encompassing the entire span, which includes the starting and ending keyframes as well as all the frames in between, you can activate the Span-Based Selection option. This can be done by accessing the Frame View menu located in the upper-right corner of the Timeline panel. Another method is to hold down the Shift key while clicking to select the entire span. By enabling the Span-Based Selection feature, users can select the motion tween by clicking any- where within it. This allows for the convenient movement of the entire animation along the tirneline as a cohesive unit, either forward or backward. To select individual keyframes whileSpan Based Selection is enabled, it is recommended to hold down the Command/ Ctrl key and then proceed to click on the desired keyframe.

MOVING KEYFRAMES VERSUS CHANGING TIME IN TWEEN SPANS

Effectively managing the timing of your animation involves manipulating keyframes and adjusting tween spans. However, this process can occasionally be challenging due to the varying outcomes that result from different selections made on the timeline and the specific dragging techniques employed. To reposition a keyframe within a tween span, ensure that only one keyframe is selected and that a small box appears next to your cursor when you start dragging the keyframe to a different position. Let us examine the provided animation, wherein a ball traverses from the left side of the Stage to the bottom edge, and subsequently moves towards the right side, forming the shape of the letter "V". The timeline of this animation consists of three keyframes, each representing the ball's position at distinct points in time.

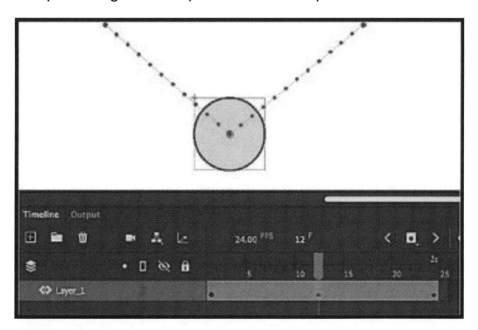

Adjusting the position of the middle keyframe alters the temporal sequence in which the ball reaches the bottom of the Stage.

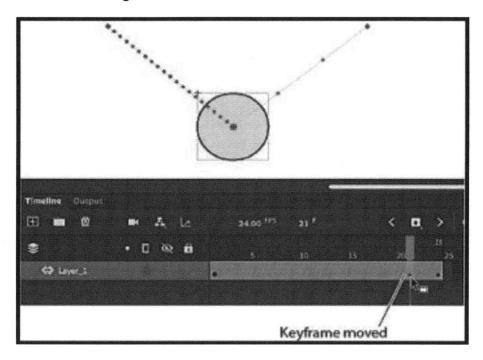

Keyframe moved

When a span of frames is chosen within a tween, the duration can be adjusted by either compressing or expanding it. This can be done by dragging the selection when the double-headed arrow is visible near the right edge of the chosen frames. A black flag is displayed to indi-cate instances where the degree of compression or expansion is a multiple of the original length (x0.5, x2, x4, and so forth).

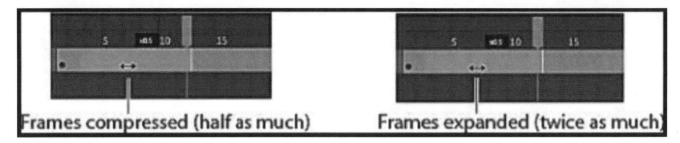

Frames compressed (half as much)   Frames expanded (twice as much)

EDITING THE MOTION PATH

The trajectory of movement that is observable on the Stage can be completely modified using the Selection, Subselection, or Free Trans- form tool.

BENDING THE MOTION PATH

The Selection tool will be used to modify the motion of the hand, transforming it from a linear trajectory to a subtly curved path.

1. Use the Selection tool to carefully manipulate the path of motion downwards, resulting in the formation of a smooth and gradual curve.

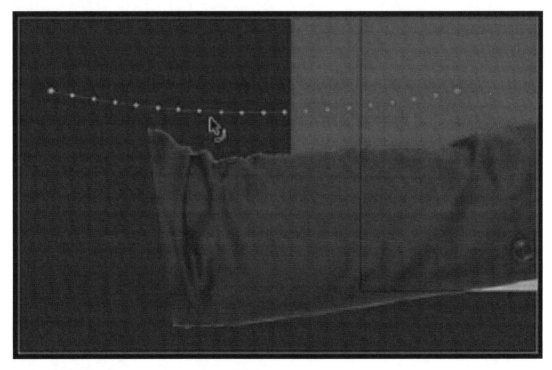

2. Take a moment to preview your animation once more. The hand now traces the curve in a smooth and graceful arcing motion.
3. Select the Subselection tool from the toolbar.

4. Use the anchor points located at both ends of the path and manipulate the Bezier handles to modify the curvature.

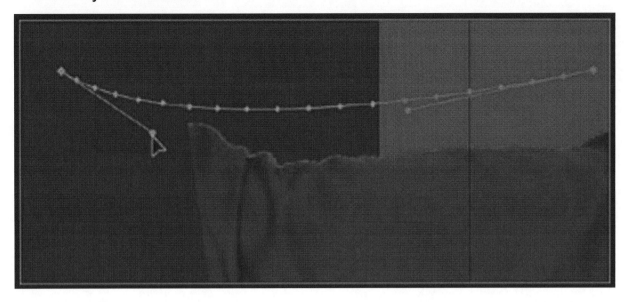

Regarding this task, it is not necessary to perform any specific edits using the Subselection tool. However, it is important to comprehend that any modifications made to the motion path will be reflected in the symbol instance. With motion tweens, there is no need to be con-cerned about aligning the registration point of the instance to a path, unlike in the case of classic tweens.

ABOUT THE MOTION EDITOR

The Motion Editor is a sophisticated panel that has been seamlessly integrated into the Timeline panel. It can only be accessed when you are actively engaged in editing a motion tween. The panel displays the dynamic alterations in the properties of your animation throughout the tween, represented bylines on a graph. Acquiring a thorough understanding of the lines' significance and comprehending how the curves manifest as visual alterations on the Stage requires a certain amount of time. However, once you have gained the ability to discern how the curves accurately depict alterations in your animation, you possess a formidable instrument at your disposal. One can make ad-justments to the property curves on the graph by either adding or removing anchor points. Additionally, the curvature of these curves can be altered with a high level of precision using Bezier techniques. The Motion Editor is exclusively accessible for motion tweens, excluding classic tweens, shape tweens, inverse kinematics with the Bone tool, or frame-by-frame animations. The Motion Editor provides users with the capability to apply advanced easing techniques to their animations, akin to the easing options found in the Properties panel.

Nevertheless, the Motion Editor provides a visual representation of how the ease you apply affects the curve of a property. It is possible to apply various easing functions to the curves of each property within a tween.

EXAMINING PROPERTY CURVES

The animation of the hand was modified by incorporating a subtle downward movement. One can achieve more advanced movements by modifying the X and Y property curves within the Motion Editor.

1. To access the motion tween in the China layer on the timeline, you can either double-click on it or right-click or select the option to Refine Motion Tween.

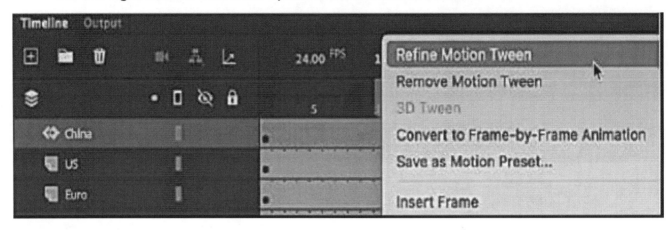

The motion tween is expanded to reveal the Motion Editor panel. Ensure that the Location category is expanded, in case it is not already expanded. The Location category comprises two properties, namely X and Y, which are each depicted by a line on the graph. The graph dis-plays time on the horizontal axis, while the vertical lines represent the selected property values (specifically, pixel values for X and Y).

2. Click on the X-proper ty to select it.

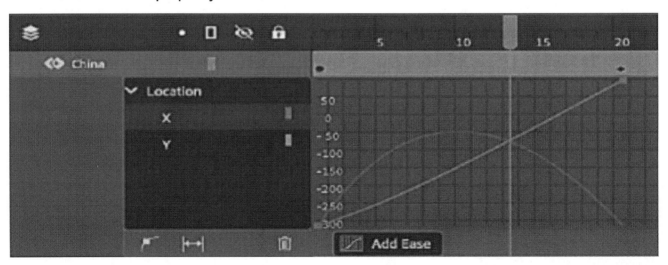

The ascending crimson line intensifies in thickness, while the contrasting line gradually diminishes in prominence. The rising red line depicts the change in the hand's X-position, which ranges from -314 to 96.

3. Select the Y property.

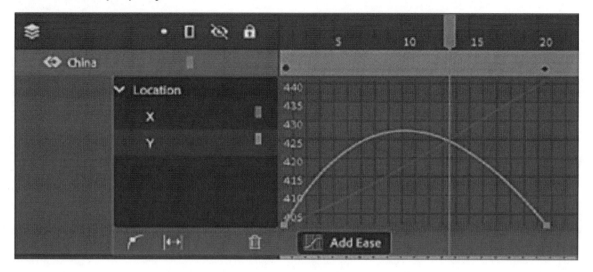

The curved line gets prominent, while the other line fades. The curving line depicts the shifting value of the hand's Y-position, which starts at roughly 402, rises to around 430, and then falls back to 402.These shifting values represent the hand's mild downward arcing motion- the one you produced by altering the motion route in the previous challenge.

EDITING PROPERTY CURVES

To modify the curvature of the property curve, add or remove anchor points. At each anchor point, you may adjust the curvature or direc-tion of the curve. For the following exercise, you'll change the X-property such that the hand stops briefly before reaching the bricks as if to size them up. Then it backs up and shoves the blocks. To produce this back-and-forth movement, you'll need to change the X-property curve.

1. In Motion Editor, choose the **X-property** from the Location category.
2. Choose the **Add Anchor Point** on Graph option.

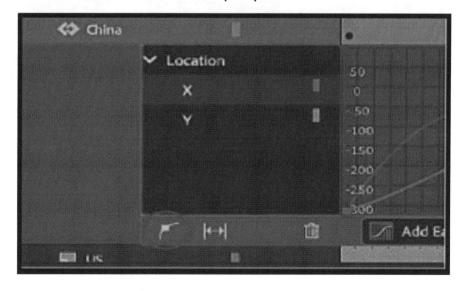

3. Hover the mouse cursor over the property curve. Your cursor switches to the Pen tool symbol with a + sign, suggesting that you may add an anchor point to the curve.

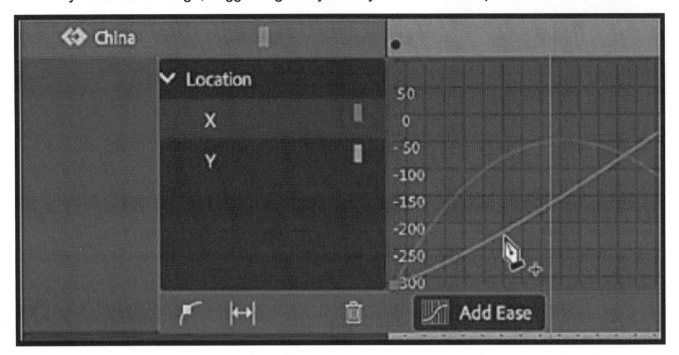

4. Drag the curve upward at frame 11 and release when the anchor point reaches about 50 pixels. This adds a new anchor point to the curve and creates a new keyframe at frame 11.

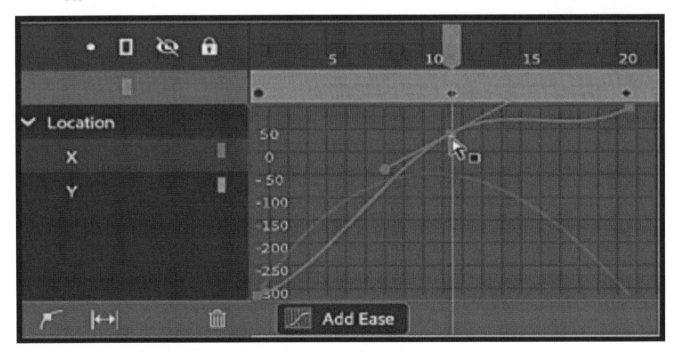

5. Choose **Add Anchor Point on Graph** again. To create a new anchor point, double-click a place on a property curve.
6. Create a new anchor point at frame 17 and move it to roughly-SO. Adding another anchor point to the graph creates a new keyframe for the motion tween.

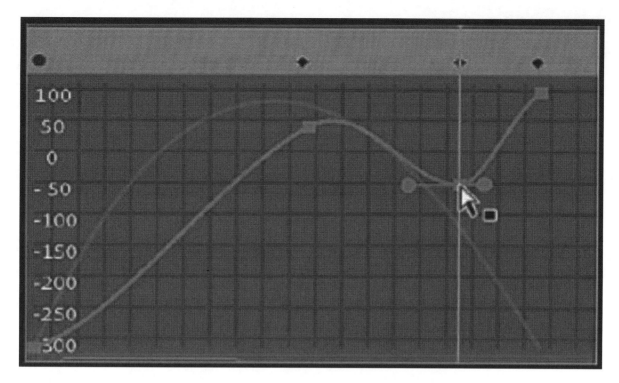

7. New anchor points have direction knobs on both sides to adjust curvature. Move the handles on each new anchor point horizontally. This will assist in building a smooth curve with one hill and one dip before reaching its ultimate value.

You can change the vertical axis property values by moving any of the anchor points, including those at the start and final keyframes. You may also relocate any of the anchor points (save the first) to other positions along the motion tween. In effect, moving anchor points to new times moves the keyframes inside the tween span. For more accurate control, nudge a specified anchor point using the arrow keys. To move the anchor point one property unit up or down, use the Up Arrow key or the Down Arrow key, respectively, or Shift-Up or Shift- Down to move it ten property units.

8. Double-click the China motion tween to close the Motion Editor. To preview your tween, hit Return/Enter.

Your newly modified X-property curve causes the hand to progress toward its end keyframe (the first hill), then withdraw somewhat as it sizes up its target (the dip), before continuing to its final destination. The motion route on the stage represents these modifications.

Hold down the Option/Alt key while moving a direction handle at an anchor point to modify its angle independently of the other handle. You may change the length of each direction handle without holding down the **Option/Alt keys**. Adjusting the length or angle of one side of a direction handle independently of the other allows you to make more dramatic adjustments to the property curve. Option/Alt-click an anchor point to remove its direction handles, resulting in a corner point with no smooth curves. Some anchor points (for example, the start and end anchor points of a property curve) do not have direction handles by default. Select the anchor point to which you want to add direction handles, then hold down the **Option/Alt keys** while pulling out a direction handle and editing its curve.

DELETING ANCHOR POINTS

If you mistakenly inserted too many anchor points, you may easily delete them (excluding the first and last). Removing an anchor point has the same impact as removing a keyframe from the motion tween. Hold down the Command/Ctrl key. When you hover over an anchor point, your cursor changes to a Pen symbol with a negative sign. Click any anchor point (other than the first and final ones). Animate re- moves the anchor point from the property curve. At this stage in the class, leave all anchor points on your project. If you do so by accident, use Command+Z/Ctrl+Z to undo the action.

DELETE PROPERTY CURVES

To delete a curve, click the trash can icon at the bottom of the Motion Editor. This will remove the tween for the chosen property curve.

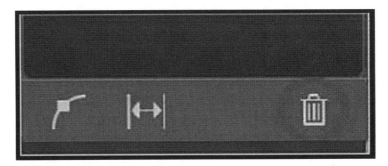

VIEWING OPTIONS IN THE MOTION EDITOR

Animate offers many viewing options for the Motion Editor, allowing you to tweak your property curves with better precision.

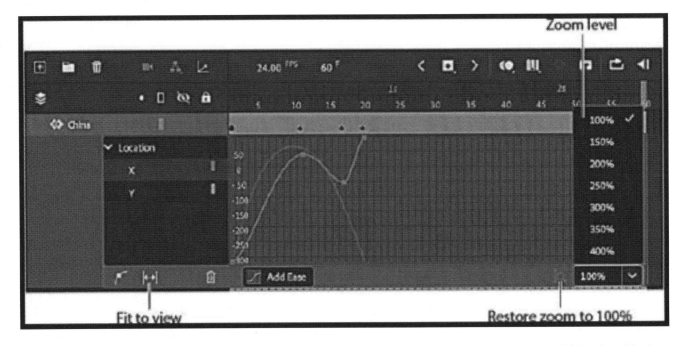

To alter the magnification, hold down the **Command/Ctrl key** while scrolling within the Motion Editor. You can choose a custom magnifi-cation level for the Motion Editor, but the lowest number is 100% and the highest is 400%.

1. To adjust the zoom level, go to the menu at the bottom of the Motion Editor. The vertical axis widens to provide a more detailed level of property values. To see where the curve begins and ends scroll up or down.
2. To revert the Motion Editor to its default perspective, click **Zoom 100%**.
3. Click **Fit to View** to enlarge the Motion Editor and fill the timeline. To return to the default view, click the icon again (this time with the name Restore View).

UNDERSTANDING PROPERTY KEYFRAMES

Changes in properties are independent of one another and do not have to be linked to the same keyframe. For example, you may have one keyframe for the location, another for the color effect, and a third for the filter. Managing many types of keyframes may be difficult, particularly if you want distinct characteristics to change at different moments throughout the motion transition. Fortunately, Animate includes a few useful tools for keyframe management. When examining the tween span, you may opt to only seethe keyframes of certain attributes. For example, you can choose simply the Position keyframes to watch when your object moves. You may also opt to display sim-ply the Filter keyframes, which will show you when a filter changes. In the Timeline panel, right-click a motion tween and choose **View Keyframes**. From the list, select the required attribute. You can choose All or None to display all or none of the attributes.

You can also put a keyframe that corresponds to the attribute you want to alter. Right-click a motion tween in the Timeline panel, choose **Insert Key frame**, and then the desired attribute.

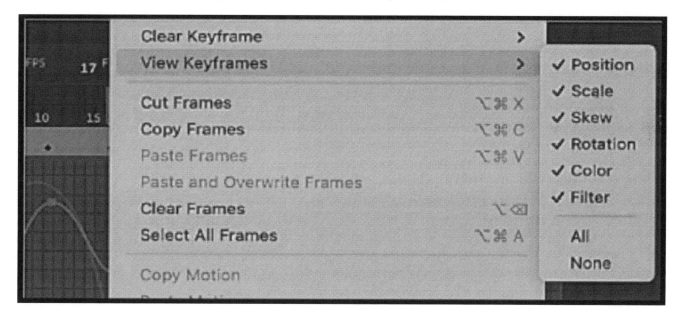

ADDING COMPLEX EASES

Now that the hand has pushed the bricks, it's time to animate them falling from the top of the planet. As the blocks fall, they bounce up and down, losing height with each bounce. The Motion Editor has a variety of eases that you can use to create realistic physics-based effects that are fast and simple to adjust.

MOTION-TWEENING THE BLOCKS

To start, you'll use a motion tween to determine where the three blocks will start and stop.

1. Drag to choose frame 21 from the US, Euro, and Yen layers. (If you're using span-based selection, hold down the Com-mand/Ctrl key while dragging.)

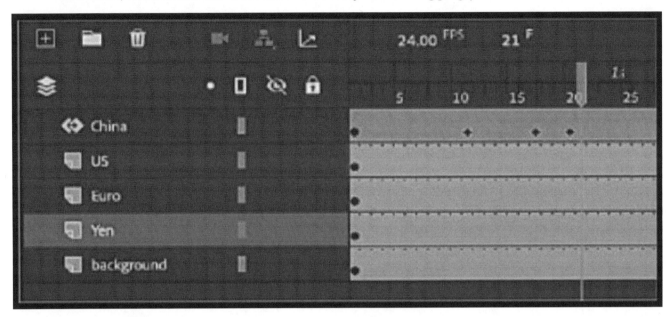

2. Insert a keyframe (F6). Frame 21 adds new keyframes to the US, Euro, and Yen layers.

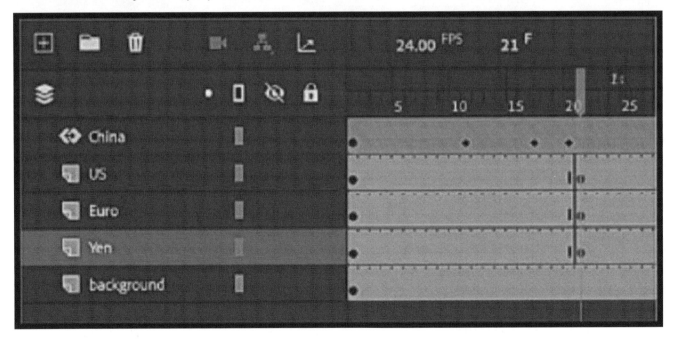

3. In the Timeline panel, pick all three keyframes. Then, right-click the Stage blocks and chooses **Create Motion Tween**. Mo-tion tweens are formed for the three blocks beginning with frame 21.

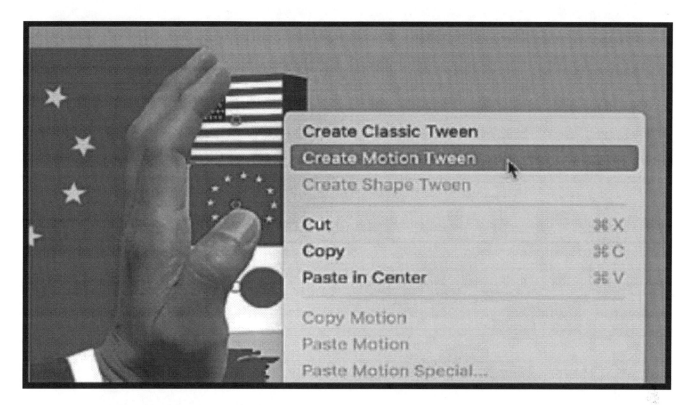

4. Move the play head to the conclusion of the timeline, frame 60.

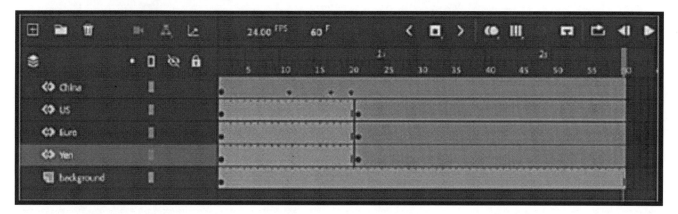

5. Use the Selection tool to move the US movie clip to the bottom-right of the Stage, at X=700 and Y=531.

6. Using the Free Transform tool, spin the clip 180 degrees clockwise to make it seem upside down.

7. Move the Euro movie clip to the bottom-right of the Stage, immediately beneath the US movie clip. Rotate it 90 degrees clockwise using the Free Transform tool.

8. To rotate the Yen movie clip instance 180 degrees clockwise, move it to the bottom-right corner of the Stage, beneath the Euro movie clip. Use the Free Transform tool.

9. Test your new motion by hitting Return or Enter. The three bricks fall gently in a diagonal path, turning as they descend. However, you'll want a more forceful, realistic fall, so the next step is to include some eases.

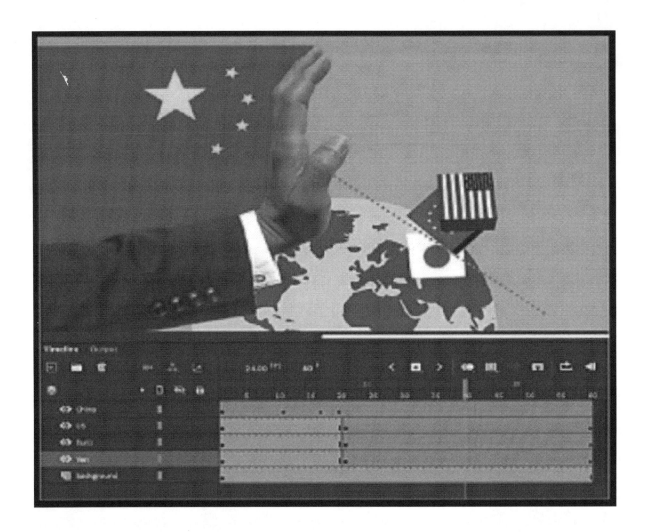

APPLYING EASES FROM MOTION EDITOR

Bounce In, one of the Motion Editor's preset ease, replicates bouncing motion. The distance to the final property value steadily de- creases as the motion tween approaches its last keyframe.

1. To access the Motion Editor, double-click the motion tween in the US layer.

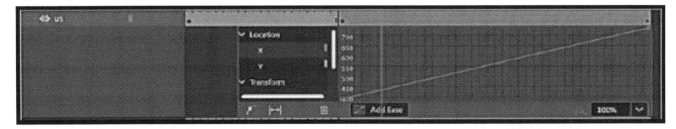

Animate widens the motion tween in the US layer to expose the Motion Editor panel. The Motion Editor includes property curves for the X and Y properties for Location, as well as the Z property for Transform > Rotation.

2. Choose the Y-property under Location.
3. To access the Ease panel in Motion Editor, click **Add Ease** at the bottom.
4. Double-click the Bounce and spring category to see the settings therein.

5. Choose the Bounce In ease preset and enter 5 as the Easing value. The Bounce In ease replicates a bounce that gradually decays as the motion tween nears its finish. The number of bounces is determined by the Easing setting for Bounce In ease.

6. Confirm the Easing setting by using Tab, and then dismiss the Ease window with Esc. A dotted line appears in the Motion Editor, overlaid on the original property curve. This is the **"resulting curve"** since it depicts the influence of easiness on the tween.

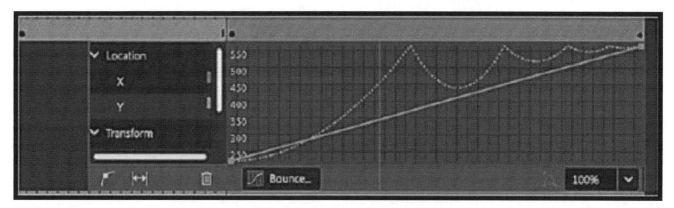

7. Test the new motion by hitting **Return / Enter.** The US instance bounces (just in the Y direction) when it falls to the ground. Take note of the route of the bounce on the Stage, as specified by the dots.

8. Expand the Motion Editor for the Euro layer and collapse the one for the US layer.

9. Select the Y-property and use the Bounce In ease. If the Easing value isn't already set to 4, set it to 4.

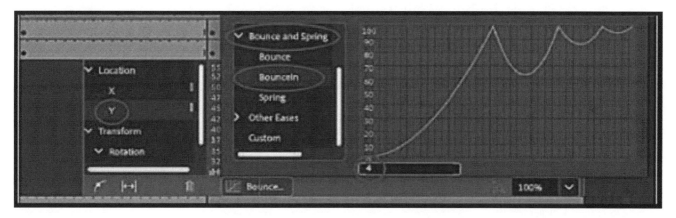

To eliminate an ease, choose No Ease from the ease category list in the Motion Editor. After you've selected an ease preset, the label on the Add Ease button changes to reflect the preset name.

10. Expand the Motion Editor for the Yen layer after collapsing the one for Euro.

11. Apply a Bounce In ease to the Y-property of the Yen instance and set the Easing value to 3.

12. Test the new motion by hitting **Return/ Enter.**

If you're seeing unusual, unexpected behaviors, make sure you've just applied the Bounce In ease to the Y-proper ty curve. You want the bouncing motion to solely affect the vertical motion, not the horizontal or rotation. When the three blocks fall, they each tumble with a unique amount of bounces. The top block bounces the most, with five bounces, followed by the middle and bottom blocks, which bounce four and three times, respectively. In the Motion Editor's Ease panel, you may traverse the ease kinds using the Up, Down, Left, and Right Arrow keys.

APPLYING A SECOND EASE TO ANOTHER PROPERTY CURVE

The Motion Editor is powerful because it allows you to handle each property curve of a single motion tween individually. For example, you may use one ease for the Y property and a separate ease for the X property. This is what you will do next - You will add an ease-out for each instance's horizontal motion while keeping the vertical motion at Bounce In ease.

1. Expand the Motion Editor on the US layer.
2. Choose the X-property under Location. The straight line is emphasized. This shows the object's linear velocity in the hori-zontal direction.

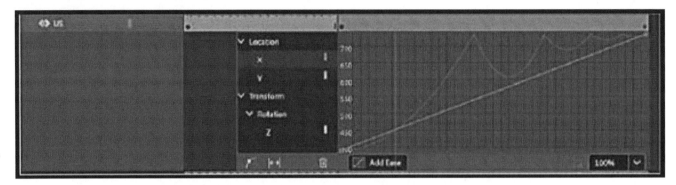

3. To access the Ease panel in Motion Editor, click **Add Ease** at the bottom.
4. Double-click the **Simple category**. The category opens, displaying the Slow, Medium, Fast, and Fastest options. The Simple categories ease impact just one side of the motion (either at the beginning or conclusion). Ease in the Stop and Start cat e- gory affects both sides of the motion transition. The other group has a more complicated ease.
5. Choose the **Fast Ease preset** and input 50 for the Easing value (if not already set to 50). The Fast ease curve is provided, which visually depicts the strength of the ease. Slower eases are shallower and closer to a straight line, whereas quicker eases have increasing curvature. The Easing value controls the intensity and direction of each ease setting. A positive number indicates ease-out, whereas a negative number indicates ease-in.

The Easing number of SO indicates a powerful ease-out motion.

6. Accept your softening selections by clicking outside the Motion Editor or using the Esc key. The dotted line represents the consequent ease of horizontal mobility. The block slows as it approaches its ultimate X-position.
7. Apply Fast eases with an Easing value of 50 to the X-property curves of the other two motion tweens (Euro and Yen).
8. To preview your new motion, hit **Return/Enter.** As the three blocks bounce to the ground in the Y direction, their forward speed progressively decreases, resulting in a more realistic animation in the X direction.
9. Select **Control> Test Movie> In Browser**. Animate publishes all of the files required to execute as an HTML5 Canvas page. Your browser loads and plays the animation.

PROPERTY CURVES VS. EASE CURVES

When you add an ease to a motion tween in the Motion Editor, the original property curve is not permanently changed. In the first segment of this tutorial, you changed the property curves of a motion tween by adding anchor points. Applying eases is similar to using a filter to change the result of an initial property. The ease may be adjusted or deleted entirely, similar to a filter. It is possible to change a property curve while still adding ease, but the effect might be unexpected.

FREQUENTLY ASKED QUESTIONS

1. What do you understand by motion tweens?
2. How do you create hand animations?
3. How do you examine and edit property curves?
4. How do you delete anchor pints and property curves?
5. How do you apply eases from motion editor?

CHAPTER 7: ADVANCED SHAPE ANIMATION AND MASKING

OVERVIEW

It is nearly impossible to talk about Adobe Animate 2024 without discussing how best you can animate shapes and use masks. Therefore, in this chapter, you will learn how to animate shapes, how to create a shape tween, how to create and use masks, and so much more

ANIMATING SHAPES

Shape tweening is another technique for animating a graphic's contours. Shape tweening is a method that interpolates the stroke and fills changes of a vector form between keyframes. form tweens allow for the seamless transition from one form to another. Shape tweening may be used for any animation that needs the stroke or fill of a shape to change, such as smoke, water, or hair.

SHAPE TWEENS AND THE ASSET WARP TOOL'S ENVELOPE DEFORMER

Shape tweening and traditional tweening use the Asset Warp tool's envelope deformer to modify the outlines of an item.

However, there are significant distinctions between the two approaches.

1. Shape t weening is only applicable to vector shapes.
2. The envelope deformer applies to both vector shapes and bitmap images. When the envelope deformer is applied to a vector shape, Animate will automatically transform it to a bitmap (known as a warped bitmap) unless you deactivate it in Preferences.
3. Shape tweening allows for adjustments to a shape's stroke and fill. The gradient fill, stroke width, and stroke color may all be adjusted.
4. A shape tween modifies the shape's contour using the Selection or Subselection tool, whereas an envelope deformer modifies the mesh bounds, distorting the visual.
5. Use shape tweening for basic forms like water droplets, hair curls, and smoke puffs. For more complex graphics with many shapes to distort, use the Asset Warp tool's envelope deformer. For example, you might use a shape tween to modify just one brow, but an envelope deformer to change the whole head, including the hair and facial characteristics.

UNDERSTANDING THE PROJECT FILES

The 08Start.fla file is an ActionScript 3.0 document with most of the visuals in place and grouped in layers. However, the file is static, and you will add the animation. This animation has four layers: a blood layer, which has a red form at the top of the Stage; a face layer, which contains the shapes of the eyes, nose, and mouth; a pumpkin layer, which contains a bitmap of the jack-o'-lantern; and a title layer, which contains the Halloween message shapes.

CREATING A SHAPE TWEEN

To get the blood trickling appearance, animate the changes in the red form at the top of the Stage. You'll use shape tweening to manage the seamless morphing in which the rectangle's curving edge gets stretched with vertical drips. A shape tween needs a minimum of two keyframes on the same layer. The first keyframe comprises a shape created using Animate's drawing tools or imported from Adobe Illus-trator. The last keyframe additionally has a form. A shape tween interpolates the smooth transitions between the first and last keyframe.

ESTABLISHING KEYFRAMES WITH DIFFERENT SHAPES

In the next stages, you will animate the blood that drips down the Stage.

1. In all four layers, choose frame 72 and then click **Insert > Timeline > Frame (F5).** The total duration of the animation is defined by adding three seconds' worth of frames to each of the four levels.

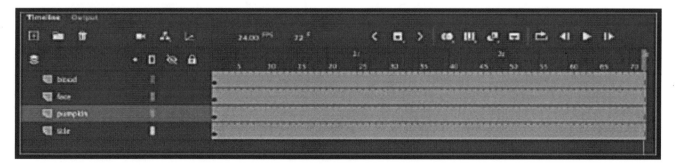

2. Select frame 40 in the blood layer and select Insert Keyframe above the timeline. The contents of the preceding keyframe (frame 1) are replicated into the new keyframe. You now have two keyframes on the timeline in the blood layer: frame 1 and frame 40. Next, in the last keyframe, modify the form of the blood.

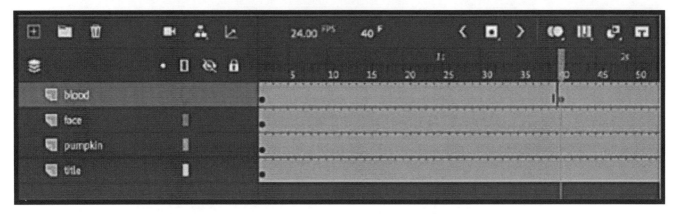

3. Select the selection tool.
4. Deselect a shape by clicking away from it. To extend a drip, move your cursor near the shape's edges and drag the curve of the red rectangle's bot tom edge down. The starting and ending keyframes now have distinct shapes-a red rectangle with a moderate curve at its bottom edge in the beginning keyframe, and an extended curve in the ending keyframe.

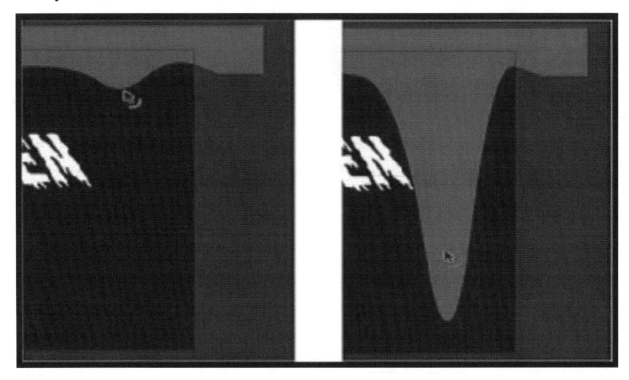

5. The top of the drip will most likely seem overly thick, so use the Selection tool to modify it. Hold down the Option/Alt key and click the drip's contours to create anchor points on each side of the bulge where the drip begins. Pull the curves inward to form the drip. You don't have to reproduce this exact screenshot, but try something close.

USING THE SHAPE TWEEN

To achieve smooth transitions, add a shape tween between the keyframes.

1. In the blood layer, click on any frame between the first and last keyframes.
2. Press and hold the Create Tween button above the timeline, then choose **Create Shape Tween**. Alternatively, you may right-click and choose Create Shape Tween, or use the Insert menu. Animate uses a shape tween between the two keyframes, as represented by a black forward-pointing arrow and an orange fill in the tween span.

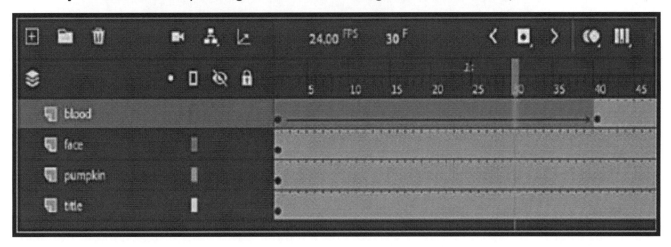

3. To see your animation, choose **Control > Play (Ret urn [macOS] or Enter [Windows])**, or click the **Play button** at the top of the Timeline window.

You'll probably be unhappy with the early outcomes. Do not worry! You'll have the opportunity to repair it later using shape tips. The red rectangle is likely to undergo some unexpected alterations as it transitions from the first to the final form, but the crucial point is that you have built a seamless animation between the keyframes in the blood layer, morphing between two shapes.

BLEND TYPES

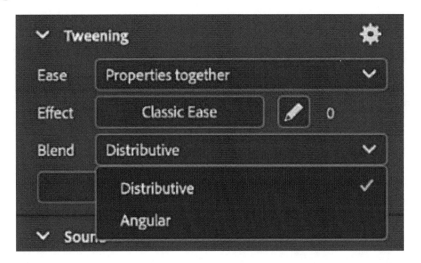

In the Properties section, you may change your shape tween by selecting either Distributive or Angular for Blend. These two settings control how Animate performs interpolations to transition shapes from one keyframe to the next. The Distributive option is the default and works effectively in most situations. It generates animations where the intermediate forms are smoother. Use the Angular mix if your forms have a lot of points and straight lines. Animate tries to keep visible edges and lines in intermediate forms.

USING SHAPE HINTS

Animate generates seamless transitions between your shape tween's keyframes, but the results might be unexpected. Your forms may undergo odd contortions, flips, and rotations to transition from one keyframe to the next. You may like the result, but more often than not, you will want to preserve control over the modifications. Form cues may aid in refining form modifications. Shape hints instruct Animate to map points on the starting form to matching points on the ending shape. Multiple shape suggestions allow you to more accurately con-trol how a form tween looks.

ADDING SHAPE HINTS

Add shape clues to the red rectangle to change how it transitions from one form to the next.

1. Select the first keyframe from the blood layer. The red form at the top of the Stage has been picked.
2. Select **Modify> Shape> Add Shape Hint** (Command+Shift +H or Ctrl +Shift +H). A red-circled letter" a "emerges on the stage. The highlighted letter denotes the first shape clue.

3. Select the **Selection tool** and ensure that Snap to Objects is selected in the Properties panel's Doc tab. Snap To items guar-antee that items snap together when moved or updated.
4. Drag the marked letter to the top-right corner of the rectangle.

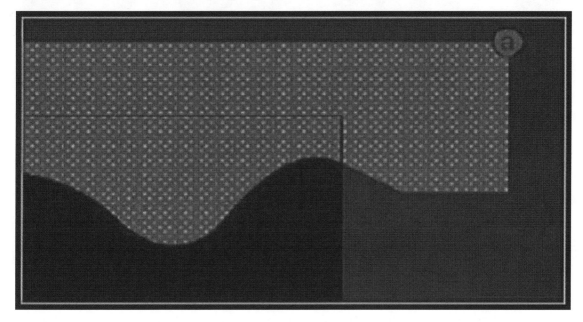

5. To generate a second shape hint, choose **Modify > Shape > Add Shape Hint** once again. A red-circled "b" emerges on the stage.

203

6. Drag the "b" form suggestion to the lower-right corner of the red rectangle. The first keyframe contains two shape sugges-tions that are assigned to various positions on the form.

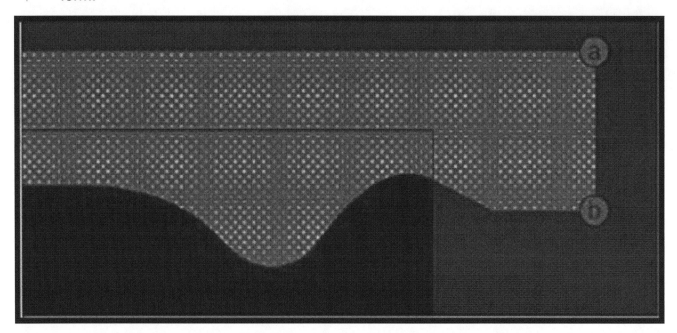

7. Choose the last keyframe of the shape tween (frame 40). A similar red-circled "b" emerges on the St age, concealing an "a" form suggestion located just underneath it.

8. Drag the highlighted letters to their respective places on the form in the second keyframe. The "a" suggestion goes in the top-right corner, whereas the "b" hint goes in the bottom-right corner of the rectangle. The shape suggestions become green, indicating that they are appropriately positioned and matched to comparable positions in the first keyframe.

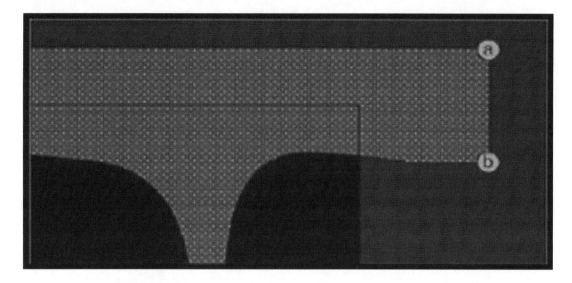

9. Select the first keyframe. Note that the original shape clues have become yellow, suggesting that they are properly placed. When appropriately positioned, the form suggestions in the first keyframe become yellow, while those in the last keyframe turn green.
10. Scrub the play head through the first shape tween on the timeline to observe how the shape clues influence the shape tween.

The shape hints cause the top-right corner of the red shape in the first keyframe to map to the top-right corner of the red shape in the sec-ond keyframe, and the bottom-right corners to map to each other. This limits the changes and keeps the regions fixed.

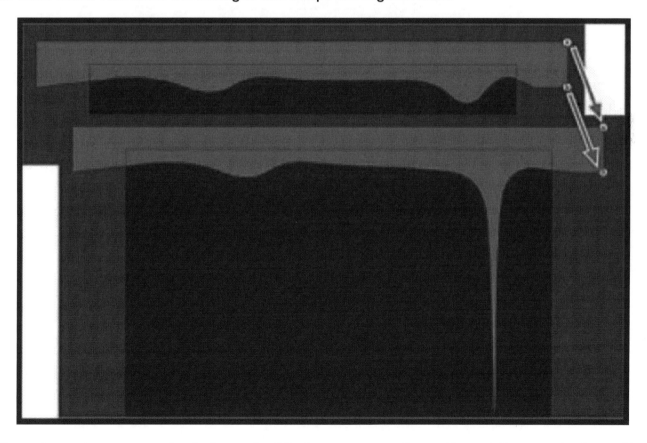

Any shape tween may include up to 26 shape suggestions. To get the greatest results, add them continuously in a clockwise or coun-terclockwise orientation.

11. Select the first keyframe again and add more form suggestions. Add "c," "d, " "e," "f ," "g," and "h" shape suggestions along the contours in a clockwise direction.

12. Select the keyframe in frame 40 and place shape suggestions "c" through "h" on the rectangle shape. Ensure they become green. The shape hints at maintaining the desired parts constant, allowing the shape tween to morph just the long drip running from the bottom.

13. Use the Selection tool to extract another drop off the bottom border of the red rectangle in frame 40, just as you did with the previous one. Take care to alter the curve between shape suggestions "e" and "f."

14. If you want additional accuracy in your curve editing, you can use the Subselection tool with the Bezier handles. This will allow you to create bulges at the bottom of the drips.

EDITING SHAPE HINTS

If you've added too many shape tips, just remove the ones you don't need. When you delete a form clue in one keyframe, it also re-moves the equivalent shape hint in the other keyframe.

- To eliminate a shape hint, choose the first keyframe in which it occurs. Right-click (Ctrl + click) and choose Remove Hint from the menu that displays.

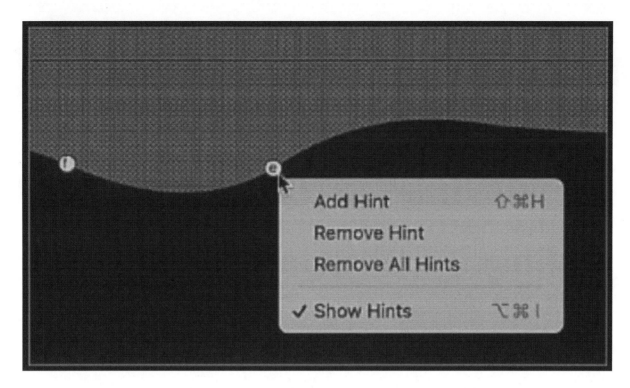

- To delete all shape indications, choose the first keyframe in which they occur. Right-click (Ctrl + click) and   choose Remove All Hints from the menu that displays.

If you have many keyframes in a shape tween and wish to add shape suggestions for each, you must keep track of which shape hints be- long to the ending keyframe and which to the starting keyframe of each tween.

CHANGING THE PACE

A shape tween's keyframes may be readily shifted around the timeline to adjust the animation's tempo or pace.

MOVING A KEYFRAME

The flowing blood animates gently over a 40-frame span. If you want the blood to alter the form more quickly, bring the key frames closer together.

1. Choose the last keyframe of the shape tween in the blood layer.

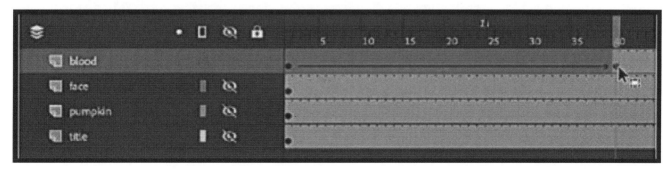

2. When dragging the final keyframe to frame 6, make sure the box symbol shows near your mouse.

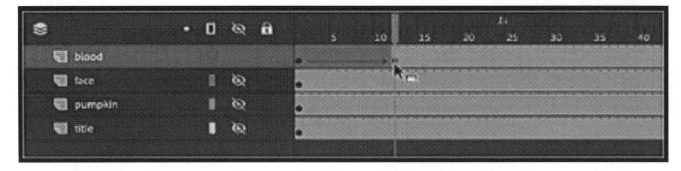

3. Press **Return/Enter** to start your animation. The blood drops swiftly before remaining motionless for the remainder of the frames on the timeline.

If you want the animation to progress slower, space the keyframes apart. For now, return the final keyframe to frame 40.

BROKEN TWEENS

Every form tween requires a starting and ending keyframe, each with a shape within it. If the final keyframe of a shape tween is missing, Animate displays the broken tween as a dotted black line rather than a solid arrow.

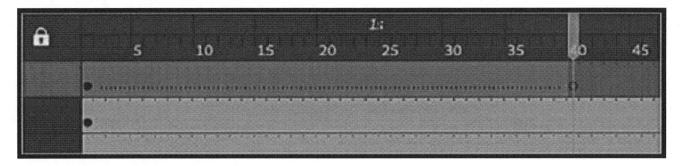

To repair the tween, put a keyframe at frame 40.

EASING A SHAPE TWEEN

Eases let you add acceleration or deceleration to your animation's motion, giving it a feeling of weight. The Motion Editor, a complex panel incorporated into the timeline that offers many ease kinds, is not accessible for shape tweens. The Properties panel allows you to add ease to a form tween. Tweens and traditional tweens may be shaped with the same simplicity.

ADDING AN EASE-IN

You will cause the blood to progressively slowdown as it drops downhill.

1. Select anywhere inside the form tween in the blood layer.
2. In the Properties panel, click the Effect button and choose **Ease Out > Cubic**. Double-click to activate the effect.

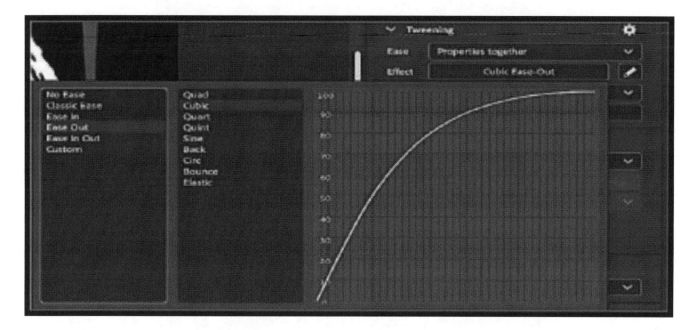

Animate creates an ease-in effect for the form tween. You may experiment with different types of ease effects, which vary in kind and severity. You'll return to making more shape tweens to complete this Halloween greeting card, but first, learn how to use mask layers. You can use sophisticated eases or even bespoke eases, just as with traditional tweens. To modify your ease curve, click the Edit Easing option.

CREATING AND USING MASKS

Masking is a method for selectively concealing and revealing items on a layer. It allows you to manage what material your audience sees. For example, you may create a circle mask and enable your audience to only look through the circular region, resulting in a keyhole or spotlight effect. In Animate, you apply a mask to one layer and place the masked content on another layer below it. For the animated Hal-loween card you'll make in this lesson, you'll need two mask layers: one for the cuts in the pumpkin to display the flashing lights inside and another to reveal the title.

DEFINE THE MASK LAYER

You will mask the face layer, revealing material in the masked layer behind it.

1. Double-click the symbol in front of the face layer's name, or select the face layer and go to **Modify > Timeline > Layer Properties.**

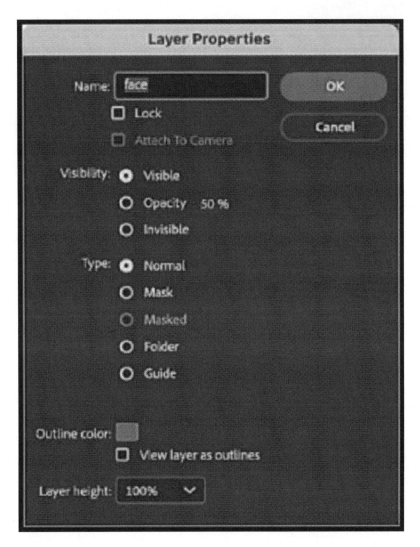

Masks do not detect strokes; therefore only use fills in the mask layer. Text made using the Text tool also serves as a mask. Animate cannot distinguish between various Alpha levels in a mask made on a timeline, therefore a semitransparent fill in the mask layer has the same effect as an opaque fill, and edges are always harsh. However, with an ActionScript 3.0 document, you can use ActionScript code to dynam-ically build masks that support transparencies.

2. Select Mask and click OK.

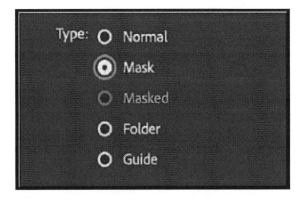

The text layer transforms into a mask layer, as shown by the mask symbol in front of the layer name. Anything in this layer will serve as a mask for the masked layer underneath it. You will not notice any changes, however, since you have not yet established a masked layer.

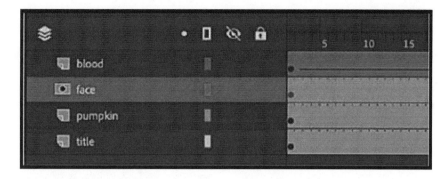

For this exercise, we'll use the white forms of the eyes, nose, and mouth as the mask, although any filled shape would do. The color of the fill does not matter. The size, placement, and curves of the form are critical while animating. The shape will serve as a "peephole" through which you may glimpse the content of the masked layer underneath. You can use any of the drawing or text tools to create the fill for your mask.

CREATING THE MASKED LAYER

The masked layer is always indented below the mask layer.

1. Select the **New Layer button** or choose **Insert > Timeline > Layer**.
2. Name the layer within.

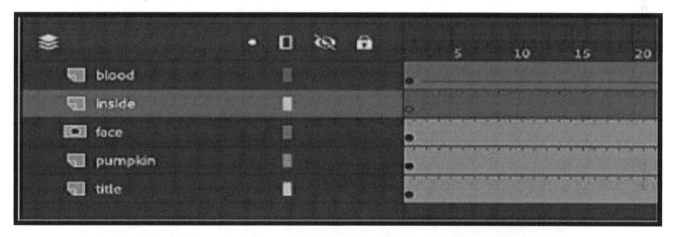

3. Drag the inner layer beneath the mask layer (called face) and slightly to the right so that it is indented.

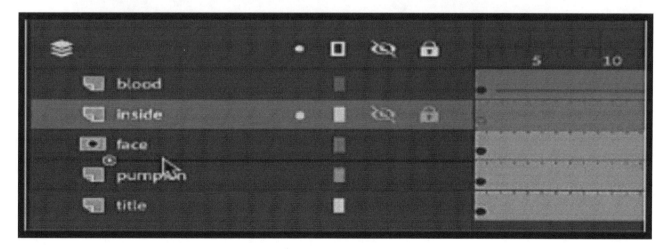

The interior layer becomes a masked layer when combined with the mask layer above it. Any material in the masked layer will be hidden by the layer above it. To convert a regular layer behind a mask layer to a masked layer, double-click it or go to **Modify > Timeline > Layer Properties** and pick **Masked.**

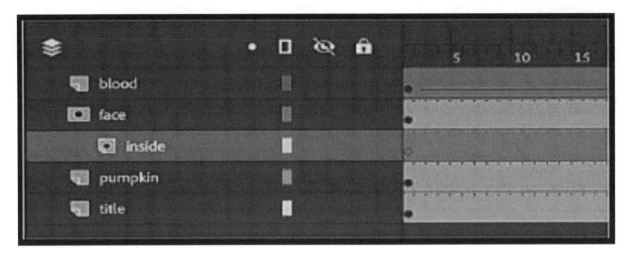

4. Select the Oval tool.
5. For the fill, make a radial gradient from light purple to dark purple.
6. Draw an oval on the inner layer (masked layer) to cover the shapes in the mask layer.

It can look weird at first-perhaps even a mistake but the consequences of the mask-masked layer pair are not seen until the layers are locked.

SEEING THE EFFECTS OF THE MASK

Lock both layers so you can observe how the mask layer affects its masked layer. Multiple masked layers may be combined beneath a single mask layer.

1. Lock both the face mask layer and the interior mask layer.

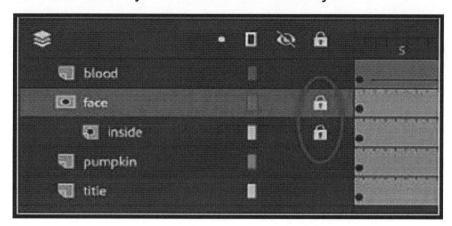

The mask and masked layers get locked. The forms in the mask layer disclose portions of the purple radial gradient in the masked layer.

2. Select **Control > Test.**

Blood seeps down the Stage above a jack-o'-lantern, its eyes, nose, and mouth revealing a weird purple interior.

TRADITIONAL MASKS

It may seem contradictory that the forms in the mask layer expose, rather than conceal, the information in the masked layer. After all, isn't a mask something we use to disguise our faces? That may be true fora facemask, but a classic mask in photography or painting functions differently. When a painter uses a mask, it covers the painting from paint splatters, allowing the underlying painting to remain seen.

Masking tape ensures that surfaces are not damaged. When a photographer employs a mask in the darkroom, it shields the photosensitive material from light, preventing those regions from becoming darker. Thinking of a mask as something that protects a lower, masked layer helps you recall what portions are covered and which are shown.

ANIMATE THE MASK OR MASKED LAYERS

The jack-o'-lantern is strange, with a purple inside. However, the customer for this hypothetical enterprise has demanded even more drama. Fortunately, you can include tweens in both the mask and the masked layer. If you want the mask to move or expand to reveal various areas of the masked layer, you may add an animation to it. You may also build an animation on the masked layer if you want the material to move beneath a mask, such as scenery passing by through a train window.

ADDING A WARPED ASSET IN A MASKED LAYER

To make the jack-o'-lantern more appealing to your customer, you'll include another masked layer with an animation. The animation will show a flame flashing back and forth.

1. To add a new layer, choose the inner (masked) layer and then the **New Layer button**. A new layer is added to the existing one.
2. Rename the new layer Flame. Note that the face (mask) layer now has two masked levels underneath it. The single mask layer affects both layers.

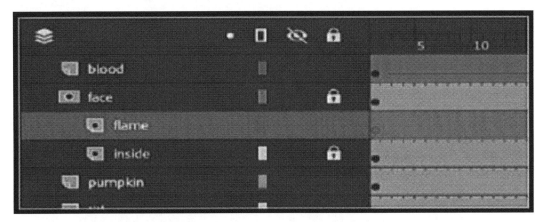

3. Hiding the layers above your flame layer will make drawing simpler.
4. Draw a flame-like shape in the flame layer. Create a new radial gradient for the fill those transitions from bright yellow in the middle to red at the edges.

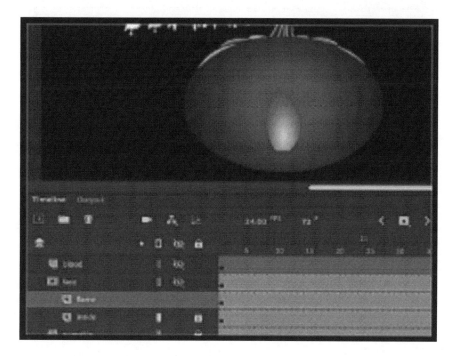

5. Select the **Asset Warp tool.**
6. In Preferences (**Animate > Preferences / Settings > Edit Preferences),** uncheck the Auto Convert Vector To Bitmap For Better Warping And Tweening option for the Asset Warp tool in the Drawing section. When using the Asset Warp tool on a basic form like this flame, it's better to leave the vector graphics intact.

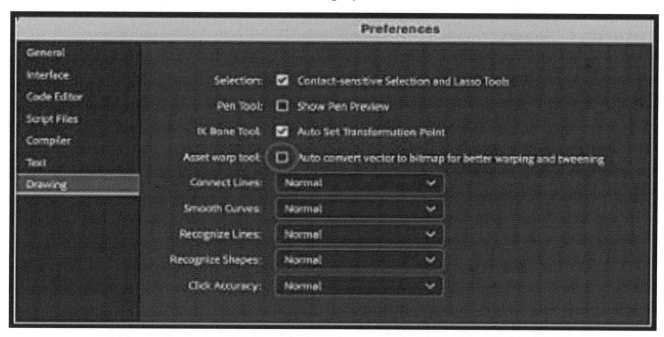

7. To pick the flame form, click it, followed by the base within the flame. Animate transforms the flame shape into a distorted object that is saved in the Library panel.

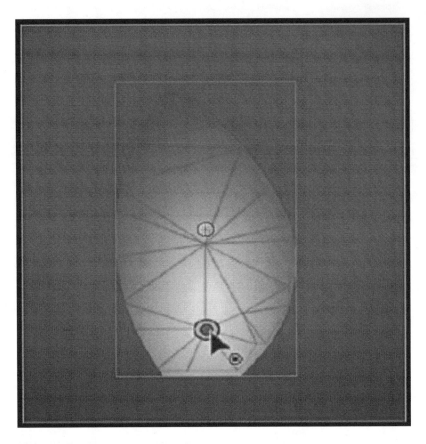

8. In the Properties window, allow Create Bones and pick Flexi as the Bone type. The Flexi option lets you distort the flame using Bezier curves.

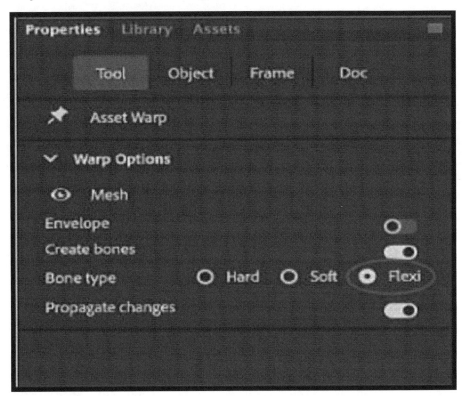

9. Drag the flame point.

Animate produces a bone from the flame's base to its tip that you may adjust to animate the flame.

ANIMATING THE FLAME

The next step is to animate the distorted item by creating flame variants and using standard tweens.

1. In the flame layer, add many keyframes (F6) between frames 1 and 72. It is not necessary to add the same amount of keyframes or place them in the same places as the figures. You will be producing various flame locations in each keyframe.

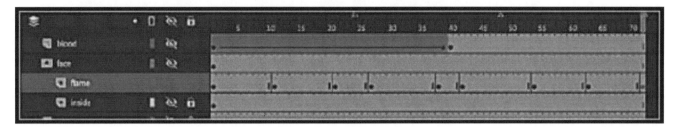

2. For each keyframe, alter the form, direction, or curvature of the flame using the bone of the warped item. Elongate the form by changing the anchor point at the tip, or move the handles to modify the direction of the curve of the bone.

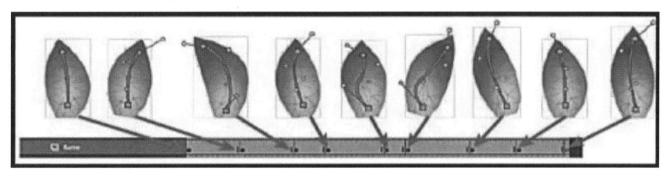

3. Select frames in between each pair of keyframes, then apply a conventional tween. Animate smoothly interpolates the changes in the warped asset flame.

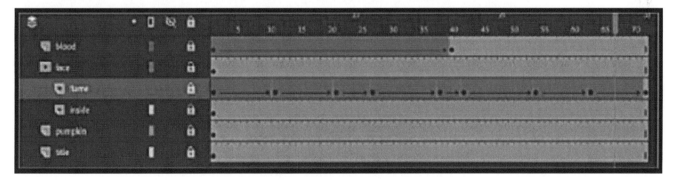

4. Lock the face layer, the flame layer, and the interior layer, and make all your layers visible.
5. Play your animation. The cutout shapes in the face layer now conceal the two layers below it: the flame layer and the inte-rior layer.

PREVIEWING ANIMATIONS USING ONION SKINNING

It might be beneficial to examine how your animation moves from one frame to the next. Seeing how the changes occur gradually allows you to make better modifications to your animation. You can do so by selecting the onion skinning option at the top of the Timeline panel. Onion skinning displays the contents of the frames preceding and following the presently chosen frame. The phrase **"onion skin"** refers to classic hand-drawn animation, in which animators use onion skin, a thin, semitransparent tracing paper. A light box flashes a light behind the designs, allowing them to be viewed through many sheets. When designing an action sequence, animators swiftly switch between sketches held between their fingers. This helps people to see how the designs flow nicely together.

TURNING ON ONION SKINNING

The Onion Skin button, located above the timeline, allows you to turn it on and off. Pressing and holding the Onion Skin button brings up more possibilities.

1. Unlock the flame layer and hide the others.
2. In the Timeline panel, choose the **Onion Skin button.**

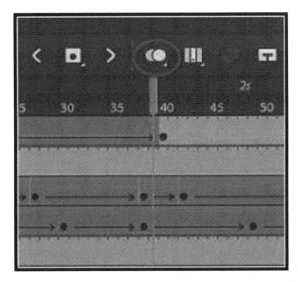

Animate displays many flame forms, each indicating a shape from a previous or future frame. Seeing numerous frames on the Stage at once helps you to compare the differences between them. The currently chosen frame is shown in red. The previous frames are repre-sented in blue, while the next frames are shown in green. The contours of the flame fade as they move away from the current frame.

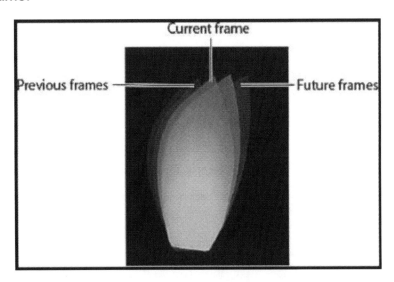

3. Animate shows markers on the timeline to bracket the presently chosen frame. The blue marker (to the left of the play- head) shows how many prior frames are shown on the Stage, while the green marker (to the right of the play head) indi-cates how many future frames are shown.

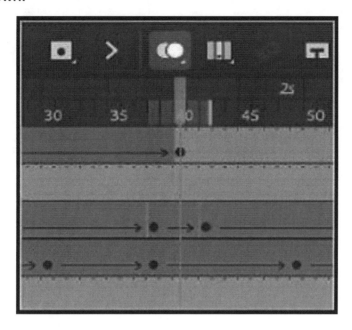

4. Adjust the play head to a different frame.

Animate retains the markers around the play head regardless of where you move it, constantly displaying the same amount of frames behind and ahead. You can also move the play head back and forth along the timeline to witness the ghostly pictures of the onion peels moving along with the animated sequence. Normal playing does not reveal onion peels.

ADJUSTING THE MARKERS

You can adjust either marker to display more or fewer onion skin frames.

- Use the blue marker to change the amount of previous onion skin frames shown.
- Use the green marker to change the number of future frames shown.
- Hold down the **Command/Ctrl key** while dragging to shift the past and future marks equally.
- To change the onion skin range to a different position on the timeline, hold down the Shift key and drag either marker (as long as it still includes the play head).
- Press and hold the Onion Skin button at the top of the Timeline panel to choose Anchor Markers. With the Anchor Markers option selected, you may move your play head around the timeline while the bracketed onion-skinned frames stay fixed in place.
- Hold the Onion Skin button at the top of the Timeline window and choose All Frames. With the All Frames option set, the brackets will automatically shift to cover the start and end frames on the timeline

ADVANCED ONION SKIN OPTIONS

The Advanced Settings allow you to adjust the blue and green color coding of previous and future frames, as well as the opacity of the onion skins.

- Hold the **Onion Skin button** at the top of the Timeline panel and choose Advanced Settings.

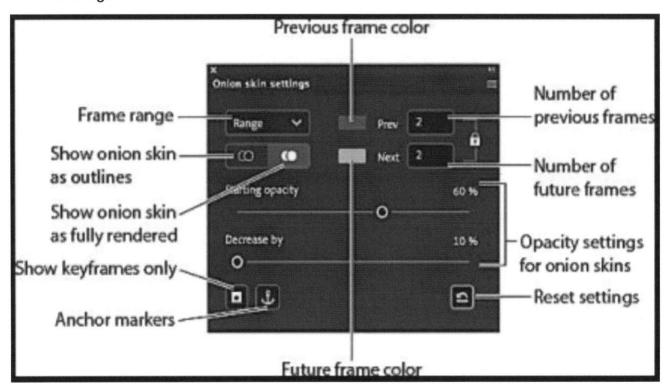

Adjust the following options to customize the appearance of the onion skin frames:

- Select previous and future frame ranges numerically.
- Use the color swatches to adjust the color of previous and future frames.
- You can see onion skin frames as outlines or completely drawn.

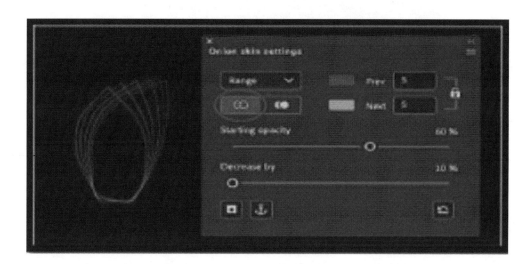

Animate remembers the most recent options entered into the Onion Skin Settings window. **Clicking the Onion Skin button above the timeline toggles onion skins with those settings on and off.**

- Use the opacity sliders to adjust the beginning opacity and fade rate of the onion skin frames.
- Show just keyframes.
- Anchor the frame markers.

SHAPE TWEENING THE FILLS OF SHAPES

Earlier in this course, you used shape tweening to adjust a form's contours or strokes. This enabled you to generate the flowing blood effect. Shape tweening allows you to animate both a shape's stroke and its fill.

ANIMATING THE GRADIENT FILL

Next, shape-tween the gradient fill of the interior layer to create the flickering effect of the flame on the pumpkin's inner wall.

1. Disable Onion Skin, unlock the inner layer and conceal the face and flame layers above it.

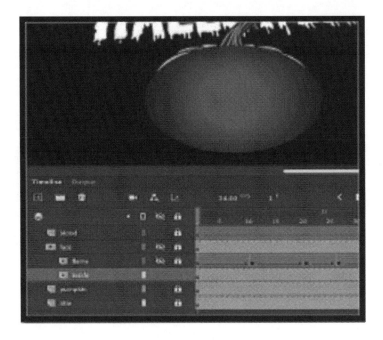

2. Select the **Gradient Transform tool**(F), which is concealed behind the Free Transform tool.

3. Select the purple radial gradient on the Stage. Control points appear over your form, indicating how the radial gradient is applied to the fill.

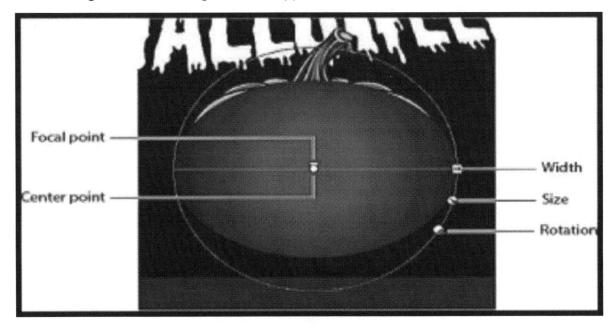

4. Adjust the settings to change how the radial gradient is applied to the circle's fill.

5. Add more keyframes to the inner layer, including one at frame 72. You don't have to have the same amount of keyframes as indicated below or follow their precise locations.

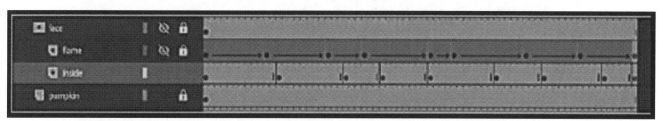

6. Using the Gradient Transform tool, change the gradient fill for each keyframe in the inner layer. The fluctuations in the purple radial gradient will resemble the moving shadow and light on the pumpkin's interior surface.

7. Apply a shape tween between the first and final keyframes (frames 1- 72).

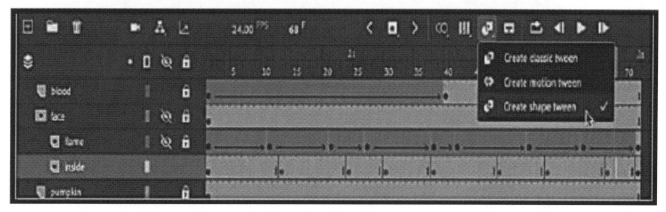

Animate creates a shape tween between all keyframes on the inner layer, seamlessly interpolating all changes.

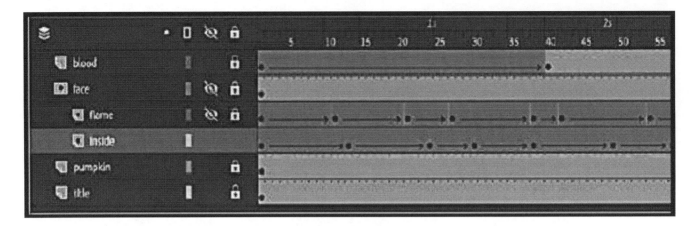

8. To play your animation, lock the inner layer, unhide the layers above it, and press Return/Enter.

The cutout shapes concealed both the flickering flame (animated with standard tweens) and the moving purple radial-gradient (animated using shape tweens). This illustrates how combining different approaches may result in a more powerful overall impression. Shape tweens may smoothly animate solid colors or color gradients, but they cannot transition between various kinds of gradients. For example, you cannot shape-tween a linear gradient into a radial gradient.

ANIMATING TEXT REVEAL

Animate a shape tween on a masked layer below the text to gradually show the "Happy Halloween" message.

1. Create a new layer and call it glow. Transfer the layer to the bottom of the layer stack.

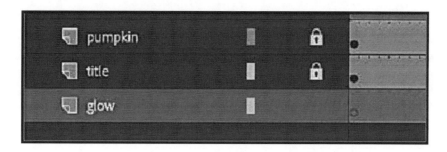

2. Hide all layers except for the glow and title layers. Lock all of your layers except the glow layer.

3. In the glow layer, add a huge white rectangle above the lettering. Create wavy curves around the bottom border of the rectangle.

4. In the glow layer, add a new keyframe at frame 72.
5. In frame 72, drag the bottom border of your rectangle's edges and wavy curves down the Stage, covering the lettering.

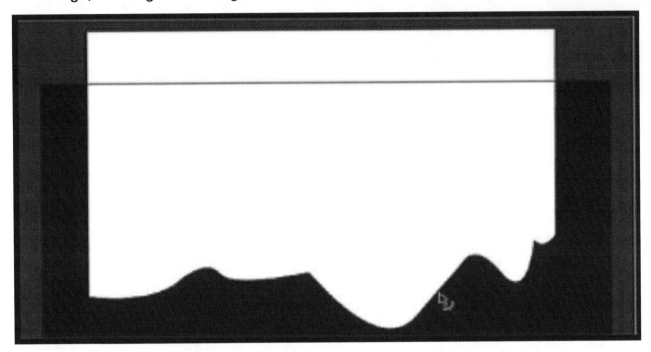

6. Add a shape tween between the beginning and end keyframes of the illumination layer.

7. In the Layer Properties panel, double-click the icon next to the title layer name and choose Mask as the layer type.
8. To modify the type of the glow layer, double-click the icon next to its name and choose Masked in the Layer Properties window. (Alternatively, slide the glow layer to the right to indent it under the title layer, and it will automatically tum   into a masked layer.)
9. Lock both layers.

10. Play your animation (Enter/ Return).

The letters from the Halloween greeting are in a mask layer, revealing the form of a tween in the glow layer. As the rectangle moves lower, the white fill shines through the letters, displaying the whole message.

EXTRA FINAL TOUCHES

As a final touch, consider replacing the glow layer's plain white fill with a linear gradient. Ali near gradient from opaque to transparent white may be used to soften the form of the tween's increasingly harsh edge.

1. Use the Color panel to create a linear gradient. On one end of the gradient, set the fill color to white with an alpha of 100% (completely opaque). On the other end, set the fill color to 0% alpha (completely translucent).

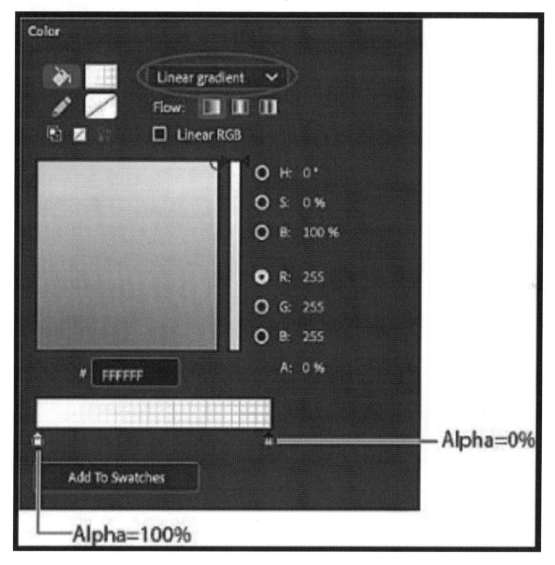

2. Use the Paint Bucket tool to create a linear gradient to your white rectangle in the glow layer.
3. Rotate and narrow the gradient using the Gradient Transform tool, placing opaque white at the top and transparent white at the bottom.

4. In the last keyframe of the illumination layer, apply the linear gradient to the form and make the bottom edge partially translucent.

5. Play your animation after locking all layers.

The gradient softens the curved edge of the form tween, resulting in a spookier, more subtle revelation of the Halloween message.

SHAPE TWEENING WITH VARIABLE-WIDTH STROKES

Shape tweening allows you to change any feature of a form, including the width of its stroke. You can modify the width of the strokes in separate keyframes, and when you use a shape tween between those keyframes, Animate generates smooth interpolations of those stroke widths. The ability to animate the width of a form's stroke, the curves of the stroke itself, and the interior fill (with solids, gradients, or transparencies)of a shape provides practically endless creative possibilities.

EXPORTING THE COMPLETED ANIMATED GIF

Your project is complete, and you will export the animated GIF for use as a Christmas message.

There are two ways to generate an animated GIF: rapid and difficult, depending on whether you want to fine-tune your animated GIF settings.

1. To quickly share and publish an animated GIF(.gif), choose **Quick Share and Publish > Publish.**

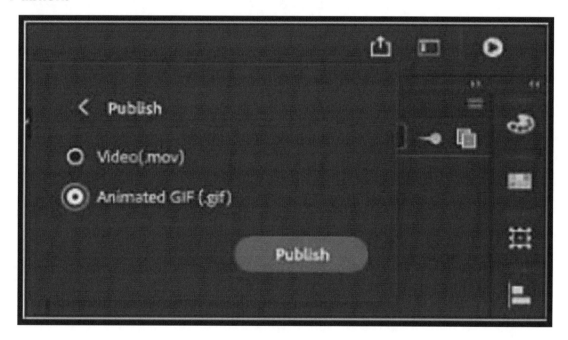

2. Click **Publish**. Animate creates an animated GIF and stores it in the same directory as your Animate file.
3. For additional flexibility over export parameters, choose **File > Export > Export Animated GIF**. Animate brings up the Export Image dialog box. It offers a picture preview as well as several optimization choices. In the Preset section, make sure the Matte option is set to Black.

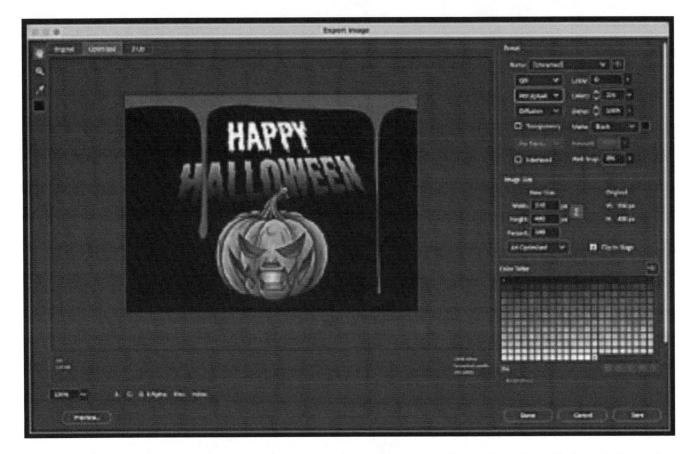

4. In the Preset box, choose **GIF** from the Optimized File Format option. Select O from the Lossy option and 256 from the Colors menu. This will greatly improve the quality of your photograph. The other two selections allow you to pick Selec-tive or Diffusion. These parameters control how the 256 colors are selected and combined to generate the final picture.

5. Keep all Image Size values at their default levels. The width and height should correspond to the original stage dimensions.

6. Under Animation, choose the looping behavior for your animated GIF. Select Forever to have your animated GIF loop indefinitely. Clicking the Play button allows you to preview the animation. You may also explore each of the 72 frames sep-arately, sliding ahead or backward one frame at a time.

7. In the Save dialog box, choose a filename and select the 08End folder to save the animated GIF.

FREQUENTLY ASKED QUESTIONS

1. How do you create a shape tween?
2. How do you use shape hints?
3. How do you move a keyframe?
4. How do you create and use masks?
5. How do you create the masked layer?
6. How do you turn on onion skinning?
7. How do you adjust the markers?
8. How do you export the completed animated GIF?

CHAPTER 8: INVERSE KINEMATICS AND BONE TOOL

OVERVIEW

In chapter six, you will learn how to create the pedaling cycle, how to disable and constrain joints, how to inverse kinematics with shapes, how to tween automatic rotations and so much more.

CHARACTER ANIMATION USING INVERSE KINEMATICS

The Bone tool enables you to create an armature that is comparable to the rig created using the Asset Warp tool. Both are composed of

joints and bones arranged hierarchically. However, here is where the similarities stop. The Bone tool uses inverse kinematics to move your armature. Inverse kinematics is a mathematical method for determining the various angles of a jointed item to reach a certain configura-tion. In inverse kinematics, when you move the child bone, the parent bone moves with it. For example, dragging a character's hand causes the upper arm to move as well. The upper arm represents the father, while the hand represents the kid.

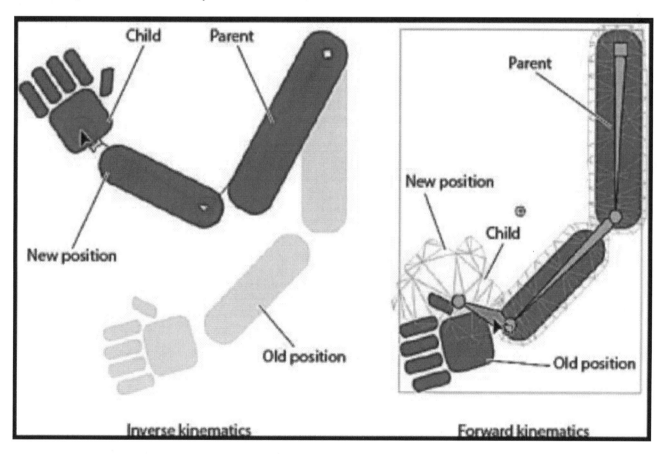

Layer parenting and current rigging using the Asset Warp tool, on the other hand, use forward kinematics, which means that moving the parent bone controls its child's bones. For example, dragging a character's upper arm causes the hand to move with it, but dragging the hand does not affect the upper arm.

KEY DISTINCTIONS BETWEEN THE BONE TOOL AND THE ASSET WARP TOOL

There are a few fundamental differences between the Bone tool and the Asset Warp tool in terms of their capabilities, how they func-tion, and how you use them, including the following:

- The Asset Warp tool utilizes forward kinematics, while the Bone tool uses inverse kinematics.
- Use the Bone tool to link movie clip symbols and vector forms. You utilize the Asset Warp tool with vector shapes or bitmaps.
- The Bone tool can only produce a single continuous armature in each layer. The Asset Warp tool, on the other hand, may generate a rig with numerous independent bones or single joints.
- Animate the Bone tool armature on a dedicated layer. Use conventional tweens to animate an Asset Warp tool rig.

BUILDING YOUR ARMATURE TO ANIMATE A CHARACTER

When animating a character with limbs and joints, first decide which parts of the character should move. At the same time, investigate how the pieces join and move. This will almost always be a hierarchical structure, such as a tree, with a root and numerous branches.

The Bone tool's construction is known as the armature. Each solid portion that makes up the armature is referred to as a bone, much as in a genuine skeleton. The armature determines where your thing may flex and how its many bones are linked. To design your armature, use the Bone tool. The Bone tool shows Animate how a succession of movie clip instances are linked, or it offers the jointed structure of a shape. A joint is a structure that connects two or more bones.

1. Examine your file to see the images for the bicycle and Ruby, the rider, which have already been produced and set on the Stage.

The components of the rider have been arranged such that it is clear how they connect. Leaving some space between the parts will make joining the bones of your armature simpler.

2. If required, add the Bone tool to the Tools panel by clicking the Edit Toolbar option, and then pick it.

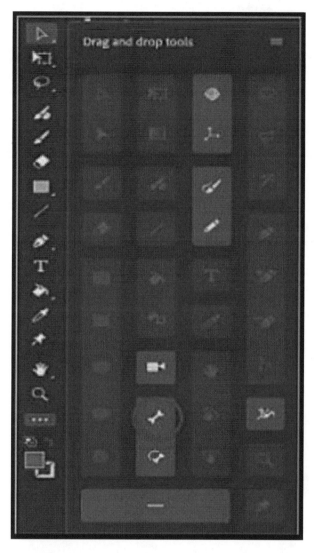

3. Click in the center of Ruby's chest and drag the Bone tool to the top of her right upper arm. Release the mouse button.

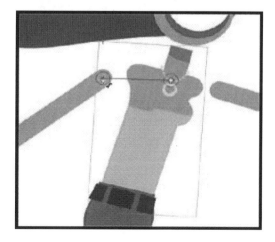

Your first bone has been defined in a new armature. Animate depicts the bone as a straight line with a square at the base and a circle at the tip joints. Each bone is distinguishable from one joint to the next. Ruby and her bicycle are visuals from Adobe's Assets Panel. There are many additional animated and static components available for usage or use in your projects.

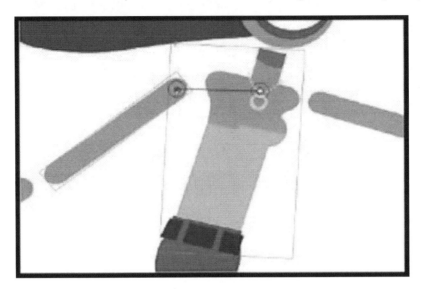

In the timeline, your freshly formed armature is immediately assigned to a new layer with a new icon and the default name, Armature_#. This layer separates your armatures from other items on the timeline, such as graphics and motion tweens.

4. Now, click and drag your first bone (at Ruby's shoulder) to the top of Ruby's lower arm (her elbow). Release the mouse button.

The first armature layer produced in a pristine file will be named Armature_1, and each subsequent armature layer will have its name in-creased by one. Don't worry if the name of your armature layer differs from the one in these screenshots.

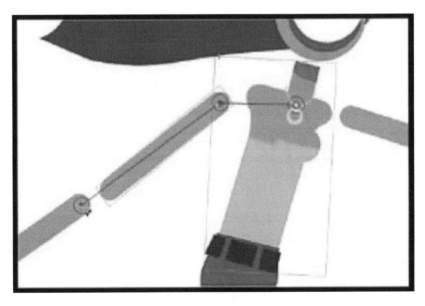

If you're having problems putting your bones because your mouse snaps to neighboring edges, you can turn off snapping. To uncheck Snap to Objects, go to the Doc tab in the Properties panel and click the magnet icon. Your second bone is defined.

5. Select the **Selection tool** and try sliding the final bone in the chain (Ruby's right forearm) up and down the Stage.

Since the bones link the whole arm to Ruby's body, moving the lower arm allows the upper arm and torso to move as well, although in an odd way.

EXTEND YOUR ARMATURE

You will proceed to assemble the armature by attaching Ruby's second arm, leg s, and bicycle.

1. With the Bone tool selected, click at the base of the first bone (in Ruby's chest) and drag it to the top of Ruby 's other upper arm. The first bone is known as your **"root bone."** Release the mouse button.

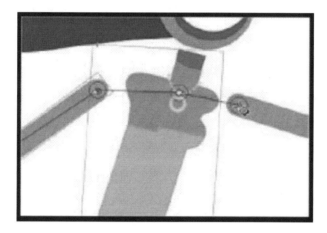

2. Continue to build additional bones in her lower arm. Your armature now extends in two directions, one for Ruby's left arm and another for her right arm.

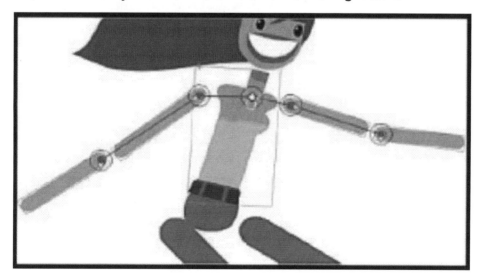

3. Drag the Bone tool to the center of Ruby's pelvis after clicking the base of the first bone (in her chest).
4. Extend the armature from the pelvis to both Rubies' lower legs. The pelvis will separate into the right and left thighs, lower legs, and black pedals. You may rearrange items to make them simpler to link.
5. Connect Ruby's torso to her head, and her pelvis to the bicycle's seat.

Your armature now joins all of Ruby's components, including her bicycle, and describes how each item may rotate and move relative to the other elements in the armature. You may question why we need to incorporate the bicycle as part of Ruby's armature. The bicycle must not move, but it must appear between her legs, with one leg behind the bicycle and the other above it. Because all of the pieces of an armature are on the same layer, one way to manage overlapping objects is to include them in the armature itself.

ARMATURE HIERARCHY

The root bone is the initial bone in an armature and serves as the parent bone for the child bones that are connected to it. A bone may have several children linked to it, as you have with your Ruby armature, resulting in an extremely intricate connection. The parent bone is located in the chest, each upper arm bone is a child, and the arms are siblings. As your armature grows more complex, you can utilize the Properties panel to travel up and down the hierarchy by using these connections. When you pick a bone in an armature, the top of the Properties window shows a sequence of arrows. You can use the arrows to navigate the hierarchy and easily choose and inspect the attributes of each bone. If the parent bone is chosen, use the down arrow to choose the child. If a child's bone is chosen, click the up arrow to pick its parent or the down arrow to select its child, if one exists. The sideways arrows lead between sibling bones.

MOVING THE BONES OF THE ARMATURE

Now that you've linked each movie clip to your bones in a full armature, you may adjust the relative location of each bone. Initially, there were gaps between the movie clips to facilitate joining them. Holding the Option/Alt key enables you to change the location of any bone in your armature.

1. To deselect the armature, choose the **Selection tool** and click on an empty region of the Stage.
2. Hold down the **Option/Alt key** and bring Ruby's right upper arm closer to her torso. You can also use the Free Transform feature. The top arm has been relocated, but the armature remains intact.

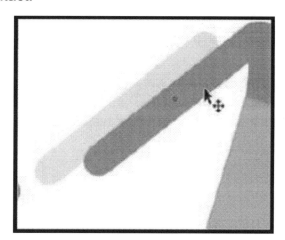

3. Hold down the **Option/ Alt key** and bring all of Ruby's body and the bicycle closer together to fill the gaps in her joints. The character and her armature should resemble the following figure.

REMOVING AND INSERTING BONES AND VIDEO CLIPS

To remove a bone, just use the Selection tool to pick it, and then hit Backspace / Delete. The bone and all of its child bones will be removed, but the film clip will remain. To delete a movie clip, select it on the St age and then hit Backspace / Delete. The movie clip and its corre-sponding bone will be deleted. To add additional movie clips to your armature, drag more movie clip instances onto the Stage in a separate layer. You cannot add additional items to an armature layer. Once the movie clip instance is on the Stage, use the Bone tool to attach it to the bones of your current armature. The new instance will be placed in the same layer as the armature.

CHANGING THE POSITION OF THE JOINT

If you want to modify the point at which one bone links to another (the joint), use the Free Transform tool to shift the transformation point. This also changes the bone's rotation point. For example, if you made a mistake and hooked the end point of your bone to the center of the following movie clip instead of the base, that body part would spin abnormally.

1. To change the location of the joint, use the Free Transform tool and pick the video clip. Move the transformation point to a new location.

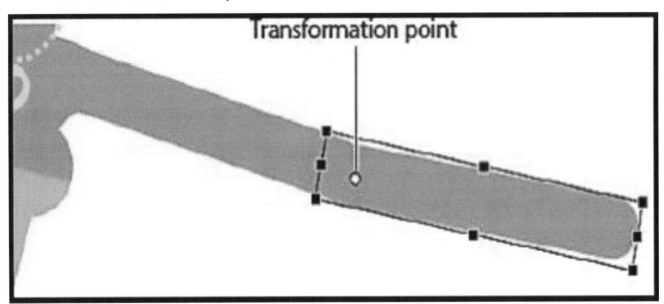

2. The bone now links to the movie clip's new transition point.

REARRANGE THE STACKING ORDER

When you create an armature, the most recent bone is moved to the top of the stack in your graphics. Depending on how you joined your bones, the different video segments may not overlap properly. For example, in the prior challenge, Ruby's legs may not have properly over-lapped with the bicycle. One leg should be behind the bicycle, while the other should be in front. To properly overlap the movie clips in your armature, use the **Modify > Arrange** command.

1. Select the **Selection tool,** then Shift-select the three video clips that comprise Ruby 's rear leg, including the pedal.

2. Select **Modify > Arrange > Send To Back** or right -click and choose Arrange > Send To Back (Shift +Com m an d +Down/Shift +Ctrl +Down).

The chosen armature bones shift to the bottom of the stacking sequence, thus Ruby's left leg is now behind the bicycle, and the bicy-cle seat protrudes from between her legs.

3. Select the two clips that makeup Ruby 's left arm and use the Modify > Arrange command to shift them back.
4. Select Rub y's head, **then Modify > Arrange > Bring To Front**, or right-click and select **Arrange > Bring To Front (Shift +Command+ Up/Shift +Ctrl + Up).** The armature's head rises to the top of the stacking sequence, bringing Ruby's head over her neck.

5. Choose the Selection tool and drag the armature around to watch how Ruby's right and left arms and legs move behind or in front of her torso. Make any necessary adjustments.

Use **Modify > Arrange > Send To Back** to send chosen graphics to the bottom of the stacking sequence, or **Modify > Arrange > Send Back- ward** to move them only one level back. Similarly, Bring To Front moves visuals to the top of the stacking sequence, whereas Bring Forward moves pictures one step higher.

CREATING A PEDALING CYCLE

Armatures make animating the pedaling action simpler since you simply need to accurately place her feet on the pedals in keyframes (known as poses), and because her feet are related to the rest of her body, the upper limbs will follow naturally.

POSING YOUR ARMATURE

In the first posture, set Ruby's starting position by placing her feet and pedals on opposing sides of the rotating action.

1. Using the Selection tool, move Ruby's right foot to the top of the pink circle, which depicts the pedaling action. Move the black pedals linked to her feet so that they are parallel to the ground. As you pull her leg and pedal, the bones that link them move as well. Do not panic if you are having problems manipulating the armature! It takes practice, and the next sec-tions will teach you additional tips and tactics for constraining or isolating certain joints for precise alignment.
2. Move Ruby's left foot and pedal to the bottom of the pink circle. Attempt to maintain the black pedal on the curvature of the circle.

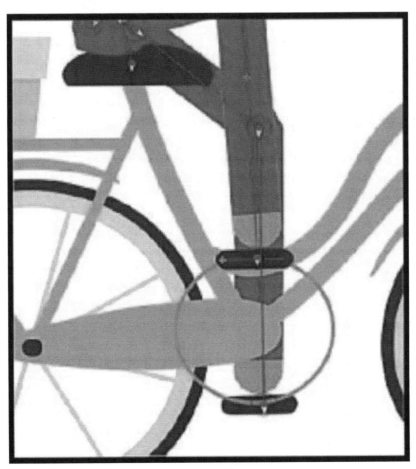

3. Position Rub y's arms on the bicycle's handlebars.

Your initial posture is finished in frame 1 of your armature layer.

ISOLATING ROTATION OF INDIVIDUAL BONES

Since the links between the bones, you may struggle to regulate their rotation when you pull and push on the armature to construct your stance. Holding down the Shift key while moving particular bones will isolate their rotation.

1. Select the back pedal under her left leg.
2. Use the Selection tool to drag the pedal. The leg moves to match the action of the pedal.
3. Hold down the Shift key and drag the pedal.

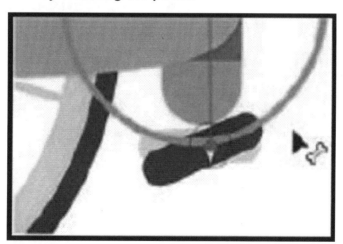

The pedal revolves around the leg while the rest of the armature remains stationary. The Shift key isolates the rotation of the currently chosen bone. Holding down the Shift key isolates the rotations of particular bones, allowing you to place your postures precisely how you want. Return to Ruby's legs and pedals and make any required modifications using the Shift key.

241

PINNING INDIVIDUAL BONES

Fixing individual bones in place is another approach to having more exact control over your armature's rotation or position. For example, the bicycle is now free to move and spin underneath the rider, therefore pinning it will secure it in place.

1. Select the selection tool.
2. Choose the bone of the bicycle near the seat. The bone gets highlighted, suggesting that it is chosen.
3. In the Properties panel, choose the **Pin option.**

The bicycle is securely fastened to the Stage in its present position. The joint is pinned, a white circle with a black dot.

4. You can also choose a joint and click it when your cursor transforms into a pushpin icon. The picked bone will be pinned. Click again to unpin the bone.

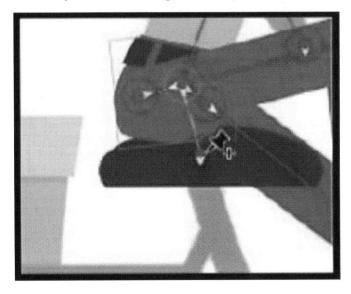

The armature motion differs when using the Pin option vs. the Shift key. The Shift key separates an individual bone from the rest of the bones that are related to it. When you pin a bone, it stays set, but you may move all of the kid bones.

DISABLE AND CONSTRAINING JOINTS

Before inserting the remaining poses, you might improve your armature to make Ruby simpler to place. The armature's joints may easily rotate, which isn't very realistic. Many armatures in real life are restricted to certain degrees of rotation. For example, your forearm may rotate up toward your bicep but not in the other way beyond it. Your hips may move slightly around your torso. These are limits that you can also apply to your armature. When dealing with armatures in Animate, you may restrict the rotation or translation (movement) of the different joints.

DISABLE JOINT ROTATION

If you move Ruby's head, you'll see that the bone that joins the torso to the pelvis may freely rotate, allowing for highly implausible poses.

1. Select the bone that joins Ruby's head and body.
2. If required, turnoff the Enable option in the Joint: Rot at ion section of the Properties window. The circle surrounding the joint at the head of the chosen bone vanishes, indicating that the joint can no longer rotate.

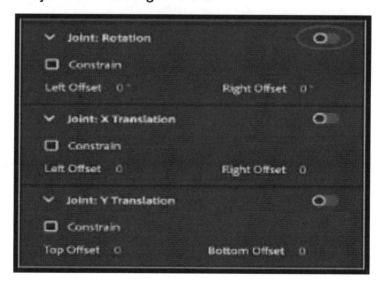

3. Now, drag Ruby's head. Her head can no longer revolve around the joint in her torso.

CONSTRAINING THE RANGE OF ROTATION

The armature needs some further work. You can enable rotation while simultaneously limiting the range of movement for different joints.

1. Choose the bone that joins Ruby's chest and her left upper arm.

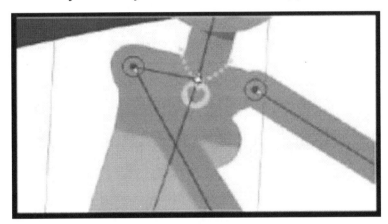

2. If required, turn off the Enable option in the Joint: Rota t ion section of the Properties window. Rotation around the thoracic joint is inhibited, limiting the upper arm's ability to move as freely as it would otherwise.
3. Choose the kid bone (the bone connecting the upper arm to the forearm).

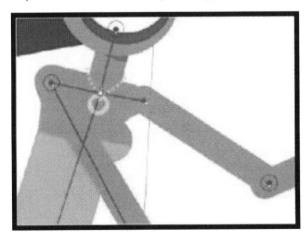

4. Select the **Constraint option** from the Joint: Rotation section of the Properties screen. The angle indication on the joint changes from a complete circle to a partial circle, indicating the lowest and maximum permitted angles as well as the bone's present location.

5. In the Properties panel, adjust the Left Offset rotation angle to -90 degrees and the Right Offset rotation angle to 90 degrees.
6. Drag the upper arm.

You can move the arm, but it can only rotate straight up or straight down, preventing your armature from being unnaturally positioned and making it much simpler to manage and place your postures.

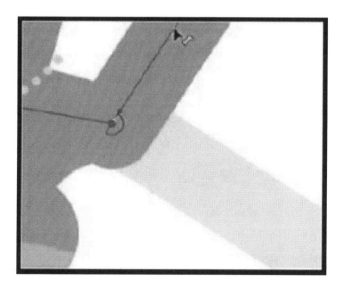

In reality, joints simply enable bones to spin. However, with Animate, you may enable joints to glide in either the x(horizontal) or y (verti-cal) direction, and you can determine the distance that those joints can travel. To allow and limit this kind of motion, use Joint: X Transla-tion and Joint: Y Translation in the Properties panel, as you would for rotation.

ADDING POSES

When working with armature layers," **poses"** and "keyframes" are practically the same thing. Your armature is now ready. You've linked your bones and added the necessary restrictions to make the armature simpler to position. Poses are inserted into the timeline in the same way that keyframes for a motion tween are.

INSERTING POSES

Remember that your objective is to create distinct stances that allow for natural pedaling action. You'll design eight more postures for Ruby's feet to approximate the circle in which they'll traverse. The whole cycle will last 48 frames, with each posture taking six frames. For this assignment, choose the Auto Keyframe option from the options at the top of your timeline. Remember that changing material on the Stage immediately generates keyframes.

USING ON-STAGE CONTROLS FOR JOINT CONSTRAINTS

You can quickly alter any joint rotation or translation limits by just utilizing the on-Stage controls that display above joints, rather than making such changes in the Properties panel. Using the on-stage controls, you can examine the limitations concerning the other bones and visuals on the stage.

Simply choose a bone and slide your cursor over the joint in its head. A circle with four arrowheads is highlighted in blue. Click it to access the on-stage controls.

To adjust the rotation limits, slide your cursor over the outside border of the circle (highlighted in red) and click it. To specify the mini-mum and maximum angles of joint rotation, click within the circle. The gray region represents the range of permitted rotation. You may also drag to adjust the angles inside the circle. Click outside of the circle to confirm your changes. To prevent rotation at that joint, click the lock symbol that appears when you roll over the center of the circle. To adjust the translation limits (up and down or side to side), slide your cursor over the arrows within the circle, which will be highlighted in red. To confine the joint's t ran slat ion in either direction, click the horizontal or vertical arrow and then drag the offsets.

1. On the timeline, pick frame 6.

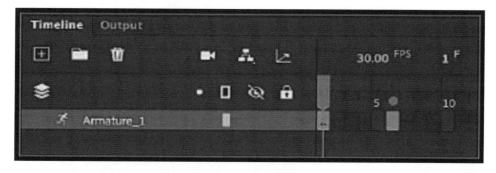

2. Make sure the **Auto Keyframe option** is on in the controls at the top of your timeline, and then adjust Ruby's feet and pedals so that the front foot/pedal is at the northwest position (around 1 o'clock) and the rear foot/pedal is on the other side. A new pose/keyframe is added at frame 6.

3. On the timeline, choose frame 12.

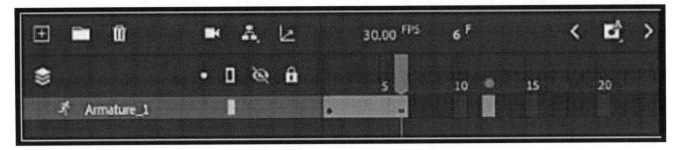

4. Move Rub y's feet and pedals such that the front foot/pedal is facing northeast (about 3 o'clock).

5. Continue to add new positions every six frames while situating Ruby's feet along the pink circle. You'll finish up with nine positions, each about every 7 minutes of a clock face, over 48 frames.

The first and last postures will be the same.

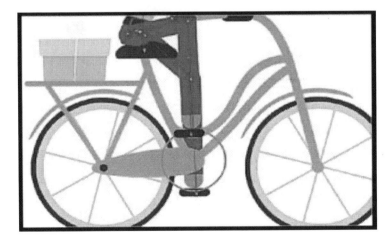

To add ease to your inverse kinematics animations, pick the animation on the timeline and then choose an ease type and strength in the Properties box. Eases may alter the animation by beginning slowly (ease-in) and finishing gradually (ease-out). You can adjust poses on the timeline in the same way that you do with keyframes in a motion tween. To add a new posture, right-click anywhere along the timeline and choose Insert Posture. Remove any posture from the layer by right-clicking it and selecting Clear Posture. To pick a posture, command- click or control-click it. Drag the posture to a new location on the timeline.

6. At the bottom of the timeline, choose **Loop Playback** (Shift + Option + L/ Shift +Alt+ L) and drag the markers to cover the full animation from frame 1 to frame 48.
7. To examine your animation loop, click the **Play button** at the bottom of the timeline (hit the **Return** [macOS] or **Enter** [Windows] keys).

To ensure that the first and final postures are similar, duplicate the first keyframe and paste it into the last frame. Hold down the Option/ Alt key while dragging the initial keyframe to frame 48.

CHANGING JOINT SPEED

Joint speed refers to the stickiness or stiffness of a joint. A joint with a low joint speed value will be slow. A high joint speed number indi-cates more responsiveness. The Properties tab allows you to change the joint speed value for each specified joint. When you drag the end of an armature, the joint speed becomes obvious. If there are sluggish joints higher up on the armature chain, they will be less sensitive and spin at a slower rate than the others. To alter the joint speed, click and pick a bone. In the Properties window, change the Joint Speed value from 0%to 100%. The joint speed does not affect the actual animation; it just changes how the armature reacts to the way you position it on the Stage, making it simpler to maneuver.

ADDING A WAVE AND HEAD NOD

Now that the pedaling motion is complete, you'll add other actions to give Ruby some personality.

1. Select frame 18, then raise Ruby's left arm to wave.

2. Select frame 24, and then straighten her forearm.

3. To finish the wave, choose frame 30 and raise Ruby 's left arm, angling her forearm toward her head.

4. Rotate Ruby's head slightly so that she offers a nod during the wave in one of the stances (you may choose).

INVERSE KINEMATICS USING SHAPES

Ruby and her bicycle are armatures built of movie clip symbols. You may also construct armatures inside forms, which is great for animat-ing things with no evident joints or segments but can still move in an articulated manner. For example, an octopus's arms lack true joints, but bones may be added to a smooth tentacle to mimic its undulating action. You may also animate other biological items, such as a snake, a waving flag, grass blades bending in the wind, or, as you will see in the following job, Ruby's hair blowing in the breeze.

DEFINE BONES INSIDE A SHAPE

Ruby's hair is shaped with a crimson fill and no strokes. To make it animate, you'll need to add bones.

1. In the library, enter the Girl Bicycle _ as sets_ folder and double -click the Ruby_Head movie clip icon.

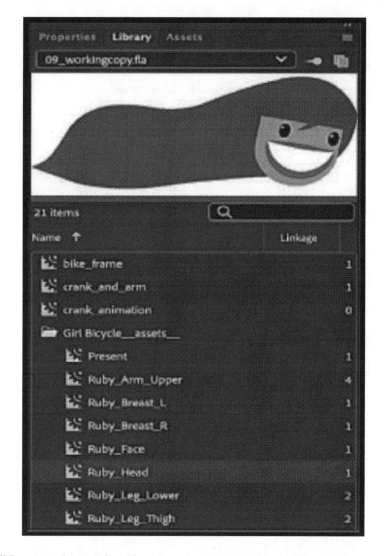

2. In symbol editing mode, notice that her hair is on the bottom layer.

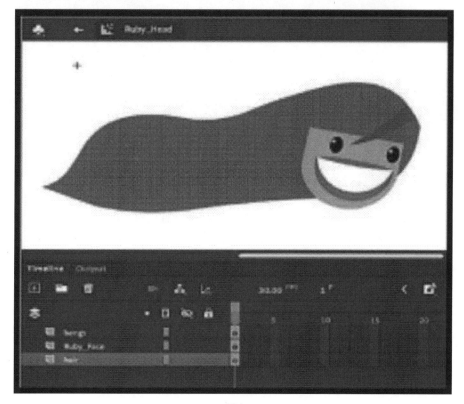

3. Choose the **Bone Tool.**
4. Click within the form, beginning from the right side, and drag a bone halfway into the hair. Animate generates an arma-ture inside Ruby's hair and assigns it to its armature layer.

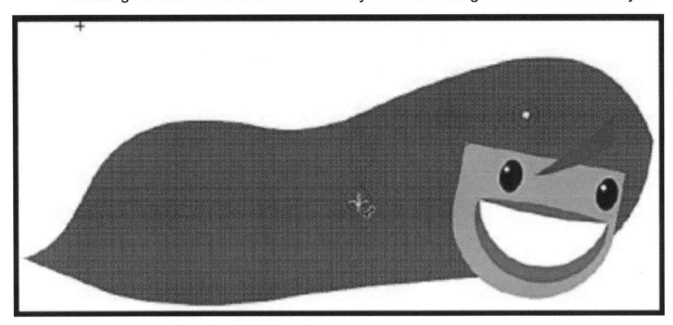

5. Click the end of the first bone, and then drag the second bone down toward the tip of the hair. The second bone is defined.
6. Continue to add bones to the hair armature until there are around four.
7. When the armature is finished, use the Selection tool to move the last bone to observe how the hair deforms in response to the armature's bones.

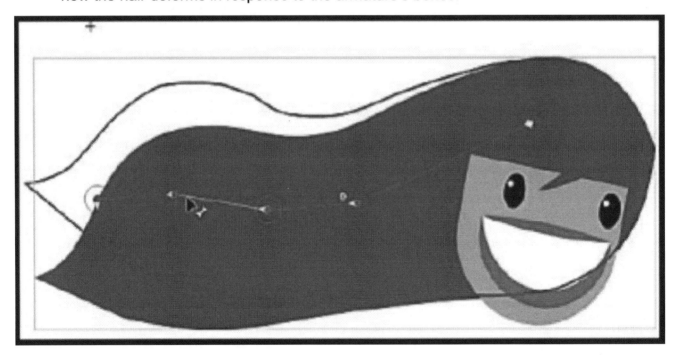

ANIMATING THE HAIR

Animating an armature within a shape is the same as animating an armature created with movie clips. Using keyframes, you may create alternative postures for your armature throughout the timeline.

1. For all three layers, select frame 40 and then choose **Insert > Timeline > Frame** (F5).

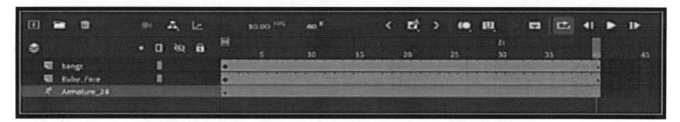

Animate adds frames up to frame 40 to the timeline. Making the number of frames in Ruby's nested animation different from the main timeline of the pedaling ensures that the animations do not synchronize, resulting in a more natural loop.

2. Set the play head on the timeline to frame 15.
3. Move the armature in Ruby's hair to deform it. To isolate a bone's rotation, hold down the Shift key while you move it. Ani- mate adds a new pose for Ruby's hair in frame 15.

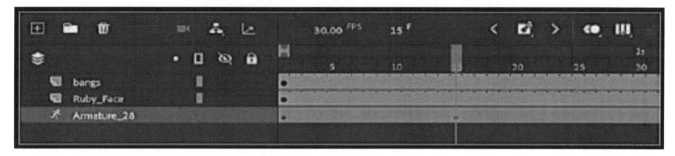

4. Advance the play head to frame 25.
5. Move the armature in Ruby's hair to a new place. Animate adds a new pose for Ruby's hair in frame 25.
6. Hold down the **Option/Alt** keys and drag the first pose to the final frame (40). Animate duplicates the first pose into frame 40, ensuring that the animation ends in the same place where it began.
7. Exit the symbol editing mode and test your movie. Because the hair animation is nested within a movie clip symbol, pressing Play/ Enter on the main timeline will not result in her hair moving. Rub y's hair waves and blows while she pedals her bicycle.

8. To finish the animation, add an armature to Ruby's bangs in the bangs layer and animate the wisp of hair fluttering around her face.

The organic control of a shape by its armature results from a mapping between the shape's anchor points and bones. The Bind tool allows you to edit the connections between the bones and their control points, as well as refine the behavior. The Bind tool must be added to the Tools panel using the Edit Toolbar option. For more information on using this advanced tool, refer to the Animate Help documentation.

SIMULATING PHYSICS WITH SPRINGINESS

You have seen how armatures may let you quickly posture your characters and objects in various keyframes to achieve smooth, realistic motion. However, you can add physics to your armatures so that they respond as they move from stance to posture. The Spring feature makes this easier. Spring mimics physics in any animated armature, including movie clips and shapes. A flexible item would generally have some "springiness" that caused it to bounce on its own as it moved and continue to jiggle long after the whole body's motion had ceased. The level of springiness varies by object- for example, a hanging rope has a lot of jiggle, but a diving board is considerably stiffer and has less bounce. You may adjust the spring's strength based on your item, and you can even specify various springiness levels for each bone in an armature to get the desired level of stiffness or flexibility in your animation. In a tree, for example, the broader branches will have less spring than the tiny terminal branches.

ADDING SPRINGINESS TO RUBY'S HAIR

Adding spring to Ruby's hair armature gives it more leftover motion after a keyframe posture. Spring strength ratings vary from zero (no spring) to one hundred (the greatest spring).

Here are the steps:

1. Double-click the Ruby_Head movie clip symbol in the library to enter symbol editing mode (if not already there).

2. In symbol editing mode, choose the last child bone in Ruby's hair.

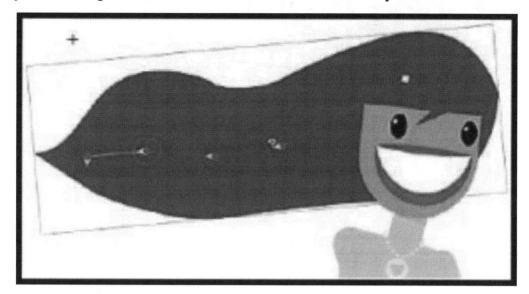

3. In the Properties panel, choose the spring section and set the Strength to 100. The final bone has the most spring strength since the tip is the most flexible element of the whole armature and would have the most independent motion.

4. Choose the next bone in the armature. Simply click it on the **Stage**, or use the arrows in the Properties window to travel up the armature hierarchy.
5. In the Properties panel, choose the **spring section** and set the Strength to 70. The center of the bone is less flexible than the tip, resulting in a lower strength value.
6. In the Properties panel, choose the next parent bone and adjust the Spring Strength to 30. The base of the hair armature is less flexible than the center, resulting in a lower strength value. The impacts of the spring feature are more noticeable when there are more frames on the timeline following the armature's final stance. The extra frames show you the leftover bouncing effect after the final stance.
7. Add frames to each layer till frame 100.

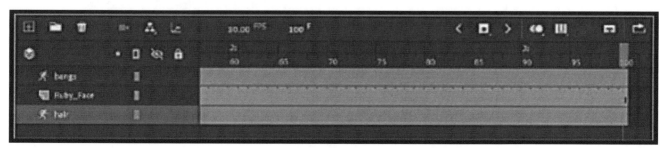

8. Test the movie.

Ruby's hair flows from one stance to the next, but even after the last pose, it sways somewhat. The back-and-forth rotation of the hair armature, paired with the addition of springiness to the bones, may imitate the effects of physical pressures on an item, making the ani-mation more lifelike. Return and experiment with various spring strength levels to find what works best for your animation.

ADD DAMPING EFFECTS

Damping refers to how much the spring effect fades over time. It would be unrealistic if the swinging of the hair went on endlessly. The swaying should gradually reduce and then cease. To regulate how quickly these effects subside, you can provide a damping value to each bone ranging from 0 (no damping) to 100 (highest damping).

Follow the steps below:

1. In the Properties panel, set the Damping value to 50 in the spring section for the hair's final bone(tip). The Damping set- ting will reduce the swinging of the hair over time.

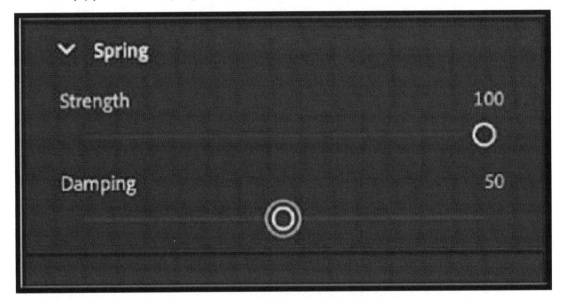

2. In the Proper ties panel, set the Damping value to 100 for the next bone(parent) in the armature.
3. Select bones with Strength values, and then apply Damping values to reduce springiness.
4.
5. Select **Control > Test** to test how different Damping levels affect Ruby's hair motion.

The hair still sways, but it stops fast. The damping levels provide weight to the armature. Experiment with the Strength and Damping parameters in your armature's Spring section to get the most lifelike motion.

TWEENING AUTOMATIC ROTATIONS

Ruby cycles and waves, her hair blowing in the wind, yet her bicycle's wheels and crank must move.

ADDING A NESTED ANIMATION OF ROTATING WHEELS

You will now animate revolving wheels inside the bicycle frame's video clip.

1. Double-click the bicycle frame on the Stage. You enter symbol editing mode for the bike_frame movie clip symbol, but you modify it in situ such that all other graphics on the Stage are darkened.
2. Double-click the rear wheel to locate the Wheel_Turning movie clip sign.
3. Select the wheel on Stage and click the **Create Motion Tween icon** above the timeline. Animate generates a tween layer and adds 30frames.

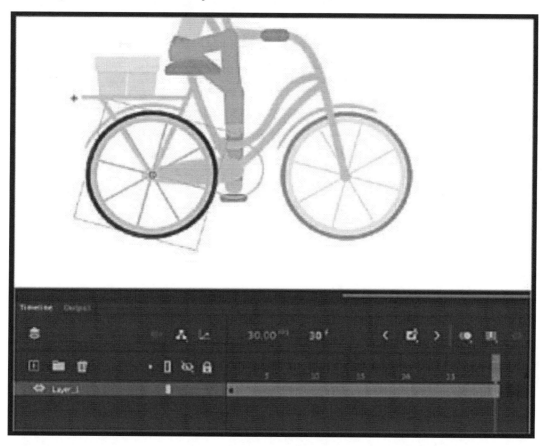

4. To rotate the tween, pick **Clockwise** in the Properties window and leave the Count at one. The wheel automatically re-volves one full clockwise revolution around its transformation point (which is in the middle).

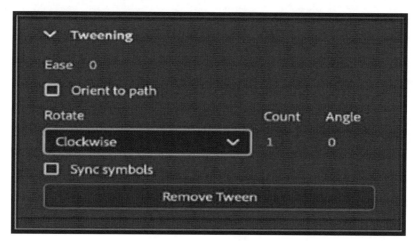

257

You don't need to generate a new tween since the Wheel_Turning movie clip for the front wheel of the bicycle already exists. Your bicycle's wheels are complete.

ADD THE CRANK ARM

Lastly, the pedals must be attached to the crank arm, which turns the gears.

1. Double-click the crank_animation movie clip icon in the library. You go into symbol editing mode for the movie clip symbol.

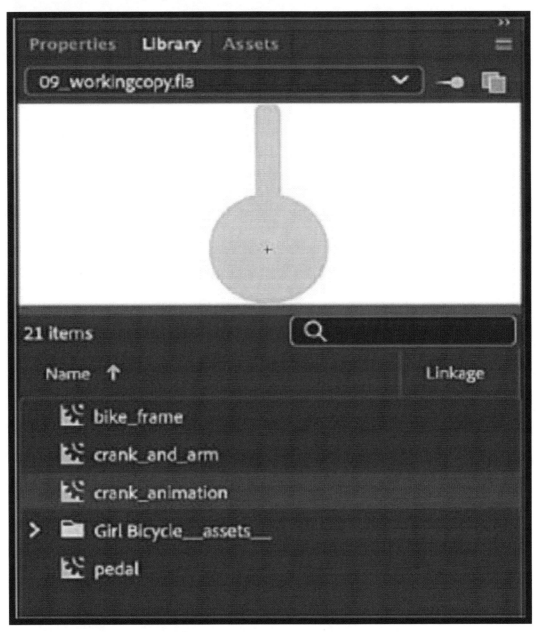

2. Select the movie clip instance on the Stage or the first keyframe on the timeline. Then, click **Create Motion Tween** above the timeline. Animate generates 30 frames in a motion tween layer.
3. Add 48 frames to the tween layer. The animation of the crank arm turning must be coordinated with Ruby's pedaling; hence the number of frames must match (48).
4. Select a t ween. In the Properties window, choose **Clockwise Rotate** and 1 for Count. Animate automatically performs a clockwise rotation for one revolution.

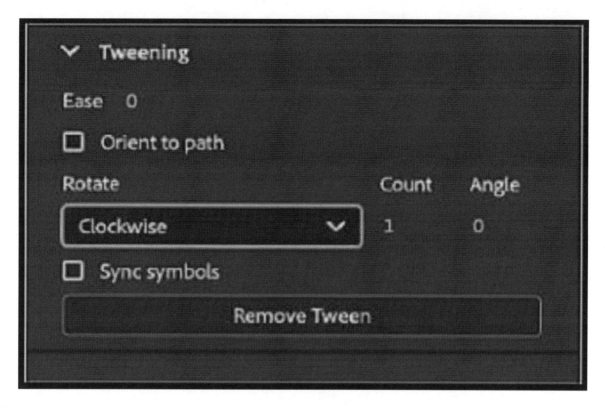

5. To create a smooth loop, make a little change between frames 1 and 48, which are identical. Drag the right edge of the tween to move it to frame 49.

6. Create a new keyframe at frame 48.

7. Remove Frame 49. You still have 48 frames for the rotation, but the finishing keyframe does not duplicate the initial keyframe, thus the loop is flawless.

8. To modify the bike_frame movie clip symbol, add the crank_animation symbol to the front_pedal layer. The instance should fit perfectly within the pink circle.

9. Copy the crank_animation instance.

10. Select the back_ped al layer and use **Edit > Paste In Place** (Command +Shift +V/Ctrl +Shift +V). The Paste In Place command places the copied items precisely where you copied them from.

11. Ensure the transformation point is in the middle of the crank, then choose **Modify > Transform > Flip Vertical**. The instance flips, and the crank arm now points downwards. If the transformation point is not in the center, you may adjust it using the Free Transform tool. Hide the layers above the back_pedal layer to see the pedal, its transformation point, and how it flips. However, the crank arm will now turn counterclockwise.

12. Select **Modify > Transform> Flip Horizontal**. The crank_animation instance flips horizontally, such that the spinning continues clockwise.

13. Right-click the icon in front of the rotation_guide layer and choose Properties.

14. In the Layer Properties dialog box, pick Guide as the type. Click OK. When you publish the project, no guidance layers appear. It appears on your timeline as an icon of a T square.

15. Exit symbol editing mode and test your video.

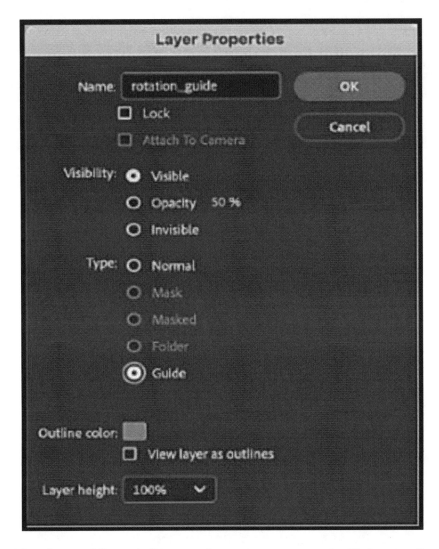

Ruby pedals her bicycle, and the rotating crank arms correspond with her motion. The pink circle that you used as a reference to place her feet and pedals no longer appears since it is in a guide layer.

RIG MAPPING

Rig mapping is a function that allows you to apply stored armatures to multiple images. For example, a walking motion may be repeated with a variety of figures. You may save your armatures and poses in the Assets panel, or you can utilize one of Adobe's numerous assets.

SAVE AN ANIMATED ARMATURE IN THE ASSETS PANEL

To save an armature animation in the Assets panel, first, save it to your library as a movie clip symbol.

1. Select the armature layer for your Ruby animation. Right-click and choose **Convert Layers to Symbol.**

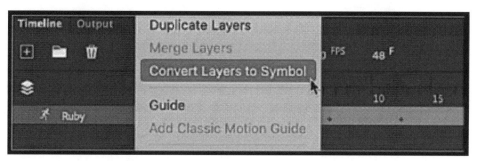

2. In the Convert Layers to Symbol dialog box, pick Movie Clip as the type and enter Ruby_bike_animation as the animation's name. Click OK. Animate stores the armature layer as a movie clip symbol that shows in your library.

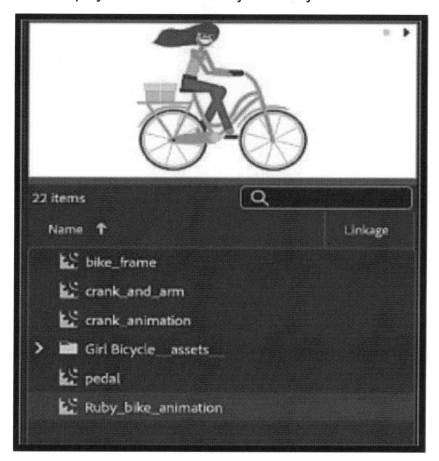

3. Right-click the new movie clip symbol and choose **Save As Asset.**

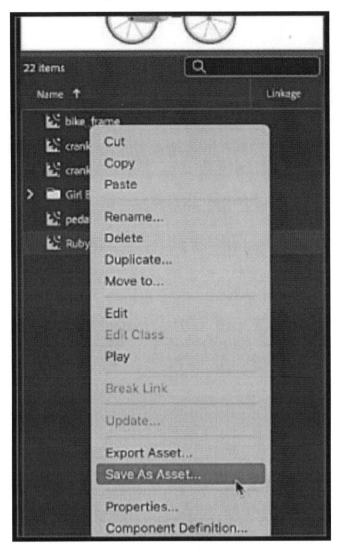

4. In the Save As item dialog box, insert keywords separated by commas to act as searchable reminders for the item. Since you want to preserve the images, armature, and animation, leaves Objects, Bones, and Motion selected. Select **Save.** Ani- mate saves the animation to the Custom tab of the Assets panel.

If you simply save Bones and Motion (and uncheck Objects), your animated armature will be saved to the Assets panel.

FREQUENTLY ASKED QUESTIONS

1. How do you inverse kinematics with bones in Adobe Animate?
2. How do you build your armature to animate a character?
3. How do you create a pedaling cycle?
4. How do you disable and constraian joints?
5. How do you add poses?
6. How do you change the joint speed?
7. How do you add damping effects?

CHAPTER 9: BUILDING INTERACTIVE MEDIA

OVERVIEW

Chapter seven focuses on interactive media, how you can create one, create buttons, prepare the timeline, navigate the actions panel, and create destination keyframes and so much more.

This is the example exercise we will be focusing on here:

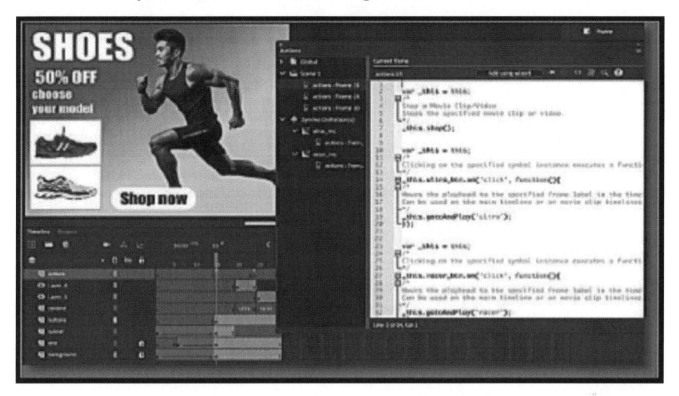

ABOUT INTERACTIVE MEDIA

Interactive media responds to the viewer's actions. For example, when the viewer clicks or touches a button, a new visual with further information appears. Interactivity may be basic, such as a button click, or complicated, receiving input from a multitude of sources, such as mouse movements, keyboard keystrokes, or even a mobile device's tilt.

ACTIONSCRIPT AND JAVASCRIPT

Animate allows you to create interaction using either ActionScript 3.0 or JavaScript, depending on the kind of page you're working on.

If you're working with an ActionScript 3.0, AIR for Desktop, AIR for iOS or Android project, you'll need to utilize ActionScript to provide interaction. The published file for an ActionScript 3.0 document with ActionScript interaction is a projector, which is a standalone file that runs on the user's computer. An AIR for Desktop document also creates a file that can be played on a PC or an AIR-enabled device. An AIR for iOS or Android document creates a mobile application. ActionScript includes instructions for an animation to react to the user. These instructions might include playing a sound, moving to a keyframe on the timeline when new images emerge, or doing a computation. In an HTMLS Canvas document, such as the one you're creating for this banner ad, you employ JavaScript, which is the same code that powers interaction on web pages in browsers. The WebGL glTF, VR 360, and VR Panorama Animate documents all employ JavaScript.

ActionScript 3.0 and JavaScript are relatively similar (both are based on an ECMA coding language standard), although they vary some- what in syntax and use. In this task, you'll use JavaScript in an HTMLS Canvas page to create nonlinear navigation, which means the movie doesn't have to play from beginning to finish. You'll use JavaScript to instruct the Animate play head to bounce about and move to various frames of the timeline depending on which button the user presses. Distinct frames on the timeline have distinct content. The user is un- aware that the play head is moving across the timeline; instead, the user sees (or hears) various materials emerge when the Stage's buttons are pressed. Don't worry if you don't believe you're a competent programmer! You don't need to be a coding ninja since Animate has an easy-to-use, menu-driven wizard in the Actions panel that enables you to install JavaScript quickly and easily.

CREATING BUTTONS

A button is a simple visual representation of anything that consumers may interact with. Users often use the mouse to click or press a button, but there are several more forms of interactions that may occur. For example, when a user rolls the mouse curs or over a button, anything may occur. A button is a kind of symbol with four distinct states or key frames that control how it looks. Buttons may take on many different forms, including images, graphics, and text. They do not have to be the traditional pill-shaped gray rectangles seen on many websites.

CREATING A BUTTON SYMBOL

Here, you'll learn how to design buttons with tiny thumbnail pictures. Buttons area specific form of symbol that is kept in the Li-brary panel.

1. Create a new layer above all other layers and call it buttons.

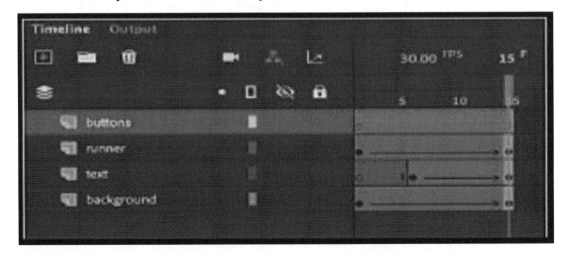

2. Lock the other layers to avoid mistakenly moving the other items on the Stage.

3. Use the Rectangle tool with a white fill and an orange stroke to draw a rectangle 90 pixels wide and 65 pixels high on the Stage's buttons layer.

4. In the Library panel, drag the vapormax ultra thumbnail bitmap to the middle of the rectangle you just created.

5. Select the rectangle and its stroke, as well as the running shoe picture, and then click **Modify > Convert to Symbol**.
6. In the Convert to Symbol dialog box, choose **Button** from the Type menu and name the symbol ultra. Click OK.

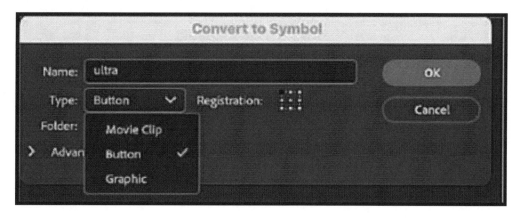

Animate generates a button symbol from the specified graphics, which are displayed in your library.

EDITING A BUTTON SYMBOL

A button sign comprises four special states, which are shown as frames on the button's timeline, as well as on the main timeline. The four frames include the following:

- The Upstate displays the button as it appears when the user does not interact with it.
- The Over states displays the button as seen when the cursor hovers over it.
- The Downstate depicts the button as it looks when the cursor hovers over it and the user pushes or touches it.
- The Hit state identifies the click able region of the button.

Working through this exercise will help you grasp the link between these states and the look of the button.

1. In the Library panel, double-click the extreme button icon. You enter symbol editing mode for the button symbol, which displays a timeline with Up, Over, Down, and Hit frames. Only the Up frame has a full keyframe.

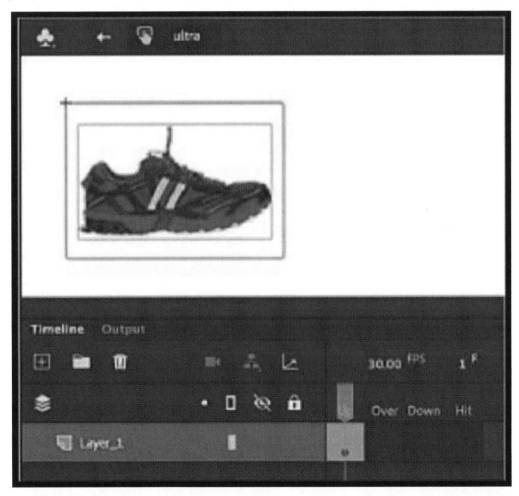

2. To expand the timeline, choose the Hit Frame and then pick **Insert > Timeline > Frame**. The rectangle and shoe graphic now spans the Up, Over, Down, and Hit states.

3. Set a keyframe in the Over frame. When the user's mouse pointer lingers over the button, the new keyframe indicates that the visuals have changed.

4. Select the stroke surrounding the rectangle by double-clicking it, and then change the color from orange to red.
5. Select the rectangles fill and change the color from white to yellow. The Up and Over keyframes are no longer identical. The button is ordinarily white with an orange stroke, but when the mouse cursor rolls over it, the Over keyframe appears, which has a yellow fill and a red stroke.

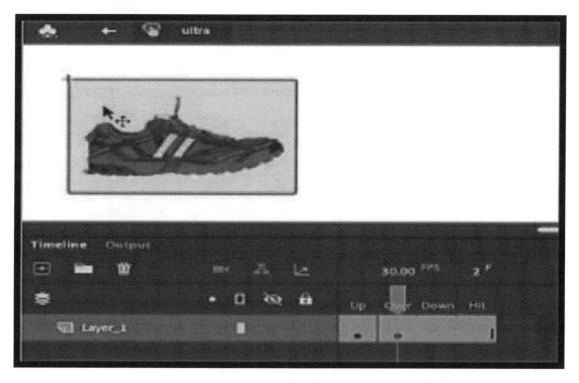

6. Click the left-facing arrow button in the Edit bar above the Stage to leave symbol editing mode and return to the main timeline. Your first button symbol is complete, but it will not respond to your cursor yet. You'll need to test your movie to observe how your button changes visually based on the Up, over, and down keyframe states.

INVISIBLE BUTTONS AND HIT KEYFRAMES

The Hit keyframe for your button symbol represents the region that is "hot," or clickable by the user. Normally, the Hit keyframe includes a form with the same size and placement as the Up keyframe. In most circumstances, the visuals that consumers view should be in the same location where they click. However, in certain complex applications, the Hit and Up keyframes may need to be different. If your Up keyframe is empty, the resultant button is referred to as an invisible button. Users cannot see invisible buttons, but since the Hit keyframe still specifies a clickable region, they stay active. You may add invisible buttons to any region of the Stage and use code to program them to react to users. Invisible buttons are excellent for generating generic hotspots. Placing them on top of various photographs, for example, al- lows you to have each photo react to a click or touch without having to create a separate button symbol for each one.

DUPLICATING BUTTONS

Now that you've made one button, replicating symbols will make it easier to develop the second.

1. In the Library panel, right-click the ultra button and choose **Duplicate**. You can also choose Duplicate from the Library panel menu.

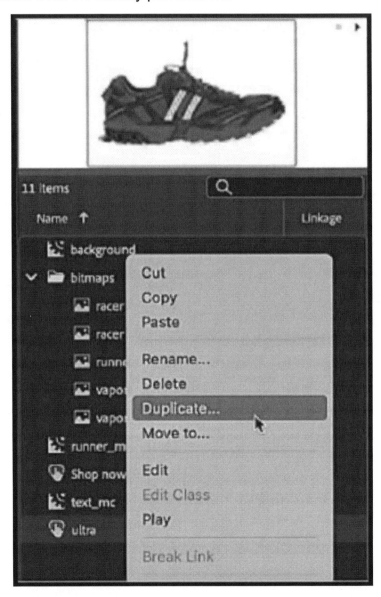

2. In the Duplicate Symbol dialog box, choose **Button** from the Type menu and name the symbol racer. Click OK.

SWAPPING BITMAPS

Bitmaps and symbols are simple to change on the Stage, which may greatly speed up your process.

1. To modify your newly replicated symbol (the racer button), double-click on its icon in the Library window.
2. Select the shoe picture from the Stage.
3. In the Proper ties panel, choose the **Swap symbol.**

4. In the Swap Bitmap dialog box, choose the other shoe thumbnail picture, racer thumbnail, and then click OK. The thumbnail you picked replaces the old one (visible with a dot next to the symbol name). Because they're the same size, the changeover is seamless. If you want to center the new bitmap in the button, shift it down slightly.
5. Move to the Over keyframe and replace the ultra-shoe thumbnail picture with the racer shoe.
6. When you're finished, go to the Library panel, create a folder called buttons, and arrange your buttons within.

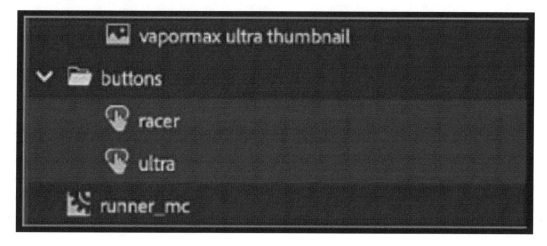

PLACING BUTTON INSTANCES

Place the buttons on the Stage and name them in the Properties window so that your code can recognize them.

1. Drag the racer button from the Library panel to the Stage on the buttons layer, beneath the existing ultra-button.

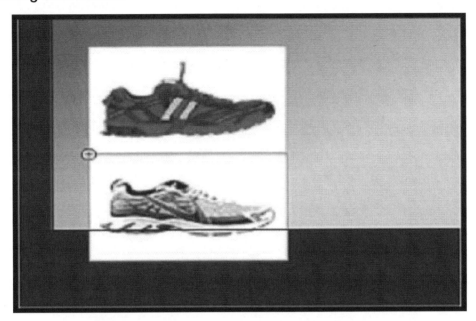

2. Select both buttons and slide them beneath the text column. The X and Y values should be around 7 and 140, respectively.

3. Move the keyframe on frame 1 of the buttons layer to the final frame (frame 15). Now, the buttons display only after the animation has finished.

4. At this stage, you may test your video to see how the buttons respond. Select File > Publish Settings. The Publish Settings panel displays.

5. Deselect the Loop Timeline checkbox on the Basic tab for the JavaScript/HTML option that is chosen on the left, then click OK. You can also use JavaScript code to pause the timeline. Normally, an Animate project loops, but for this banner ad, you want the animation top lay once and then cease.

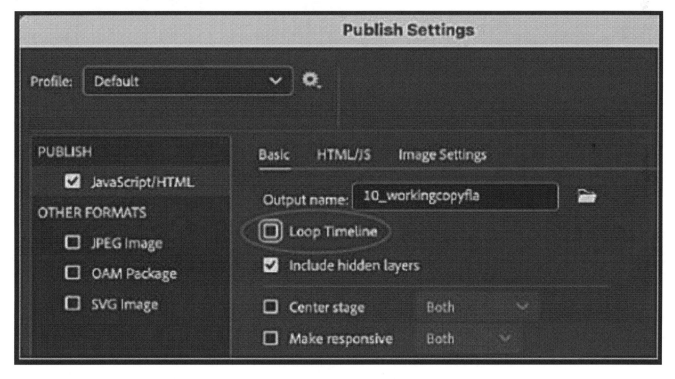

6. Select **Control > Test**. You may disregard any warnings that appear in the Output window.

The animation runs in the newly opened browser, and your two buttons appear at the conclusion. Take note of how the buttons change as your mouse cursor moves over them.

If your browser returns a blank screen when you test your video (**Control > Test**),ensure that you are connected to the internet. If not, access the Publish settings (**File > Publish Settings**). Select the HTML/JS tab and uncheck Hosted Libraries. The Hosted Libraries option connects to external JavaScript code, so your published files do not need to contain it; nevertheless, you must be connected to the internet for your project to function. However, you have yet to give instructions for the buttons to accomplish anything. That portion occurs after you've named the button instances and learned a little code.

NAMING BUTTON INSTANCES

Label each button instance so that your code can refer to it. Beginners often overlook this critical step.

1. Click an empty portion of the Stage to deselect all of the buttons, and then choose just the first one.
2. In the Properties window, enter ultra_btn as the instance name.
3. Name the other button racer_btn. Animate is quite finicky, and a single mistake may prohibit the whole project from func-tioning properly.

NAMING RULES

Naming instances is an important step in constructing interactive projects using Animate. The most typical error committed by beginners is failing to name, or mistakenly name a button instance. Instance names are significant because ActionScript and JavaScript use them to refer to specific objects. The instance names do not correspond to the symbol names in the Library panel. The names on the Library panel are just organizational reminders.

Instance naming adheres to these fundamental conventions and recommended practices:

- Avoid using spaces or special punctuation. Underscores are OK to use.
- Don't start a name with a number.
- Know the difference between uppercase and lowercase letters. ActionScript and JavaScript are case-sensitive.
- End the button name with _btn. Although not needed, it helps in identifying the items as buttons.
- Do not use words designated for ActionScript or JavaScript commands.

PREPARING THE TIMETABLE

You will add extra frames to the timeline to make place for more material.

1. Select frame 30 for all of your layers.
2. Select **Insert > Timeline > Frame** (FS). You can also right-click and choose Insert Frame. Animate adds frames to all of the specified layers up to the desired point, frame 30.

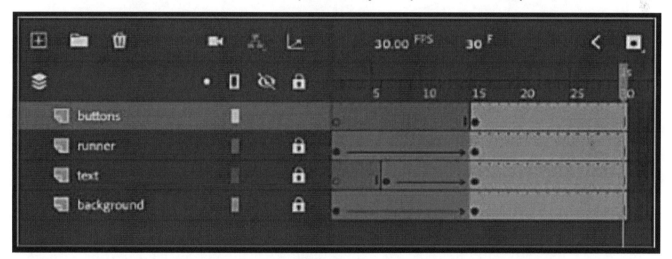

CREATING DESTINATION KEYFRAMES

When the user presses each button, Animate will move the play head to a new point on the timeline based on the code you'll enter. Before adding the code, you will design all of the timeline choices that your user can choose.

INSERTING KEYFRAMES WITH DIFFERENT CONTENT

You will create four keyframes in a new layer and fill them with information about each of the running shoes.

1. Add a new layer at the top of the layer stack and call it content.

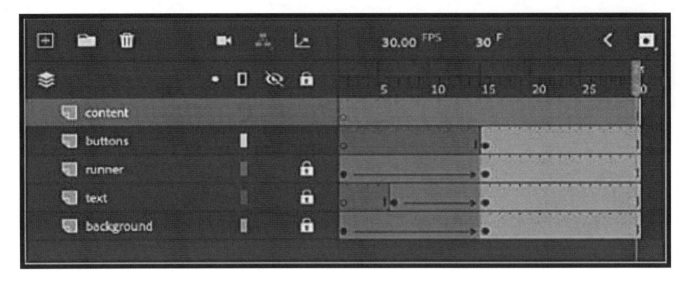

2. Select frame 20 from the content layer.
3. Insert a new keyframe at frame 20 (**Insert> Timeline > Keyframe**, press F6, or use the Insert Keyframe button above the timeline).

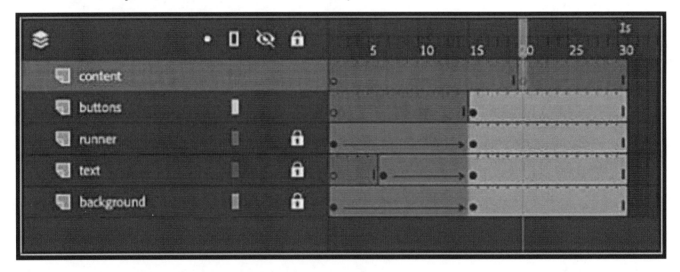

4. Add a new keyframe at frame 25. The content layer of your timeline now has two new empty keyframes.
5. Unlock the runner layer and then choose frame 20.
6. Select **Modify> Timeline > Convert to Blank Keyframes** (F7). A blank keyframe occurs at frame 20 of the runner layer. This frees up space on the stage to display more information about the chosen running shoe.
7. Choose the empty keyframe at frame 20 of the content layer.
8. In the Library panel, drag the vapormax ultra bitmap to the Stage.
9. Position the bitmap where the runner used to be and rotate it to provide some motion. In this example, the Transform panel displays a -24-degree rotation, while the Properties panel's Position And Size section should display X=6 5 and Y=-52.

10. Use the Text tool to write a description next to the shoe picture. Add the words Vapormax Ultra in the typeface and size of your choice.

11. Choose the empty keyframe on frame 25 of the content layer.

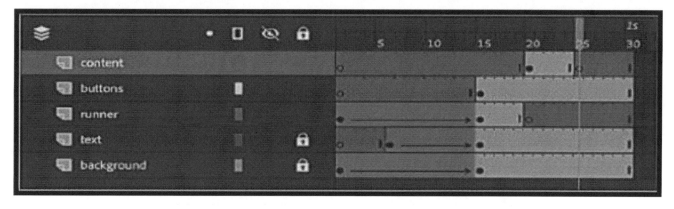

12. Drag the racer bitmap from the Library panel onto the Stage.

13. Position and rotate the bitmap in the same way as the last shoe.

14. Add the term **"Racer"** next to this shoe.

The content layer now has three keyframes: the first, at frame 1, is empty; the second, at frame 20, has the Vapormax Ultra shoe; and the third, at frame 25, contains the Racer shoe.

PUTTING LABELS ON KEYFRAMES

Frame label s are the names you provide to keyframes. Instead of referring to keyframes by frame number, you use their label, which makes code simpler to understand, write, and modify.

1. Select frame 20 from the content layer.
2. In the Label section of the Properties panel, type ultra in the Name box. A little flag symbol appears on the keyframe.

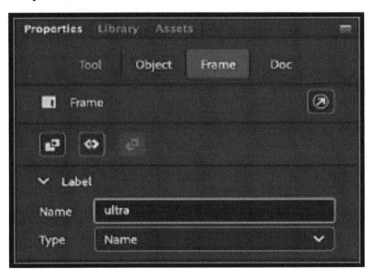

3. Select frame 25 from the content layer.
4. In the Label section of the Properties panel, type racer into the Name area. Alit tle flag symbol appears on the keyframe.

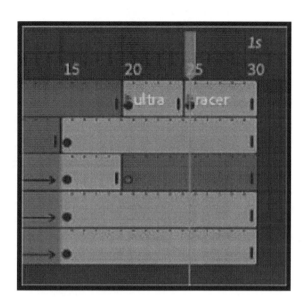

NAVIGATING THE ACTIONS PANEL

The Actions section is where you'll enter all your code. If you are using an HTML5 Canvas page, you must input JavaScript. If you're work-ing with an ActionScript 3.0 document, you enter ActionScript. To open the Actions panel, go to **Window > Actions** or choose a keyframe on the timeline and click the **ActionScript panel button** in the upper right corner of the Properties panel.

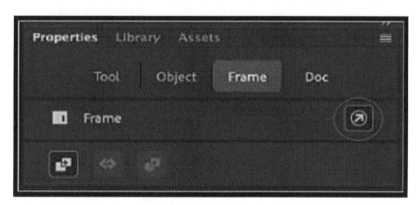

You can also right-click any keyframe and choose Actions. The Actions panel provides a flexible environment for inputting code, as well as several tools for writing, editing, and viewing code.

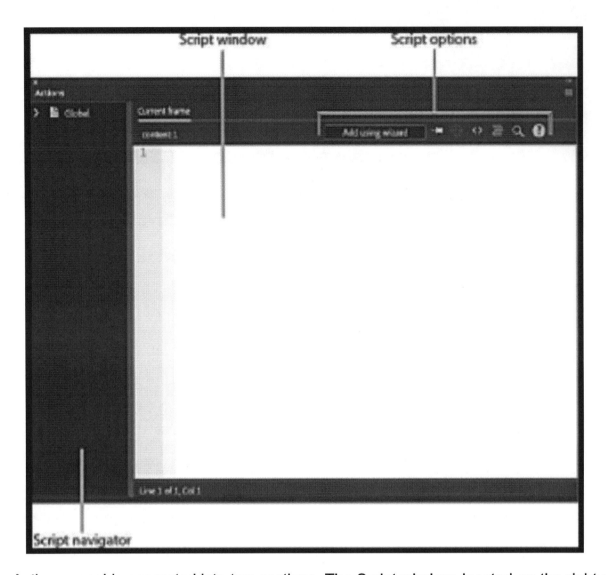

The Actions panel is separated into two sections. The Script window, located on the right side of the Actions panel, is a blank slate on which you may freely write code. You type Action Script or JavaScript into the Script window exactly as you would in a text editor. The Script navigator is on the left and displays you where your code is situated. Animate sets code on keyframes on the timeline, thus the Script navigator is especially handy if you have a lot of code dispersed over several keyframes and timelines. The current line number and column number (or character in the row) of the text insertion point are shown at the bottom of the Act ions panel by Animate. The upper-right corner of the Actions panel offers buttons for searching, replacing, and inputting code. The Add Using Wizard button is also available.

ADDING JAVASCRIPT INTERACTION USING THE ACTIONS PANEL WIZARD

Now that you have numerous keyframes on the timeline, your video will play from frame 1 to frame 30, displaying all of the shoe options. However, with this interactive banner ad, you'll want to stop the video at frame 15 to allow your visitors to choose a shoe model.

STOPPING THE TIRNELINE

Use the stop () action to stop your animated movie. A stop () action simply stops the movie from progressing by pausing the play head.

1. Add a new layer on the top and call it actions. JavaScript and ActionScript code are often inserted on keyframes through- out the timeline.
2. Set a keyframe at frame 15 of the actions layer.

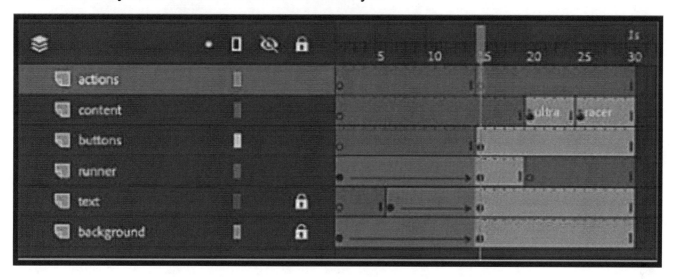

3. Select frame 15 and launch the Actions panel (**Window > Actions**).
4. Select the **Add Using Wizard button**. The wizard opens on the Actions panel. The wizard takes you step by step through the code-writing process. The first field contains the code that you generated using the wizard. The wizard allows you to incorporate JavaScript into HTML5 Canvas, WebGL gITF Extended Version, VR Panorama, and VR 360 documents. For Ac-tion Script , utilize the Code Snippets section.

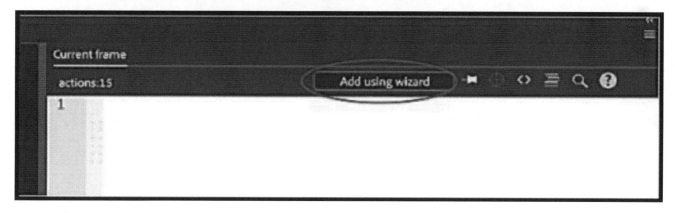

5. Step1 prompts you to choose an action, or behavior, from a list. Scroll down the list under Pick an Action and Pick Stop (the options are alphabetized). Another menu appears on the right.
6. Select This Timeline from the option that appears next. Code appears in the action window. The halt () action will be applied to the current timeframe.

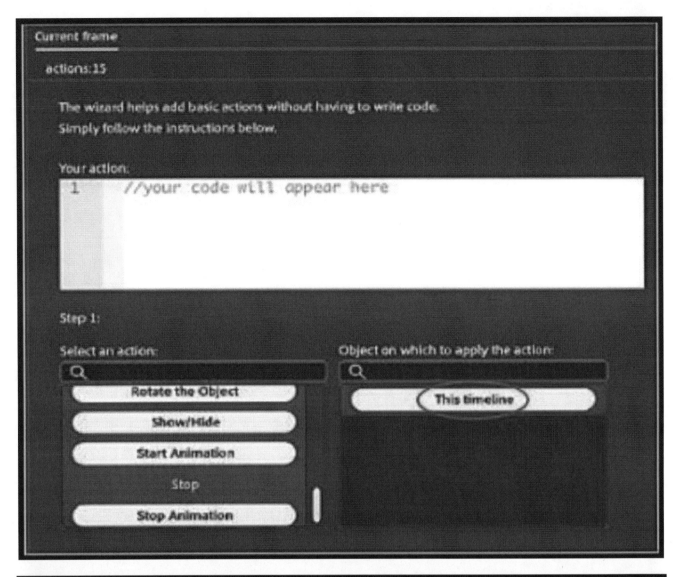

7. Click Next. Step 2 appears in the wizard.
8. Step 2 asks you to choose the trigger that will result in your desired action. Choose with this frame. Additional code is added to relate to the current timeframe. You want the stop () action to be triggered as soon as the timeline starts, thus the suitable trigger is when the play head reaches the current frame.
9. Click Finish and Add.

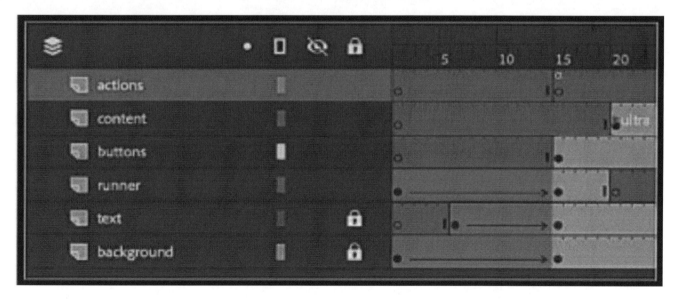

The completed code is added to the Script window in the Actions panel.

The code is:

- var _this = this.
- _this.stop();

The first sentence declares a variable, or reference, named _this, which relates to the current timeline. The second sentence refers to the current timeline and initiates the halt () operation. The semicolon after each sentence serves as a period, indicating the end of the com-mand. The light gray code that starts with /* and ends with*/ is known as a multiline comment, and it simply describes what the code does. It serves as a reminder for you and other developers. Well-commented code is vital. It will save you hours of difficulties when you return to a project and is regarded as best practice for developers. In the timeline, a little lower case "a" is added to frame 15 in the actions layer to show that code has been introduced.

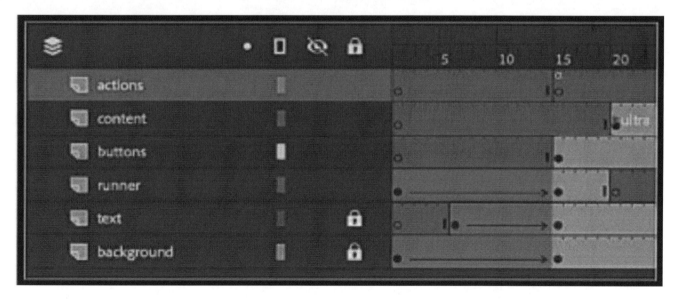

ADDING ACTIONS FOR A BUTTON CLICK

At this point, you've got code that pauses the timeline at frame 15. You will now create an action for when a button is clicked. The wizard refers to the button click as a trigger, but JavaScript and ActionScript refer to it as an event. Events are incidents in your movie that An-imate can recognize and react to. Events include mouse clicks (or taps), mouse movements, and keypresses. Pinch and swipe actions on mobile devices are also events. These events are generated by the user, although some may occur spontaneously, such as the successful loading of data or the finish of a sound.

Here are the steps:

1. Select frame 15 from the actions layer.
2. If you haven't already, open the Actions panel.
3. Place your text cursor on the last empty line of your Script window. You will add more code to the existing code.
4. Select the **Add Using Wizard button.** The wizard opens on the Actions panel.
5. Step 1 requests the action. Scroll down and choose Go to Fra me Label and Stop.
6. Select This Timeline from the option that appears next. The action will take effect within the current time frame.

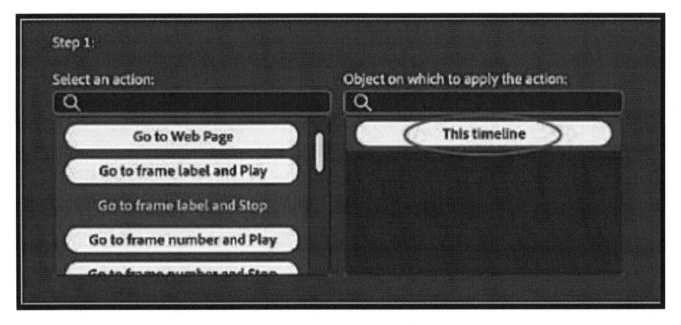

7. Replace the green highlighted characters in the action window with the name of the label where you want the play head to go. Replace enter Frame Label with Ultra. The frame label name appears in green and should be enclosed by a set of single quotes.
8. Click Next. Step 2 appears in the wizard.
9. Step 2 requests the trigger that will initiate your chosen action. Select **"On Mouse Click."** On Mouse Click is an event that occurs when you push and then release the on-screen button. Another menu appears on the right.

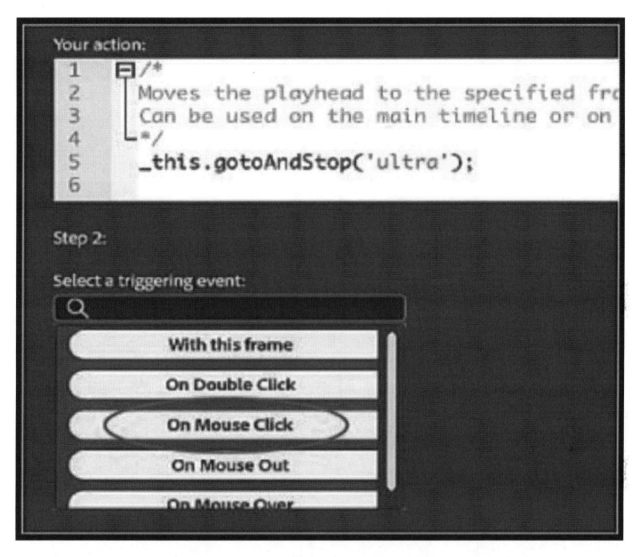

10. The wizard requests the object for the triggering event. Select ultra_btn, the button associated with the first shoe, whose information is presented in the keyframe called ultra.
11. Click Finish and Add. The completed code is added to the Script window in the Actions panel. The code is made up of the trigger 'click' and a function that collects all of the code that is performed when the trigger is activated. You must identify the function's starting and closing curly braces. This function just has one statement (a gotoAndStop () action to shift the play head), but functions may have several statements.

```
actions:15                    Add using wizard       📌  ⊕  <>  ▤  Q  ❓
1
2       var _this = this;
3     ╔ /*
4     ║  Stop a Movie Clip/Video
5     ║  Stops the specified movie clip or video.
6     ╚ */
7       _this.stop();
8
9
10      var _this = this;
11    ╔ /*
12    ║  Clicking on the specified symbol instance executes a function.
13    ╚ */
14    ╔ _this.ultra_btn.on('click', function(){
15    ╔ /*
16    ║  Moves the playhead to the specified frame label in the timeline or
17    ║  Can be used on the main timeline or on movie clip timelines.
18    ╚ */
19    ║  _this.gotoAndStop('ultra');
20    ╚ });
21
22
```

12. Select **Control > Test.** Animate opens your browser and displays your project. Click the first button. Animate recognizes the button's click trigger and changes the play head to the ultra keyframe, where the Stage displays information on the Vapormax Ultra shoe.

If you feel confident, you may attempt to speed up the process of reproducing the code for the other button. Copy the code from the Script window and paste it. Change just the button and frame label names. It will be quicker than going through the wizard, and it will be your first step in identifying and learning various aspects of JavaScript code, allowing you to ultimately create code yourself.

13. Close the browser and return to Animate.
14. Select frame 15 of the actions layer and reopen the Actions panel if it is not already open.
15. Continue to add actions and triggers to the current code for the other button. The next button should perform agotoAnd· Stop() action on the racer keyframe.

If you want to utilize frame numbers instead of frame labels, keep in mind that the JavaScript library used by Animate starts counting frames at 0, thus the first frame of your timeline will be O rather than 1. ActionScript and JavaScript for WebGL glTF and VR documents, on the other hand, start counting timeline frames from 1. For this reason, frame labels should be used wherever feasible.

CHECKING FOR ERRORS

Debugging is a vital activity for both experienced and rookie developers. Even if you take additional precautions, mistakes will leak into your code. Fortunately, the wizard helps to minimize typos and typical mistakes. If you type code by hand, a few pointers may help you avoid, catch, and identify problems.

- In ActionScript 3.0 documents, Animate shows code errors in the Compiler Errors panel (**Window > Compiler Errors**) with a de-scription and location. If a compiler error occurs anywhere in your code, none of it will operate.
- Make use of color hints in the code. Animate changing colors for keywords, variables, comments, and other language features. You don't have to know why they're different, but the varied colors might help you figure out where there could be any missing punctuation.
- To improve code readability, use the Format Code button in the Actions panel's upper-right corner. You can modify the formatting options in **Animate > Preferences > Edit Preferences > Code Editor (macOS) or Edit > Preferences> Code Editor (Windows).**

CREATING THE "SHOP NOW" BUTTON

A banner ad's most important feature is its ability to drive interested people to the advertiser's website. You'll need to add another button to achieve that. The **"Shop now"** button you build next will launch a website in a new browser window or tab.

ADDING ANOTHER BUTTON INSTANCE

The example lesson file includes a "Shop now" button in the Library section.

1. Choose frame 15 from the buttons layer and unlock it if it is locked.
2. Drag the "Shop Now" button from the Library panel to the stage. Place the button instance underneath the runner, posi-tioned at the bottom border of the Stage.

3. In the Properties panel, set the X and Y values to 114 and 238, respectively.
4. In the Properties tab, give the instance the name shop now_btn.

ADDING CODE FOR THE "SHOP NOW" BUTTON

The action will be "Go to Web Page," and the trigger will be a button click or touch.

1. Select frame 15 from the actions layer.
2. If you haven't already, open the Actions panel.

3. Move your text cursor to a new line following the final line of code in your Script window. You will add code to the existing code.
4. Select the Add Using Wizard button. The wizard opens on the Actions panel.

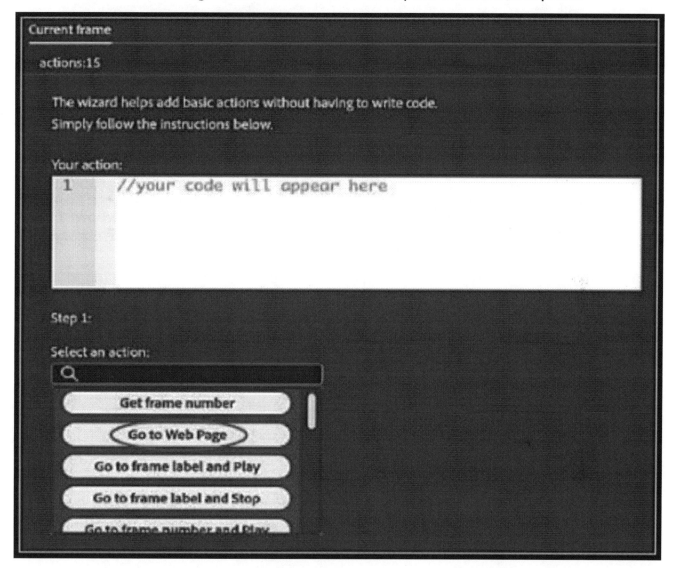

5. Step 1 requests the action. Select Go to Web Page. In a genuine project, you would change the green highlighted text in the code preview window with the URL of the advertiser's website. For this project, you may use the default URL, which is Adobe's website.
6. Click Next. Step 2 appears in the wizard.
7. Step 2 requests the trigger that will initiate your chosen action. Select **"On Mouse Click."** On Mouse Click is an event that occurs when the user presses and then releases their mouse over the button, or when they tap the button. Another menu appears on the right.
8. The wizard requests the object for the triggering event. Choose shop now_btn.

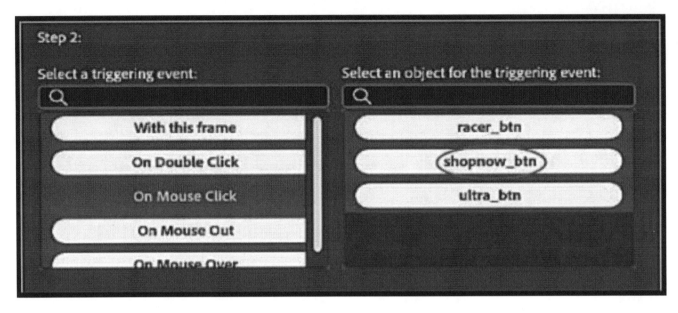

9. Click Finish and Add. The code to add the "Shop now" button has been added to the script. Don't worry if the line numbers in the screenshot don't match those in your code.

10. Try out your movie. When you click the "Shop Now" button, the Adobe website opens in a new browser tab or window.

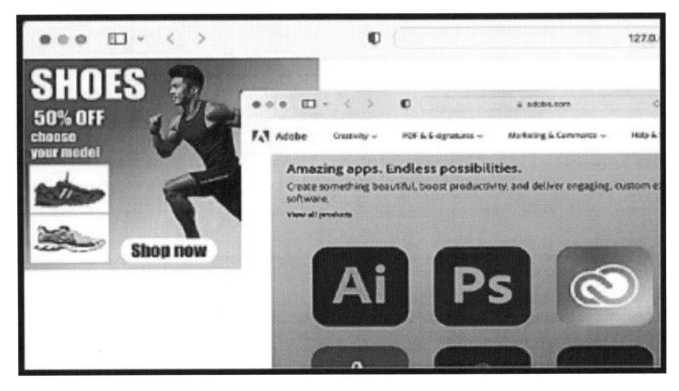

THE CODE SNIPPETS PANEL

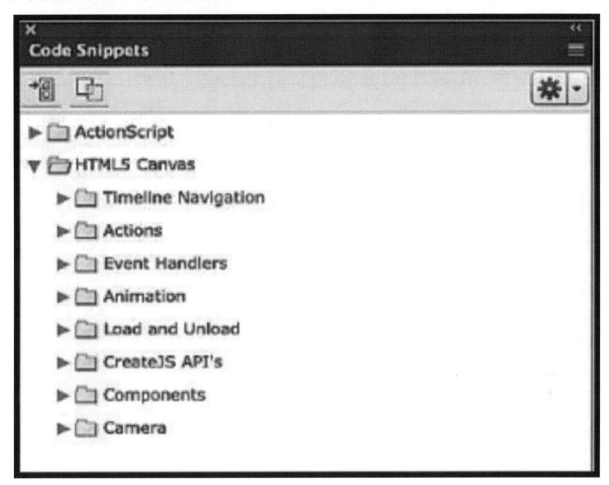

Animate has another panel, the Code Snippets panel (Window > Code Snippets), which allows you to add ActionScript 3.0 and JavaScript code. The panel is arranged into folders for various types of interaction. Simply expand the folder you want and choose the action. Ani- mate will help you through any more details. The Code Snippets panel also allows you to store your code and share it with other develop-ers. Beginners should use the Add Using Wizard option in the JavaScript Actions section.

PLAYING ANIMATION AT THE DESTINATION

At this point, this interactive banner ad utilizes the gotoAndStop() function to display information in various keyframes throughout the timeline. But say you wanted the running shoe picture to animate into the Stage rather than appear abruptly- how would you play an animation when a user presses a button? One method is to use the gotoAndPlay() action, which changes the play head to the frame number or frame label and then continues playing from there.

CREATING TRANSITION ANIMATIONS

Next, you'll make a brief transition animation for each shoe. The transition animation will show the shoe entering the stage from the right edge. Then you'll modify your code to tell Animate to go to each of the first keyframes and play the animation.

1. Move the play head to the extreme frame label and then pick the keyframe in the content layer.
2. Create Motion Tween by right-clicking both the chosen image and the text on the Stage, or use the Create Tween option above the timeline.

3. Animate asks whether you want to design a symbol to represent the motion tween options. Click OK.

Animate builds a distinct tween layer for the instance so that it may continue with the motion tween.

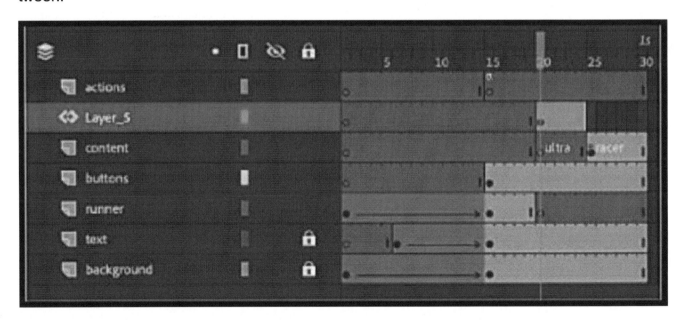

4. Move the instance off the Stage and to the right until it is no longer visible.
5. Move the play head to the conclusion of the tween span, at frame 24.
6. Place the instance back on the Stage where it was previously. The motion from frame 20 to frame 24 creates a powerful introduction.

7. Make a similar motion tween for the second shoe in the keyframe, labeled racer. Don't test your movie just yet. To make this work, you'll need to change the JavaScript code in the following task.

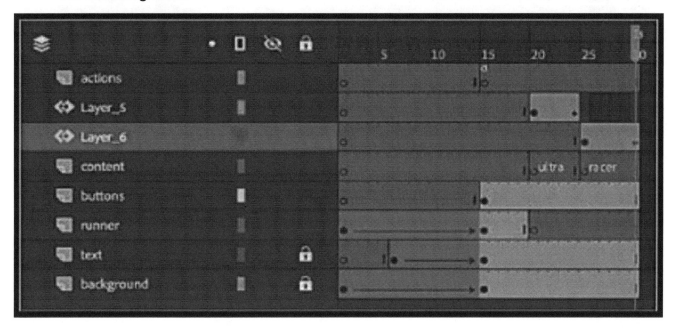

USE THE GOTOANDPLAY() ACTION

The gotoAndPlay() action movies the Animated play head to a given frame on the timeline and starts playing from there. To do many substitutions quickly and easily, use the Find and Replace command in the Actions panel. Click the Find button in the upper-right corner, then Find, followed by Find and Replace from the menu to the right of the Find Text box.

1. Open the Actions panel by selecting frame 15 on the Actions layer.
2. In your JavaScript code, convert the first two gotoAndSt op() actions to gotoAndPlay() actions while leaving the argument unchanged:
- Replace gotoAndStop('ultra') with gotoAndPlay('ultra').
- Replace gotoAndStop('racer') with gotoAndPlay('racer ').

For each button, the JavaScript code now sends the play head to a certain frame label and starts playing from there. Ensure the function for your **"Shop now "** button remains the same.

STOPPING THE ANIMATIONS

If you test your video now (Control > Test), you'll see that each button navigates to its appropriate frame label and begins playing from there, but it continues to play, displaying any remaining animations further down the timeline.

The next step is to instruct Animate to stop.

1. Choose frame 24 of the actions layer, the frame immediately before the racer labeled keyframe on the content layer.
2. Right-click the frame and choose **Insert Keyframe**. A new keyframe is added to the actions layer. We'll utilize the new keyframe to add a stop () action before the second animation begins.

3. Open the Actions panel. The script window in the Actions panel is blank. Do not panic! Your code hasn't vanished. Your event listener code is on the actions layer's first keyframe. You have chosen a new keyframe to which you will add a stop (} action

4. In the script window, type the following: this.stop(};If you like, you may use the Add Using Wizard panel to add the stop()

   action to each keyframe. Animate will stop playing when it reaches frame 24.

5. Create a keyframe at frame 30. If you wish to quickly and easily replicate the keyframe containing the stop () action, drag it to a new spot on the timeline while holding down the Option /Alt key.

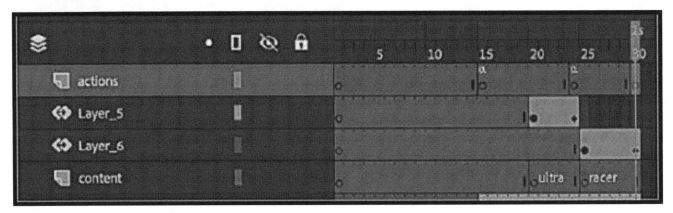

6. In this keyframe, add another stop () action to the Actions panel.
7. To test your video, go to **Control > Test.**

Each button navigates to a new keyframe and triggers an animation of a running shoe sliding onto the stage. After the animation, the film pauses and waits for the spectator to press another button.

PIN CODE ON THE ACTIONS PANEL

It might be difficult to change or examine code that is distributed over numerous keyframes on the timeline. The Actions panel allows you to retain code from certain keyframes "pinned" to it. Click the Pin Script button at the top of the Actions panel, and Animate will open a new tab with the code now visible in the Script window.

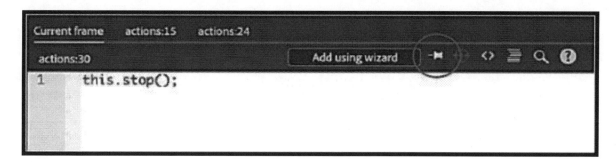

The tab will be tagged with the frame number where your code is located. You may pin many scripts, making it easy to switch between them. To proceed with the remainder of this lesson, unpin all of the scripts so that just the Current Fra me tab appears.

ANIMATED BUTTONS

Presently, hovering your mouse cursor over one of the running shoe buttons causes the red stroke and yellow fill in the box to appear. But imagine if the mouse hover produced an animated effect. It would add vitality and complexity to the interaction between the user and the button. Animated buttons show an animation in the Up, Over, and Down keyframes. The trick to making an animated button is to embed a video clip inside a button symbol. Create an animation inside a movie clip symbol, and then insert it into the Up, Over, or Down keyframe of a button symbol. When one of the button keyframes is shown, the animation in the video clip begins.

CREATING ANIMATION IN A MOVIE CLIP SYMBOL

Your button symbols in this banner ad include a bitmap of a shoe in its Overstate. You will turn the bitmap into a movie clip symbol and then construct an animation inside that movie clip.

1. Open the Library panel and expand the buttons folder. Double-click the icon for the extreme button. You enter symbol editing mode for the button symbol **"ultra."**

2. Select the shoe bitmap from the Over keyframe.
3. Rig h t- click and choose **Convert to Symbol**. A Convert to Symbol dialog box displays.
4. Choose Movie Clip as the type, and then enter ultra_mc as the name. Click OK. You now have a movie clip instance inside the Over keyframe of your button icon.

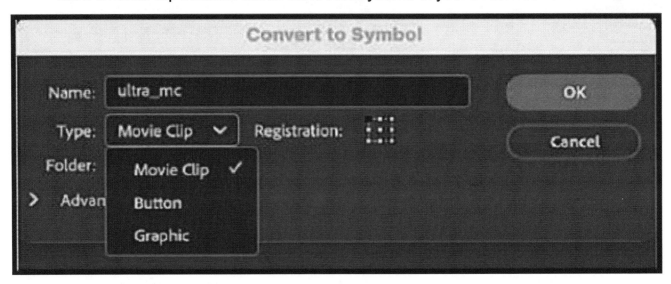

5. Double-click the movie clip instance to make changes in place. Consider how the Edit bar above the Stage displays the nest-ing of symbols.
6. **Right-click the shoe bitmap and choose Create Motion Tween.**

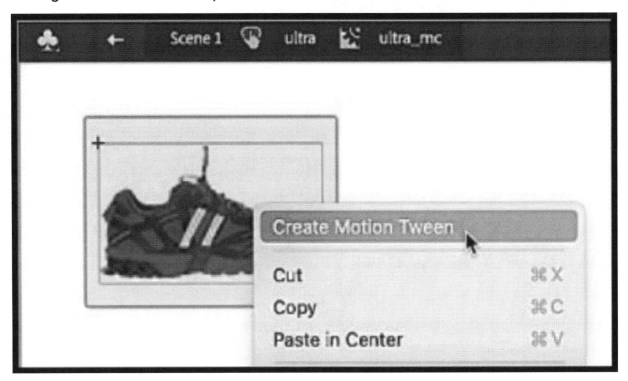

7. When the dialog box comes asking for approval to convert the selection to a symbol, click OK. The shoe bitmap is turned into a symbol and put in a motion tween layer. Animate adds one second's worth of frames to the timeline.

8. Drag the end of the tween span back until the timeline contains just 10 frames.
9. Advance the play head to frame 10.
10. Choose the Free Transform tool and increase the shoe until it fills, or perhaps breaks, the box in which it is placed. Ani- mate makes a seamless transition between smaller and bigger instances within the 10-frame tween period.

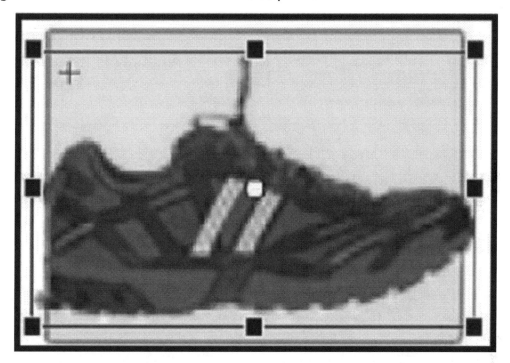

11. Create a new layer and call it actions.
12. Insert a new keyframe into the last frame (frame 10) of the actions layer.

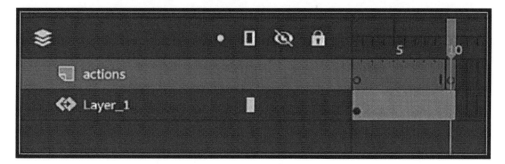

13. Open the Actions panel (Window > Actions) and type this.stop(); into the Script window.

Adding the stop O action in the last frame guarantees that the fade-in effect only appears once. The last keyframe on frame 10 of the actions layer has a little "a," suggesting that code is connected there. If you want an animated button to repeat its animation, remove the stop O action after the movie clip's timeline.

14. To exit symbol editing mode, click the Scene 1 button in the Edit bar above the stage.

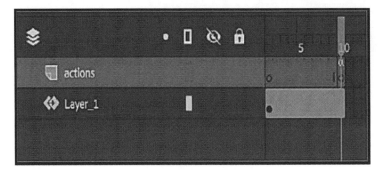

15. Select

When your mouse cursor lingers over the first shoe button, the picture of the shoe expands gradually, adding emphasis. You can add JavaScript code to either the main timeline or a movie clip's timeline. Movie clips are the sole symbols that enable interaction.

16. To animate the racer button's Over state, create an analogous motion tween and conclude it with a stop () action.

FREQUENTLY ASKED QUESTIONS

1. How do you create interactive media?
2. How do you create a button symbol?
3. How do you name rules?
4. How do you navigate the actions panel?
5. How do you add javascript interaction using the actions panel wizard?
6. How do you create the "Shop Now" button?
7. How do you use the code snippets panel?

CONCLUSION

As you reach the end of this comprehensive journey into the realm of animation and interactive design, it is essential to reflect on the path you've traveled and the knowledge you've gained. The world of animation is vast and intricate, a domain where creativity meets technology, and where imagination is given the tools to come alive. Throughout this exploration, you have delved into the depths of a powerful tool that not only bridges the gap between artistic vision and technical execution but also empowers you to bring your most ambitious ideas to life.

Animation is more than just a sequence of images brought together to create movement; it is a form of storytelling that transcends language and culture. It is a medium through which emotions, ideas, and narratives are conveyed with a universality that few other forms of expression can match. The journey to mastering this craft is one that requires not only technical proficiency but also a deep understanding of the principles that underpin animation. These principles, rooted in both the art of storytelling and the science of motion, are the foundation upon which every successful animation is built.

At the beginning of this journey, you were introduced to the basics—the tools, the interface, and the initial steps required to create simple animations. These foundational skills are the building blocks of your creative process, the elements that allow you to start turning your ideas into tangible projects. As you progressed, you encountered more complex concepts, from classic tweens to motion tweens, and from shape animation to advanced masking techniques. Each of these concepts added a layer of depth to your understanding, enabling you to create more sophisticated and refined animations.

The power of animation lies in its ability to evoke emotions and convey messages with subtlety and nuance. Whether you are animating a simple character or creating an intricate interactive experience, the choices you make in timing, spacing, and movement can profoundly impact how your audience perceives and engages with your work. Mastery of these elements is what separates a good animation from a great one, and it is a skill that develops over time with practice and experimentation.

One of the most significant aspects of this journey has been the exploration of interactive media. The ability to create content that not only moves but also responds to user input opens up a new dimension of creativity. Interactive media is not just about creating animations that entertain; it is about crafting experiences that engage, educate, and immerse the user. This dynamic form of content creation is becoming increasingly important in a world where audiences expect to interact with digital content rather than passively consume it.

In mastering these techniques, you have learned to balance creativity with functionality. Animation, at its best, is a seamless blend of artistry and technology, where each frame is crafted with intention, and each movement serves a purpose. This balance is particularly evident in interactive media, where the user experience is paramount. Creating animations that are not only visually appealing but also intuitive and user-friendly is a challenge that requires both creative vision and technical expertise.

As you have seen, the world of animation is not static; it is constantly evolving. New technologies, techniques, and trends continually reshape the landscape, offering fresh opportunities for innovation and creativity. Staying ahead in this field means being open to learning and adapting, continuously refining your skills and embracing new tools and methods. The journey of an animator is one of lifelong learning, where each project presents an opportunity to explore new ideas, push the boundaries of what is possible, and grow as a creative professional.

In addition to the technical skills you have acquired, this journey has also been about developing a creative mindset. Animation is as much about problem-solving as it is about artistry. Each animation presents unique challenges, whether it is figuring out how to convey a complex idea in a few seconds or finding the most efficient way to animate a detailed scene. Developing the ability to think critically and creatively is crucial for overcoming these challenges and finding innovative solutions.

Throughout this process, you have likely encountered moments of frustration and triumph, times when the animation seemed to come together effortlessly and times when it felt like a struggle to get things just right. These experiences are all part of the creative journey. They teach you patience, perseverance, and the importance of iteration. Animation is rarely perfect on the first attempt; it is through revision and refinement that the best work is produced. Embracing this process, with all its ups and downs, is key to developing as an animator.

Another vital lesson from this journey is the importance of collaboration. While animation can be a solitary pursuit, it often involves working with others, whether it is in a professional studio environment or as part of a collaborative project. Understanding how to communicate your ideas effectively, take feedback constructively, and work as part of a team is crucial for success in this field. Collaboration brings fresh perspectives and ideas, making the final product richer and more well-rounded.

As you move forward, it is essential to keep pushing your creative boundaries. The skills and knowledge you have gained are a foundation upon which you can build even more complex and innovative projects. Experiment with new techniques, explore different styles, and continue to challenge yourself. The world of animation is vast, and there is always more to learn and discover.

In the realm of interactive media, the possibilities are particularly exciting. The integration of animation with interactive elements opens up a world of creative potential. Consider how you can use the skills you have acquired to create experiences that are not only visually engaging but also deeply immersive and interactive. Whether you are interested in game design, interactive storytelling, or educational content, the tools and techniques you have learned will serve you well in these endeavors.

As you reflect on this journey, it is important to recognize how far you have come. From the basics of getting started to the intricacies of advanced animation techniques, you have gained a deep and comprehensive understanding of this powerful tool. More importantly, you have developed the confidence to apply these skills in your creative projects. Whether you are working on personal projects, professional assignments, or collaborations, you now have the knowledge and expertise to bring your ideas to life with confidence and precision.

Looking to the future, the skills you have acquired will continue to be relevant and valuable as the field of animation evolves. As new technologies emerge and new creative challenges arise, your ability to adapt, learn, and innovate will be crucial to your success. The world of animation is one of constant change, but with the foundation you have built, you are well-equipped to navigate this dynamic landscape.

In conclusion, the journey through animation and interactive media is one of endless possibilities. It is a journey that has taken you from the basics to advanced techniques, from simple animations to complex interactive experiences. Along the way, you have developed not only technical skills but also a creative mindset that will serve you well in all your future endeavors.

As you continue to explore the world of animation, remember that the most important tool at your disposal is your creativity. The software and techniques you have learned are powerful, but it is your imagination, your ideas, and your vision that will truly bring your animations to life. Keep experimenting, keep learning, and most importantly, keep creating. The world of animation is waiting for your unique contribution, and with the skills and knowledge you have gained, you are ready to make your mark.

This journey is just the beginning. The world of animation is vast, full of opportunities to learn, grow, and create. As you move forward, take with you the lessons you have learned, the skills you have developed, and the passion that drives you to create. The future of animation is in your hands, and with it, the power to inspire, entertain, and connect with audiences around the world. Embrace this opportunity, and let your creativity soar.

Made in the USA
Las Vegas, NV
19 December 2024

14765502R00180